IRON HORSE

Lou Gehrig in His Time

IRON HORSE

Lou Gehrig in His Time

RAY ROBINSON

W · W · NORTON & COMPANY
New York · London

Lines from *You Can't Go Home Again* by Thomas Wolfe. Copyright 1934, 1937, 1938, 1940 by Maxwell Perkins as the Executor of the Estate of Thomas Wolfe. Harper & Row, Publishers, Inc.

Printed in the United States of America.

The text of this book is composed in Cheltenham Book,
with display type set in Beton Bold Condensed.
Composition and manufacturing by The Haddon Craftsmen, Inc.
Book design by Jacques Chazaud.

First Edition

Library of Congress Cataloging-in-Publication Data

Robinson, Ray, 1920 Dec. 4–
Iron horse : Lou Gehrig in his time / Ray Robinson.
p. cm.
1. Gehrig, Lou, 1903–1941. 2. Baseball players—United States—
Biography. 3. New York Yankees (Baseball team) I. Title.
GV865.G4R63   1990
796.357'092—dc20
[B]   89–29272

ISBN 0-393-02857-7

W.W. Norton & Company, Inc., 500 Fifth Avenue, New York, N.Y. 10110
W.W. Norton & Company, Ltd., 37 Great Russell Street, London WC1B 3NU

1 2 3 4 5 6 7 8 9 0

For Tyler

Contents

Photographs appear following pages 90 and 194.

Preface:
A Letter from Lou

In the early 1930s, when Lou Gehrig was in the midst of his remarkable consecutive-game streak, I was in my pre-teen years, a worshipper and celebrant from afar. I suspect there were many other youngsters, not necessarily New York kids, who were also captivated by his achievements.

True, he was not baseball's dominant personality in that era, for it was Babe Ruth, as implausible a sports figure as was ever born, who occupied that role. But through all the years of Yankee hegemony I preferred Gehrig, even as he played and lived constantly in the bulging shadow of Ruth.

In popular parlance, Gehrig was the designated crown prince to Ruth's kingship. Ruth, the incomparable Bambino, was everybody's Sultan of Swat, even to those who had only a modest interest in the national pastime.

If everybody loved the Babe and recognized his homely features on sight, I was more taken with Gehrig's diffidence, his dimpled smile, his surface calm, his unmistakable Boy Scout aura. If Gehrig was destined to play second banana to the larger-than-life Zeus who preceded him in the batting order of the Yankees' Murderers' Row, I still chose Gehrig over the Babe. I wanted my heroes to be less flamboyant than Ruth, less outrageous, less self-centered, preferring the stubborn day-by-day dedication of Gehrig.

While the Babe connected for higher-than-heaven home runs, Gehrig settled for screaming line drives. Even when the Babe minced across the street, on those celery-stick legs, he won cheers. When he struck out, as he often did, it was with the panache of a Shakespearean actor, and he was applauded to the echo as his bat lashed the air unmercifully. Who ever heard of a baseball player striking out to the accompaniment of cheers! Did they cheer for Lou when he went down on strikes?

When Ruth winked or when he croaked his familiar "Hi, keed" to friends and strangers alike (names of teammates seemed to escape him), he was adored on the spot. When Gehrig signed his autograph in a neat script that fit his personality, he won only modest approval.

While Ruth hit 259 of his homers in Yankee Stadium, of a lifetime accumulation of 714, Gehrig hit 30 Stadium homers in 1930, the most ever hit in one year in that park, until Roger Maris hit 30 in 1961.

But despite Lou's productivity at the Stadium, the right-field bleachers, where many of Gehrig's blasts nestled, were named after the Babe. The section was popularly referred to as Ruthville. Nobody ever heard of anything called Gehrig Gardens.

"Gehrig was the guy who hit all those home runs the year [1927] that Ruth broke the record," wickedly wrote columnist Franklin P. Adams. Always it was the Gargantuan silhouette of Babe intruding on Lou. Even after Babe bowed to the years, others took the spotlight from Lou. When Gehrig experienced his four-home-run game in Philadelphia, the headlines were devoted instead to the retirement of John J. McGraw. Still later it was Joe DiMaggio, exuding a remarkable sense of class and grace, who managed to look better in Yankee pinstripes than Lou.

In Gehrig's time ball players were encumbered in heavy, sweaty wool uniforms that were about as chic as old bloomers hanging on clotheslines. Suited up, Gehrig looked bovine, unathletic. His appearance earned him the uncomely nickname of "Biscuit Pants." But shouldn't one win points for modesty, decency, and determination? I thought so, and of all the Yankees, it was Lou I cherished the most.

There was something else. Gehrig had enrolled in 1921 at Columbia, a school that also produced Eddie Collins, the Hall of Fame second baseman who maintained his pristine reputation even through the Black Sox scandal. My father attended Columbia when Collins was there and, though he wasn't much of a baseball fan, he understood the greatness of Collins. His pride in Columbia caused him to nurse special feelings for Gehrig, too. He'd often leave his law office in the Woolworth Building early on spring afternoons, so he could watch Gehrig play on Columbia's South Field.

"Lou used to hit tremendous fly balls off the steps of Low Library and off the walls of the Journalism Building," my father informed me. He judged such blows could have traveled 500 feet from home plate, on the Amsterdam Avenue side of South Field. There was another story he told that had Gehrig bouncing a baseball off the white-haired head of Columbia's dean, Herbert Hawkes, as that gentleman took a stroll some 150 yards away.

South Field, then the site of Columbia's baseball and football games, nestled among the red brick and gray stone buildings, most of which were student dormitories. A two-acre oasis of grass and dirt occupying two blocks at Broadway and Amsterdam Avenue between 115th and 116th streets, it was Columbia's concession to intercollegiate athletics and intramural play, before a banker named George Baker donated many verdant acres of elbowroom at the northern tip of Manhattan, overlooking the Hudson River. In such an anachronistic urban playground did Gehrig, an awkward kid in threadbare knickerbockers, first display his athletic skills as a collegian.

My father's stories reinforced my admiration for Gehrig. In my eleventh year, I was determined to meet the Quiet Hero, a fitting appellation bestowed on Gehrig by Frank Graham, a veteran sportswriter who had covered the Yankees for many years.

My early journalistic efforts were for the student newspaper of P.S. 165. Located on the West Side of Manhattan, at 109th Street, off Broadway, the school was surrounded by corner newsstands that sold twenty daily papers. I never failed to stop at those stands, especially when the World Series was being played, for the front pages shouted out the names of the starting pitchers and featured the determined faces of Bob "Lefty" Grove, Vernon "Lefty" Gomez, "Wild Bill" Hallahan, Charlie Root, and other greats and near-greats. When my father brought the *New York Sun* home in the evening I would clip out those pictures and lovingly paste them in my scrapbook, already jammed with those of Ruth and Gehrig and more exotic personalities, such as Fritz Ostermueller, John "Blondy" Ryan, and the great John Peter "Honus" Wagner, then a coach with the Pirates.

I yearned to interview Gehrig for my school paper. So one day I sat down with a friend and composed a letter to Lou, which we mailed to the Gehrig home in New Rochelle, New York. We held out scant hope he would respond, for he was, after all, the greatest of first basemen. Surely, he would have little time to waste with such tiny hero-worshipers.

Our certainty of failure was soon proved wrong when a handwritten letter arrived several days later. I can still remember the careful penmanship, considering the enormous size and strength of the writer. Yes, said the letter, Lou Gehrig would be happy to chat with us. "Just use this letter to come to the clubhouse," Lou wrote.

Within twenty-four hours my friend and I made the trip by uptown subway to Yankee Stadium, where the Washington Senators were scheduled to play the Yankees. We played hooky that day and suffered for it the next day, but it was a very small price to pay for an audience with Larrupin' Lou!

The May day was cloudless, the skies Columbia blue, of course. In those days games began at 3:30 in the afternoon but we arrived at the ballpark around one o'clock. Foolishly, we assumed the prized letter would be an instant ticket of admission. But the bulky gendarme guarding the Yankee clubhouse door informed us otherwise.

"You can wait here," he said, waving his pudgy arms in the direction of the entire borough of the Bronx. So, respectfully, we waited.

The game began, with the Yankees falling behind, and we listened for giveaway crowd noises that might hint at Yankee rallies. Once there was a growling roar that we interpreted, wishfully, as a Gehrig homer with the bases loaded.

Now the sun started to go down and we hoped the game was coming to an end. But the Yankees of those years were known as the team of "Five O'Clock Lightning," a handy summation for their penchant for late-inning uprisings. We were tired and thirsty but had little more in our pockets than return fare for the subway. Then, suddenly, all was quiet within the ballpark and people started emerging in small clusters. The game had ended. Soon, we hoped, we'd see Gehrig.

As earnest reporters we learned the Yankees had won and that George Pipgras (so many Yanks in the twenties and thirties had P's in their last names—Peckinpaugh, Pennock, Pipp, Paschal) was the winning pitcher.

We tried to estimate how long it would take Gehrig to shower and dress. Other youngsters also lingered around the clubhouse exit, but, with our precious letter, we felt smugly superior to all of them.

When Lou finally appeared, he was hatless, coatless, tieless; his thick brown hair—no blow-dry in those simpler times—was still damp from the shower. He had the kind of deep tan that today's players have forfeited to night games. He walked right by us, at a fast pace, heading down the street to his car, which was in a special parking lot for Yankee personnel. We set out after him in breathless pursuit.

"Mr. Gehrig, Mr. Gehrig!" we called. He stopped and turned. He looked gigantic to two eleven-year-olds. "We have a letter that you sent us."

He was curious and advanced toward us. My friend boldly handed him the letter. Gehrig gazed at it, recognizing his own handwriting.

"Did you boys enjoy the game?" he asked.

"We couldn't get in," my friend informed him.

"Oh, I'm very sorry," Gehrig said. "You should have told me you were coming. I would have left tickets for you." The voice, somewhat high-pitched and true to the accents of New York, was pleasant.

"Could we interview you now, Mr. Gehrig?" I asked, refusing to accept the failure of a mission.

"I'm afraid not," he answered, "I'm in a hurry to get home."

"But we waited all afternoon," my friend insisted, as bold as an apprentice could be.

Lou smiled, the same infectious grin that we'd seen in our scrapbooks.

"I wish I'd known you were here," he offered. He sounded like he meant it. He reached into a pants pocket and withdrew two crumpled tickets.

"Let's make it another day," he said, handing us the tickets. "I'll be happy to see you then."

"Thanks, Mr. Gehrig," my friend and I said, as we admired the tickets.

"Did you boys really wait all afternoon?" Lou continued.

"Yes, we did, Mr. Gehrig," I said, feeling he'd reverse himself and grant us an interview right there, as darkness descended on the Bronx.

"I'm really very sorry," he repeated. Then, with a wave of his hand, he entered his car. We watched as he quickly drove away, into the traffic leading away from the Stadium.

"He's some great guy," my friend said to me. I nodded in silent agreement.

But we never made it back for that promised interview.

The last time I saw Lou Gehrig was on July 4, 1939, at Lou Gehrig Appreciation Day at Yankee Stadium. John Kieran, the *New York*

Times sports columnist, wrote a splendid inscription on a trophy presented to Gehrig by his teammates. This is how it went:

We've been to the wars together,
We took our foes as they came;
And always you were the leader,
And ever you played the game.

Idol of cheering millions;
Records are yours by sheaves;
Iron of frame they hailed you,
Decked you with laurel leaves.

But higher than that we hold you,
We who have known you best;
Knowing the way you came through
Every human test.

Let this be a silent token
Of lasting friendship's gleam
And all that we've left unspoken
        —YOUR PALS ON THE YANKEE TEAM.

June 3, 1941, was my graduation day from Columbia. Gehrig died the day before. Walking across the campus, I recalled my father's stories about Lou's long home runs on South Field. At a moment that should have been joyous, I felt a strange melancholy.

What visions burn, what dreams possess him,
Seeker of the night?
The faultless velvet of the diamond,
The mounting roar of 80,000 voices
And Gehrig coming to bat . . .

—THOMAS WOLFE,
You Can't Go Home Again, 1934

1

After the Called Shot

If a single episode encapsulated the essence of Lou Gehrig's achievements, while underlining his perennial supporting role to Babe Ruth, it was that moment in the 1932 World Series when the Babe's "called-shot" home run was infused into baseball mythology.

Stepping to the plate after the Babe's grand, risky gesture had brought the house down, Gehrig hit his own follow-up home run, an enormous fly, sailing along on the wings of the breeze off Lake Michigan, clearing the high flagpole and landing in the temporary right-field stand.

But no artist has ever been inspired to paint an oil impression of Lou's home run, while several have depicted on canvas Ruth's blast.

Ironically, Gehrig is now best remembered not for the committed way he played the game, but for the way he departed it on that lugubrious summer day in 1939 when he waved farewell to the fans at Yankee Stadium because he was stricken in the prime of life with an incurable disease.

But to understand the nobility of that moment, which has inspired so many people ever since while nudging Gehrig toward sainthood and ensconcing him in American folklore, we must recover Gehrig the player and Gehrig the man.

When the Babe and Lou played in their fourth and final World Series together in 1932, Ruth, at thirty-seven, had just enjoyed his last forty-home-run season (with forty-one).

At the age of twenty-nine in 1932, Gehrig was at the peak of his physical powers and skill. He could eagerly look forward to finishing out the decade as he had begun. Early in June of that year, Gehrig drove four straight home runs out of Shibe Park, in Philadelphia.

In the weeks preceding the '32 Series with the Chicago Cubs, Ruth complained of various afflictions in his muscles and knees. Notwithstanding his purported miseries, he was determined to play in his seventh Series with the Yankees. Only once, in 1926, had the Yankees ever lost a Series with Ruth—and Gehrig—in the lineup.

In the National League, the Cubs came home in front of Pittsburgh by four games under the late-season prodding of Charlie Grimm, who succeeded Rogers Hornsby as manager in August. They were a sound baseball team, with reliable hitters such as outfielders Hazen "KiKi" Cuyler and Riggs Stephenson, second baseman Billy Herman, and catcher Charles "Gabby" Hartnett.

It is worth noting that Joe McCarthy, the Yankee manager, was panting for victory over the Cubs. He had a good motive since he'd been fired by the Cubs, after finishing first in 1929, then second in 1930.

Now in 1932, a Yankee flag under his stout belt, McCarthy had become the first manager to win pennants in both leagues. There was no doubt in his mind that revenge was at hand, for he had Ruth, still powerful if somewhat less vibrant than usual in his eighteenth season, and a young Hercules like Gehrig to lead the destruction.

As the 1932 Series approached, Gehrig, unlike Ruth, was in peak condition. However, the same could hardly be said for his country. If it was the best of times for Lou, it was one of the worst of times for America.

New York's patrician governor, Franklin Delano Roosevelt, was only a month away from winning the White House from Herbert Hoover. But despite the depressed economy and an imminent election, many were preoccupied with baseball, in keeping with the axiom that presidential campaigns never arouse the enfranchised until the last out of the World Series.

The Babe was as politically sophisticated as an earthworm, though he had once posed for pictures with a cigar stuck in his mouth and a tilted brown derby on his head as his way of endorsing fellow Catholic Al Smith for the presidency in 1928. As apolitical as Ruth, Lou had gone along with "campaigning" for Smith, as he joined in several pro-Smith group portraits.

Ironically, it was one of Babe's widely publicized quotes that helped bury Hoover's reputation. While conducting his annual salary negotiation with Colonel Jacob Ruppert, the Yankees' owner, Ruth was berated for asking for more money than President Hoover made. Mr. Hoover, a rich man who could have bought and sold the Yankees, received $75,000 a year. "Hell, I had a better year than Hoover did, didn't I?" the Babe shot back. The country roared, along with Ruth. Mr. Roosevelt couldn't have said it any better.

As the Yankees headed for Chicago for the third Series game on October 1, after walloping the Cubs 12–6 and 5–2 in Yankee Stadium, the country was assuredly in a state of mass misery. Three years after the great Wall Street crash, sixteen million were jobless. Every city had its Hoovervilles, miserable tar-paper or packing-case shacks that dotted urban landscapes. Thousands sold apples for nickels on street corners, sometimes spitting on the fruit to make it shine. "Brother, Can You Spare a Dime" qualified as the mournful national anthem. Despite such widespread distress, the World Series could be counted on to distract the country, if only for a precious week.

With no invading eye of television to bring games home to

millions in the evening, the Series was a newspaper and radio event. Many of the most talented journalists surfaced in the press box at Series time—the Heywood Brouns, Westbrook Peglers, Damon Runyons, and Grantland Rices. And through radio, baseball became a welcome antidote for millions eager to forget empty iceboxes and rebellious stomachs. People paused at work, in school, and at play, during each afternoon, to catch the latest news from the ballpark.

The *New York Times,* for example, like almost every newspaper, carried the account of each contest on its front page, ordinarily full of the financial gloom of the time, as well as the encroaching menace of Adolf Hitler. Inside the paper, in the sports section, would be supplemental features, columns, and box scores. Then, as now, this glut of words afforded readers a chance to argue the relative merits of the teams, the managers, the game strategy, the peculiar skills of the pitchers, and the dynamism of the sluggers.

The difference between the press coverage of the Series in the thirties and today's media barrage is that, in Gehrig's time, little was reported about the scandalous behavior or private peccadilloes of the heroes.

Ruth was a Rabelaisian character, who engaged mightily in every vice—overeating, overdrinking, womanizing, late hours, gambling—known to man. He could be loud, crude, coarse, boorish, lustful, loutish—the perfect example of an adult delinquent. Yet his public image painted him as a warm, generous, lovable, colorful, ingenuous boy who delighted in visiting ill youngsters in hospitals and promising to hit homers for them.

"When Ruth belched," writer Jim Kahn once said to Red Smith, "all the loose water in the showers would fall down." But Babe's belches and other gastronomical excesses were rarely recorded by the game's historians.

The truth, of course, was somewhere in between such hyperbolic extremes. But reporters who traveled with Ruth and other night-crawling, roistering Yankees rarely dropped a hint in press accounts about such off-field activities. What's more, most of the writers were pals of the players. It wasn't cricket to tell tales away from the sun-baked playgrounds.

Gehrig, for example, was partial to practical jokes and physical slapstick, unacceptable behavior in better social circles. He enjoyed crushing straw boaters on people's heads and once actually urinated over the terrace of his songwriter friend Fred Fisher's West End Avenue apartment in order to "break a batting slump." But writers preferred to describe him as a twenty-four-hour-a-day paradigm of virtue.

With millions drawn to the fall spectacle, Ruth attracted as much attention as a glamorous movie star. When the Yankees arrived in Chicago the Babe, a despised rival, was surprised to be greeted at the LaSalle Street Station as if he were a benevolent potentate. Perhaps Chicagoans suddenly warmed toward him because he'd committed an error in the first game and had failed to produce a home run.

Gehrig, meanwhile, with a homer in the first game and three hits in the second, had assumed the role of destroyer, even as he remained invisible to those fans who crowded around Ruth. Occasionally, he would sign an autograph or smile at someone shouting his name. But he remained in the background, a spear-carrier by choice.

The benign Chicago welcome turned threatening in the hours before the third game. The Babe was spat upon in front of the Edgewater Hotel and motorcycle cops were called on to clear the way for him and his wife, Claire. Benefiting from his supporting role, Gehrig was not a target.

It hadn't been Lou's style to engage in the rampant bench jockeying, with its accent on physical shortcomings and racial and religious prejudices. Not the most verbal of men, he was content to let his bat do the talking. It had been his habit, as he visited each American League city (there were eight teams in 1932—New York, Chicago, Boston, Philadelphia, Cleveland, Detroit, Washington, and St. Louis), to stand behind the batting cage before a game, receiving and trading innocuous insults with teammates and foes. This was part of the mores of baseball—a facet of the game's social environment that few outsiders were ever privileged to share. Such aimless barbs served to establish a link between all players, helping to pass the daylight hours and reduce pre-game tensions.

One of the few examples of Gehrig's spoken humor, if it was indeed that, occurred in a pre-game bantering session earlier in his career. When Gehrig was still a rookie with the Yankees, the club was on its annual spring exhibition jaunt. Reaching Waco, Texas, they had some thirty-five players suited up. The Brooklyn Dodgers were companion travelers, playing the Yanks each day. When the Dodgers took fielding practice, many of the Yankees sat on top of their dugout, for there wasn't enough room for them inside the temporary Waco quarters. The old wooden grand-stand was so close to the field that the fans had to be protected by a huge wire net. Gehrig and several others were perched on the roof, forced to listen to the caustic comments of the spectators. "Hey, we're so damn close to these fans they're gonna throw epithets at us," one of the Yankees cracked. Hearing this, Gehrig observed, "Aw, they can't hit us with anything. The wire screen will protect us." Some players felt that Lou, not yet a full-blown adult, was dead serious. Others insisted it was proof of his wry humor.

Considering Lou's generally quiet ways, it was unusual for him to participate in the Yankees' verbal assault of the Cubs that occurred during the third Series game. Remarks from the Yankee dugout flew thick and fast, generating equally quick ripostes from the Cubs.

In batting practice, the Babe and Lou provided an effective nonverbal rebuttal as well, pumping repeated drives into the temporary wooden right-field bleachers.

After this display Ruth, who felt Wrigley Field was made to order for him, bellowed he'd "give half his salary to play in this dump."

"He's on fire today," said Gehrig to a newspaperman. "He ought to hit one today, maybe a couple."

The agitation in the rival dugouts stemmed chiefly from what the Yankees perceived to be a slight to Cubs' shortstop Mark Koenig, their former teammate, who had joined Chicago in August. The Yanks regarded the Cubs as a bunch of cheapskates and tightwads for failing to reward Koenig properly for his role in the Cubs' pennant chase. Over the last thirty-three games of the schedule Koenig batted .353 and fielded brilliantly, yet the Cubs voted him only a half share of their Series money. It would have cost each Cub only $75 to bestow a full share on Koenig.

Lou had a relationship with Koenig going back to 1925, the year his consecutive-game streak started. That season, Koenig advanced to the Yanks from St. Paul of the American Association, so the two men shared the experience of breaking in together as fellow infielders. In the World Series of 1927 the reputedly light-hitting Mark outhit Lou, .500 to .308, which was the source of no little amusement between them. Generally, Koenig, a good-humored man, was popular with his Yankee teammates and certainly with Lou.

Therefore, as the jockeying went on at Wrigley Field, Lou gleefully entered into it, for not only was he "emitting harpoons dipped in blood" (in the words of writer Stanley Frank) in behalf of his old buddy Koenig, he was supporting the Babe, too. Though this participation was somewhat out of character for Lou, the level of viciousness was such that he couldn't stay submerged in the background.

In quick retaliation for the abuse, Ruth stepped up in the first inning and pounded a three-run homer. Lou followed in the third inning with a shot into the right-field bleachers, making the score 4–1. But the Cubs rallied to tie the game in the fourth inning.

In the fifth, when Ruth faced pitcher Charlie Root, the hooting from the Cubs reached new heights. In answer, with each successive pitch Ruth gesticulated with his right hand as he stepped away from the batter's box. With a count of two balls and two strikes, the Babe again stabbed his index finger in the direction of the center-field bleachers. Was he signaling that he was about to deposit a home run into that area, or was he reminding everyone that the next pitch could be hit out of the park?

Whatever Babe's intent, he hit the next pitch, a change-up curve low and away, into the deepest section of the center-field bleachers. Some swear it was the longest home run ever hit at Wrigley Field.

The act of hitting a baseball often thrown at the blinding speed of 90 to 95 miles per hour has been adjudged the single most difficult task faced by any athletic competitor. Now here was the Babe not only promising to hit the darn thing—but also swearing out an affidavit on it! Chutzpah to the nth degree!

As the Babe created his own legend, Gehrig remained an innocent, enraptured bystander. Kneeling in the on-deck circle, he had a perfect perspective on the Babe's vaudeville act. Later he said that Ruth shouted to Root that he was "going to hit the next pitch down your goddamn throat," a promise the Babe failed to keep, since the homer landed far from Root's windpipe.

Ruth trotted around the bases triumphantly, his great stomach shaking with laughter. When he reached home plate, Gehrig gripped the Babe's outstretched hand. Beaming, Ruth winked at Lou.

"You do the same thing," he chuckled.

Lou nodded, then stepped to the plate to face an obviously ruffled Root, as the crowd fretted in the background.

Batting from the left side, Lou gave the impression of enormous strength and of total confidence. He stood relaxed, a picture of concentration, his thirty-six-ounce bat resting inches off his left shoulder. His body rocked back and forth once or twice, a gentle rolling movement without jerkiness. His knees were bent slightly, with legs parallel and committed to an open stance. Occasionally, he would waggle his bat around in a semicircle. Throughout, his eyes were trained steadily on every movement of the pitcher.

Root's first delivery, a fastball right at Lou, was full of bad intentions, forcing him to hit the dirt. Brushing himself off, Lou quickly stepped back in. On the next pitch, as Lou swung with all of the might in his two-hundred-pound body, the ball went soaring into home-run territory. He had carried out the Babe's friendly advice.

If anybody bothered to notice, it was Gehrig's second home run of the game. "The Babe took a host of Walter Mittys with him as he rounded the bases," historian Bruce Catton has written. But Gehrig never seemed to arouse such fantasies in the fans.

That game is remembered best for Ruth's "called shot." In reality, it was Gehrig's Series. Ruth batted .333, with two homers and six runs batted in. Gehrig blasted out nine hits, batted in eight runs, scored nine times, and had three homers and a double, ending with a .529 average.

Yet Gehrig's on-field performance, often rated the best in Series history, was obscured by the Babe's theatrical performance. Lou's postmortem was typical. He mused, seemingly without envy, on what Babe had wrought. "What do you think of the nerve of that big monkey," Gehrig asked. "Imagine the guy calling his shot and getting away with it!"

Some years before this, Marshall Hunt, in the New York *Daily News,* had characterized Lou as being "unspoiled, without the remotest vestige of ego, vanity or conceit," a man who never chose to put himself forward.

Lou's reaction to Babe's homer was ample proof that Hunt was correct.

2

A Boy in the City

At the turn of the century America was a land of Pollyan-naish innocence, full of vast, unpopulated spaces, with an enormous potential for growth. From 1891 to 1910 a great wave of immigrants—over fifteen million of the "wretched refuse" from Germany, Italy, Ireland, England, and Russia—flooded Castle Garden and New York Harbor's Ellis Island, gateways of hope.

"I'd give a million dollars to know what they came for," remarks the fisherman in John Dos Passos's novel *Manhattan Transfer.*

"Just for *that,* Pop," responds the young man in the stern of the boat. "Ain't it the land of opportunity?"

Indeed, America was all of that.

Primitive moviehouses, with five-cent admission fees, were mushrooming over the country. Illustrator Charles Dana Gibson's tiny-waisted "Gibson Girls" were every woman's ideal. James J. Jeffries was the best heavyweight fighter in the world. Little boys read Mark Twain's *Tom Sawyer* and *Huckleberry Finn,* and little girls pored over Louisa May Alcott's *Little Women.* Wilbur and Orville Wright assembled a twelve-horsepower aircraft, with a wingspan of thirty-three feet, that stayed in the air for twelve seconds. Not to be outdone, Henry Ford created his first automobile.

But if America was a place of unexcelled promise, there were also disquieting signs. Baltimore's muckraker Upton Sinclair rudely reminded people that there was an unequal distribution of wealth in the United States. And Negroes, who lived mainly in the South, could have their lives squeezed out at the ends of lynch-mob ropes if they looked at a white woman. When an anarchist named Czolgosz gunned down William McKinley in Buffalo, in 1901, the old Rough Rider Teddy Roosevelt became president.

In New York, the race for taller skyscrapers was on in earnest and the age of the horse was fast coming to an end, to be replaced by cable cars, trolleys, and taxis. At Child's, a popular chain of low-priced eating places, New Yorkers could sip hot soup or devour a cruller with a cup of coffee, for a nickel.

On hot summer nights families often slept on rusty tenement fire escapes, frequently sharing the space with tired geranium plants. During the day knickered boys played games in the gutter on gooey tar surfaces that popped under the sun. Excavation ground along on the city's first real subway and the Great White Way barely extended past Forty-second Street.

In 1903 the first World Series—a best five out of nine—was played, with the Boston Red Sox beating Pittsburgh in eight games before a total of one hundred thousand people. The winner's share was $1,182 for each Boston player.

But it was a handsome collegian from Bucknell, Christy Mathewson of the New York Giants, who towered over the baseball world from Coogan's Bluff at 155th Street, overlooking the Harlem River in Manhattan. In 1905 Mathewson hurled three World Series shutouts against the Philadelphia Athletics.

Johnny Evers, the middle name in the popular baseball poem—extolling the virtues of the ball going from "Tinker to Evers to Chance," shortstop, second baseman, and first baseman, respectively—began his Cubs career in 1902, while Ty Cobb was a year away from the start of his tempestuous baseball odyssey.

The New York Yankees, known as the Highlanders or Hilltoppers, after Hilltop Park, the highest elevation in Manhattan, arrived in New York from Baltimore in 1903, playing in relative obscurity as poor country cousins to the Giants of John McGraw.

Destined to become baseball's religious shrine, Yankee Stadium was twenty years away from gestating into "The House that Ruth Built." Only four years before, in 1899, Columbia College moved uptown to Morningside Heights, from east of Madison Avenue on 49th Street. Seth Low, a reformer and one-time president of Columbia University, was mayor of New York City. He promised to bring decency into city government.

Henry Louis Gehrig was born into this America on June 19, 1903, at 1994 Second Avenue in the lower-middle-class section of Manhattan's Yorkville. Germans and Hungarians, most of whom spoke only a few words of English, were Yorkville's chief residents. The quota of immigrants from Germany was almost as large at the time as that of all Eastern and Mediterranean Europe combined. Lou's parents, Christina Fack and Heinrich Gehrig, were part of that favored group.

Christina was born in 1881 in Wiltser, Schleswig-Holstein, a province of pre–World War I Germany, near the German-Danish border. She emigrated to the United States in 1899. Heinrich was born in Adelheim, Baden, in 1867 and came to America in October 1888. Heinrich originally settled in Chicago, then moved to New York City, where he met Christina. The two were married in 1900.

Christina and Heinrich, both Lutherans, had four children, the first born in 1902. Only Heinrich Ludwig—Henry Louis, the second born—survived past infancy. He weighed almost four-

teen pounds at birth, a reflection, perhaps, of the size and sturdi-
ness of his parents, the statuesque Christina weighing close to
two hundred pounds. Two girls, Anna and Sophie, both died in
little more than a year. A second boy, Lou's only brother, also
died shortly after birth.

Lou Gehrig was raised in a dirt-poor household precariously
close to the poverty level. Lou was not, his mother protested
when her son became famous, "a product of the slums." But she
acknowledged that money had been scarce and hand-me-down
clothes the order of the day.

Heinrich Gehrig, or "Pop" as he was called, had certain me-
chanical skills. In the proper frame of mind, he could be expected
to support Christina and his young son through his work as an
art-metal mechanic. Such a job required steady nerves, as one
pounded various patterns into sheets of metal. When he worked
Heinrich was paid well. But jobs were not easy to come by and his
zeal for employment was limited by his intake of beer or the
mercurial state of his health. Heinrich reported in ill on more
days than one would care to record—an irony considering his
son's later commitment never to miss a single day at his post with
the Yankees.

Under such circumstances, Christina had to work steadily.
She scrubbed, washed, cleaned, cooked, toiled as a maid, took in
the laundry of rich folks, and developed a reputation as a baker.

Since most of Christina's neighbors were also poor, it was
necessary for her to roam outside of her home area to obtain
work. Her services as a cook, specializing in authentic German
dishes like whole roast pig, sauerbraten, roast geese and duck,
and pickled eels, kept the family going.

At an early age Lou was recruited to deliver the laundry that
his mother took home to clean. He never had much money in his
pockets outside of the trolley fares she gave him. Later, when Lou
was with the Yankees, his teammates chided him about his par-
simonious habits. But there was reason for his frugality.

"He's got the first dollar he ever earned," Yankee pals
chorussed, when Lou began to earn decent money. As unkind as

the remark was, it was also prophetic, for years later a postal savings certificate made out to Henry Louis Gehrig and dated October 1, 1914, when Lou was eleven years old, was discovered among his possessions. The amount: one dollar. How Lou earned the dollar, nobody knows, but the likelihood is that it was for one of the many odd jobs he performed as a boy.

With his frequent excursions to saloons and turnvereins (German gymnasiums that accented muscle development), Heinrich was inattentive toward Lou. However, as Heinrich watched his son develop a powerful physique, he became determined to turn Lou into the strongest kid in the neighborhood. He took Lou to his turnverein, introducing him to the many wonders of the weights, parallel bars, and pulleys.

Heinrich also bought Lou a catcher's mitt one Christmas. The gesture went awry, for the mitt was designed for right-handers, while Lou was destined to become a left-handed first baseman. Heinrich Gehrig simply was not aware of such pesky nuances, for he knew nothing about baseball.

Pop Heinrich's attention to Lou's muscular development notwithstanding, Lou drew closer to his mother. She was the family's breadwinner, always encouraging Lou to work hard in grammar school. She had notions that one day her son might become an architect, an accountant, or possibly an engineer. Despite her domineering, smothering traits, Christina was loving and kind toward her son. "He's the only big egg I have in my basket," she once said, in explaining her affection for Lou. "He's the only one of four who lived, so I want him to have the best." It was hardly surprising that Lou became the quintessential momma's boy, with a worshipful attachment to his white-haired, bosomy mother.

If Lou was not exactly a starving urchin out of a Dickens novel, he was forced to work harder and longer than other youngsters, with his labors often intruding into his play time. However, he managed to participate in those games that were in season—soccer, basketball, football, and his favorite, baseball. He ran with surprising speed for such a heavy-thighed boy and was quite expert at street games, such as marbles and chucking snowballs. Indoors he showed skill at checkers and billiards, a game that had been popularized by the wizard, Willie Hoppe. He also took great pride in never missing a day of grade school, even when he was sick.

When Lou was five years old, the Gehrigs left Yorkville, with its dominant German-American flavor, and settled in Washington Heights, where Christina felt the boy could grow up with more air in his lungs and space to roam. The Highlanders made their home not far from where the Gehrigs located, further whetting Lou's appetite for baseball. He attended Public School 132 at 183rd Street and Wadsworth Avenue and was graduated in 1917, at the height of the American involvement in World War I.

At the site of 181st Street and the Hudson River, later to become the approach to the George Washington Bridge, Lou and his friends often dove into the water from a steep precipice, although they had been constantly warned away from such derring-do by concerned parents. Once when Lou, with the aid of a powerful trudgen stroke, made it to Fort Lee Ferry, on the New Jersey side at the bottom of the Palisades, he was rewarded for his efforts by having his ears boxed soundly by his father.

Gehrig's playmates in the Washington Heights section were mostly of Irish, Hungarian, and German extraction. In such an environment he was subjected to some baiting about his German roots. He was known as "Heinie," "dumb Dutchman," or "Kraut-head," in the cruel ways children often employ in dealing with one another. The immigrant experience could often generate pride. It could also produce feelings of shame that were easily ignited through thoughtless indignities. However, Lou's size and his muscles, easily apparent because he rarely wore excess clothing, usually precluded fisticuffs. Other kids did not have to be honor students to realize he could mop up the street with them, if they chose to start anything.

At twelve Lou was a "shy, harassed, worried youngster, in castoff clothes," wrote sportswriter Paul Gallico, "who collected wonderful souvenir picture cards that came with the Sweet Caporal cigarettes that his Dad smoked, or in certain types of penny candy he got as an infrequent treat." On the coldest winter days Lou never wore an overcoat or a hat. His standard garb was a khaki shirt, khaki pants, and a pair of heavy brown work shoes.

As tales of World War I atrocities filtered back to America, Gehrig's neighborhood intimates became increasingly bold with insults. Anyone of German descent could be vilified as a "dirty Hun" or, at the least, as a spy for the despised Kaiser Wilhelm II.

After President Woodrow Wilson proclaimed that America had to enter the war to "make the world safe for democracy," many young men from farms, mills, and offices, who hardly knew where France and Germany were, began arriving on foreign shores in their itchy doughboy uniforms. In such an atmosphere, young Lou, with his German-speaking parents, became vulnerable. Having left Yorkville, Lou had been removed from the security of a neighborhood where there were many "Dutchmen" like himself. Now he was a Dutchman, and a poor one at that, in hostile territory.

Such anti-German hysteria was so pervasive that even veteran ball players like "Heinie" Groh of Cincinnati and "Heinie" Zimmerman of the Giants preferred not being called by their nicknames. They were more pleased to be addressed as Henry.

Boys of Lou's economic and social background did not customarily go to high school after graduation from grammar school, but Lou's mother doggedly insisted that he get a "good education" and not become a "bummer." So Lou was enrolled in Manhattan's High School of Commerce, at 155 West 65th Street. An all-boys school, Commerce was devoted to teaching the fundamentals of bookkeeping, typing, and clerical and secretarial work. Not too many of its students went on to college, though one of Commerce's famous graduates, Billy Rose, the prominent theatrical impresario, learned enough about typing at Commerce to become the secretary to Bernard Baruch, adviser to President Franklin D. Roosevelt.

It was at Commerce that Lou prepared himself to become the quintessential urban product, sprouting from the grassless

sidewalks of New York to play baseball better than most steel-
workers, farmers, millhands, garage mechanics, and country
boys had ever dreamed of playing it.

When Gehrig entered Commerce, the Great War had already
enlisted the services of several baseball stars. Hank Gowdy, a
catcher for the Boston Braves, was the first to depart for "Over
There," followed by many others, including outfielder Eddie
Grant of the Giants, who was killed in France's Argonne Forest.
The battlefield also ensnared Christy Mathewson, who received a
commission in the Chemical Warfare Service. While inspecting
trenches in France he accidentally inhaled a large amount of
poison gas and died in 1925 of tuberculosis, a direct result of
damage to his lungs. Casey Stengel enlisted in the navy and was
put in charge of the Brooklyn Navy Yard baseball team, hardly a
grueling way of sweating out a war.

Despite many losses of personnel to the war, and a feeling
beginning to surface in the country that players were evading
service, baseball decided to go ahead in 1918. Because theater
and film people had been declared "essential" to the war effort,
for morale-building purposes, baseball expected the same exemption. However, by early summer the government decreed
that all healthy, single, draft-age players should participate in
some type of military service or work in an industry essential to
war preparedness, beginning on September 2. Baseball appealed,
but the decision that the game was "nonessential" (like other
sports and amusements) was upheld, the only concession being
a two-week delay so that the World Series could be played. In the
World Series the Red Sox, with pitcher Babe Ruth winning twice,
defeated the Chicago Cubs.

Shortly before Lou completed his high school years the Cincinnati Reds toppled the Chicago White Sox, five games to three,
in the 1919 World Series. Subsequently, eight players on the
White Sox, including their illiterate slugging outfielder "Shoeless
Joe" Jackson and pitchers Eddie Cicotte and Claude "Lefty" Williams, were accused of taking bribes to throw the games. These
eight men, labeled the "Black Sox," were never convicted in any

courtroom, but all of them were banished from organized baseball for life by the newly appointed commissioner, Judge Kenesaw Mountain Landis, who had been hired by the frightened baseball owners to restore the game's reputation. In the first hours of the tumultuous Roaring Twenties, baseball's unassailable purity was at stake.

Many young men, including Gehrig, followed the sensational newspaper headlines about the alleged Black Sox sellout. "Say it ain't so, Joe," a remark supposedly uttered by a distraught youngster as Jackson departed from the grand jury room in Chicago, reflected the nation's sadness over the sullying of its favorite pastime.

"Nineteen-nineteen was the beginning of America's loss of innocence. After the Black Sox scandal there was a great deal of cynicism," said Studs Terkel. "Babe Ruth salvaged the game but the owners didn't like him."

By 1918 Ruth's slugging, not his pitching, was the talk of the American League. The war had decreased the pool of players available so that many of those remaining were pressed into service at more than one position, and Ruth began to play in the outfield. He promptly hit eleven homers for the Red Sox, tying Tilly Walker of the Athletics for the home-run title. In 1919, before the Black Sox Series played itself out, Ruth hit twenty-nine out of the park, for his first home-run title. Gavvy Cravath of the Phillies, in the National League, hit only twelve the same year, but managed to top his league. Wally Pipp led the American League in homers with twelve in 1916, and again in 1917 with nine. Such numbers were picayune in comparison to the explosions about to erupt off Ruth's bat, and he would go on to revolutionize baseball.

Lou was still doing all that he could to help out at home. He worked in a nearby grocery store on Saturdays; during weekdays he worked before and after school. When many other boys were off having fun and vacationing out of the hot city in the summer, Lou put in long, often tedious hours, which often caused him to arrive late for Commerce football practice sessions. One time when Lou showed up with his face blackened with grime, his friends kiddingly suggested that he must have been down in a coal mine. But Lou explained that his father had been ill and so he had to take over his job as a janitor.

Lou's best pal in those days was Mike Sesit, who later attended Columbia and ultimately became a cardiologist. The two were almost inseparable, often spending time together at a Yorkville turnverein at 85th Street and Lexington Avenue, where they engaged in gymnastics. "Lou was about 158 pounds then, mostly belly and ass," Sesit once recalled.

Curiously, when Lou hung on the horizontal bars at the turnverein, his muscle control was noticeably poor and there were times that he complained of sharp pains in his back and legs. "His body," said Sesit, "behaved as if it were drunk." For a young man in such superb physical shape, this was a strange state of affairs.

When Sesit and Lou occasionally had money in their pockets, which wasn't often, they patronized the German coffee shops *(Konditorei)* in the area, indulging themselves on pastries and cakes. They also sometimes stole rides on the trolleys, risking not only disciplinary action from the police but from Lou's father, who had always made it clear to his son that he wouldn't condone such behavior. When the two were arrested one day, Sesit suspected that Lou's father later beat him.

One summer when Lou obtained office work with the Otis Elevator Company in Yonkers, Otis put together a company ball team that played regularly in a Yonkers city league. Lou was their sixteen-year-old southpaw pitcher, playing the infield when he wasn't on the mound. In one of these games he became embroiled with an umpire over a questionable call, almost coming to blows with the umpire, unusual behavior for a young man who had been brought up by his parents to respect authority. (As a major leaguer, Lou was never so far removed from the transient tempests of the ball field that he wouldn't argue with umpires. But never again would he challenge an umpire with his fists.)

Lou earned his first money for ball playing with the Minqua Baseball Club (a tribe of the old Tammany organization), which was sponsored by the Assembly District Democratic Club of West 181st Street. The Minqua team played at places like Floyd Bennett Field in Brooklyn and the Bronx's Reservoir Oval, against semi-pro clubs from Morristown, New Jersey, and from the Bronx. The Minquas played for a $35 guarantee, with the batterymates receiving the munificent sum of $5 each. Lou usually pitched, since first basemen didn't earn as much, and caught when a lefty mitt was available. He appeared seventh or eighth in the batting order.

In the Commerce *Caravel* yearbook of 1921 Lou is pictured with his football teammates, including Sesit, two blacks, and a mix of German-American, Italian, and Jewish youngsters. The caption under the photo spelled his name "Gherig," an error that would be set right in the years to come.

One of those who tried out for the Commerce football team with Lou was a boy named Leonard Lyons, who was about half Lou's size. When Lyons tried to tackle Lou in practice, he was almost buried. Thereafter, Lyons settled for instruction in field-goal kicking from Lou, who excelled at the drop-kicking art and was pleased to teach his small friend. (In later years Lyons became an entertainment columnist for a New York newspaper.)

Money troubles remained a constant fact of life in the Gehrig family. His clothes were still scrubby hand-me-downs, he didn't own an overcoat, and he always brought his lunch—usually an apple—to school. Despite such meager pickings, Lou willingly shared the fruit with his pal Ed Rosenthal, a mortician's son, who became the valedictorian of Gehrig's class and, in due course, the founder of Warner Communications.

There were few days in the fall and spring when Lou and Rosenthal missed having a catch in Commerce's schoolyard, for Rosenthal loved baseball almost as much as Lou did. Each day the two boys brought their baseball gloves to school. In Lou's case, the tattered glove was one of his few prized possessions.

Rosenthal lived with his well-to-do parents above a funeral parlor at 121st Street and Lenox Avenue. He often invited Lou to his home for a meal, but Lou lived too far away for such a venture, so he never had an opportunity to visit with the Rosenthals, who had heard so much about him from their son.

A future Attorney-General of New York, Louis Lefkowitz, also attended Commerce when Lou was there. He remembers Lou as a loner who, when not playing sports, was generally content to stay by himself.

In the classroom Lou was only a fair student, but the principal had a fondness for him and pushed him along in his studies. Lou took a typing class with Mollie Silverman, who also taught English to her students. Invariably, Lou sat in the last seat of Silverman's classroom, his eyes glued to the typewriter in front of him. Now in her nineties, Mollie Silverman Parnis recalls how hard Lou worked at his typing. "He could hit a baseball without missing a stroke," she said affectionately, "but his thick fingers just couldn't seem to find the right keys on the typewriter." In the first years of Lou's major league career, when he traveled outside New York to other American League cities, he never failed to send Mollie Silverman a bouquet of roses from each locality.

During Lou's last year at Commerce his mother took a full-time job cooking and cleaning at the Sigma Nu fraternity house at Columbia. The trip from Washington Heights was long, but the connection with Columbia soon yielded dividends for, while working at Sigma Nu, Christina made the acquaintance of Bobby Watt, who had just returned to Columbia after serving in the air corps during the war. Watt, Columbia's graduate manager of athletics, was on hand one day when Commerce's football team played De Witt Clinton High School at Columbia's South Field on Morningside Heights. Watt was impressed as Lou gave an excellent account of himself in the Commerce backfield, running, kicking, and passing with skill. Equally impressed was Frank "Buck" O'Neil, hired away from Syracuse to coach Columbia's footballers.

Both Watt and O'Neil suggested to Lou's parents that he might seek his higher education at Columbia. Watt was primarily interested in Lou's football prowess, for he wanted to reverse Columbia's gridiron fortunes, only several years after the school

had restored the game to its agenda. Although football and baseball were both major sports at Columbia, it was rare for a young
man to be scouted for his baseball skills. That Watt was taken
with Lou as a football prospect was quite ironic, for Lou had
already reaped a certain measure of prominence in a high school
baseball game that took place in June 1920 in Chicago.

Under Coach Harry Kane, Commerce had assembled a talented group of baseball players. Of all of them, Kane felt Lou was
special. Kane had early spotted Lou's inability to hit curve balls
thrown by left-handed pitchers and he'd worked with him to
overcome the flaw. Now Kane would get a chance to see if his
student had learned his lessons, for the New York *Daily News*
was sponsoring a special inner-city high school baseball game
between the top teams from Chicago and New York—and Commerce had been chosen to represent New York.

When the announcement was made that Commerce would
meet Chicago's Lane Tech at Wrigley Field, the home of the Chicago Cubs, Lou was beside himself with excitement. But it was
necessary, Coach Kane told his boys, for each of them to obtain
their parents' approval to go to Chicago.

After Mom Gehrig returned from work, it was customary for
all three Gehrigs to sit down together for the evening meal. Lou
wasn't certain how his parents would react, but he wasted little
time telling them about the wonderful baseball game in Chicago
and the trip to that city.

"I can't go," said Lou, "without your consent. I hope you'll
give it to me."

Christina flushed with anger. "This baseball is a waste of
time," she said brusquely. "It will never get you anywhere."

"But I want to go, Mom," said Lou, tentatively. "All the other
boys are going."

"I don't care about *other* boys," Christina snapped.

The family discussion, heated at times, went on for several
hours. Lou's mother kept emphasizing that baseball was a
"bunch of nonsense" and a "game for bummers." It could only
end up, she said, keeping Lou from his studies. Pop was not as

recalcitrant as Mom, but he agreed that baseball was a waste and a "peculiar game" for a young man to spend so much time at.

"Coach Kane thinks I'm very good," said Lou.

"You should go to college, instead of this baseball," Mom said.

"I will, Mom," said Lou. "But I want to go to Chicago, too."

Finally, Lou was able to pry loose his mother's grudging consent. But she insisted, as part of her bargain, that the school had to be responsible for Lou while he was in Chicago.

"Thanks, Mom," said Lou, who knew Coach Kane would gladly accept such a compromise.

Most of the unsophisticated Commerce boys had never traveled more than fifty miles from their homes. Now Lou and his teammates headed for Chicago to play a single ball game before thousands of strangers. Each of them, carrying his own glove and equipment, would be sleeping in Pullman berths for the first time and eating in fancy dining cars offering the finest railroad food. At their destination, they would be lodged in hotel rooms.

Word that Commerce's ball players were aboard swept through their train. The way the other riders greeted them they could have been European royalty or reigning movie stars such as Charlie Chaplin and Doug Fairbanks. But they were just kids with names like Bunera, Johnson, Jacobs, Schacht—and Gehrig.

Even a former president of the United States, William Howard Taft, who was then sitting on the Supreme Court, was aboard. Taft had always had an interest in baseball, and as president he had inaugurated the tradition of throwing out the first ball, in 1910, in Washington's home opener.

"I'm looking forward to seeing you boys play," said the jovial Taft, who was introduced to each Commerce boy by Coach Kane.

"They'll give you a good show," promised Kane.

The comic Joey Frisco, also on the train, performed his popular soft-shoe routine and told some jokes. The boys were an appreciative audience for the vaudevillian.

At Wrigley Field, when Commerce's players emerged from

the visitor's dugout, they were greeted with a mixed reception from the ten thousand fans in the stands. When the Cubs played the Red Sox at Wrigley Field in the last World Series game in 1918, twenty-seven thousand people were present. That ten thousand would show up for a high school contest was a sign that baseball was about to enter a postwar era of enormous growth.

Soon the game would be dominated by a new muscular breed of sluggers, men like Ruth, Rogers Hornsby, Lewis "Hack" Wilson, Chuck Klein, Jim Bottomley, Jimmie Foxx, and Gehrig himself. These men, swinging uninhibitedly from the heels and aided by more tightly wound balls, plus a ban on the unsanitary spitball, would become the game's next heroes. Even Ty Cobb, the most creative contact hitter in history, would register twelve homers in 1921, his highest total.

Lou came into the game with Lane Tech with a reputation as a solid high school hitter, but in his first five times at bat he failed to hit safely. With Commerce ahead by 8–6 in the ninth, Lou had one more chance to show what he could do, as Commerce loaded the bases on two walks and a fumbled grounder.

He watched the first pitch go by without swinging, then swung vigorously at the next pitch, sending the ball on an arc toward right field and Sheffield Avenue. The ball finally came to rest on the front porch of a small house facing the ballpark. This grand slam made the final score 12–6, giving Commerce a magnificent victory. Some of Lou's biographers, seeking to magnify the drama, have suggested that the homer tied the score at 6–6. It was dramatic enough without any scoring adjustments.

The game was played in a carnival atmosphere, with motion picture cameras grinding, two bands playing, and photographers jamming the sidelines. The next day's papers joined in with gusto, applauding Commerce's emerging slugger: "Gehrig's blow would have made any big leaguer proud, yet it was walloped by a boy who hasn't yet started to shave," bubbled the *Chicago Tribune,* underneath a seven-column banner headline. The *New York Times* erupted with "the real Babe Ruth never poled one more thrilling." But just as Commerce's yearbook had mangled the spelling of Lou's name, so did the *Times*: In its story he was "Gherrig."

The sponsoring newspaper, the New York *Daily News,* was expectedly ecstatic about the high school heroics. Their entire back page featured photos of Lane Tech's conquerors, with one shot of the Commerce boys riding in an open-air bus, most of them grinning from ear to ear.

There was further hoopla after the event. When the second section of the Twentieth Century Limited pulled into New York's Grand Central Terminal at 11:15 the morning after the victory, five thousand people waited to greet its valuable cargo. Though the train was two hours late, the crowd remained calm until the boys stepped off the train, at which point all five thousand let loose with everything but rebel yells.

As the boys were whisked up Park Avenue by bus, the Hebrew Orphan Asylum Band provided musical accompaniment. In Commerce's auditorium, the superintendent of schools lavishly praised the young men and talked of their experience in "wild and woolly Chicago."

He also slipped in a mention of one particular home run by one particular batter.

3

Roar, Lion, Roar

When Gehrig was graduated from Commerce High School in 1921, there were few college football or baseball scouts scouring the country for talent. Potential stars were not pursued relentlessly or seduced the way they have been in the last half-century. In the twenties college baseball was barely subsidized, and in many schools it was not a major sports activity. Few college teams played extended schedules and the major leagues depended primarily on a network of high and low minor leagues to train talent.

However, word about Gehrig did not escape the attention of many college alumni and athletic directors, for his Wrigley Field home run wasn't a clandestine act. It had been headlined in New York, as well as in the Chicago newspapers. The whispers about this young man with thighs as big around as a bull's stomach had reached many athletics departments. Gehrig already seemed to possess a geyser of talents, even if at times he was as awkward as an uninvited guest at a lawn party.

Trying to shepherd his school out of the sports doldrums, Bobby Watt was eager for Gehrig to matriculate at Columbia. Indeed, he helped Lou gain admission by arranging for him, after graduation from Commerce, to obtain sufficient credits to meet the high standards of the school through preparation at the college's extension department. After several months of intensive study, Gehrig completed his extension course satisfactorily and passed the college board examinations. He was then granted a football scholarship.

Fifteen years before Gehrig arrived at Morningside Heights, Edward Trowbridge Collins, from Millerton, New York, played football and baseball at Columbia. In 1907 he coached the baseball team. He went on to become a Hall of Fame second baseman with the Philadelphia Athletics and Chicago White Sox. When the Black Sox scandal exploded, Collins was part of the blameless faction not involved in the fix. With Collins preceding him, Lou would become the second Columbia Lion to distinguish himself in baseball.

But even before Lou set foot on a Columbia diamond or gridiron, he was cast in the most unlikely role of dissembler. Several major league baseball scouts, having seen Lou play at Commerce, began sniffing around the Gehrig household. Overtures to Lou were made by Arthur Irwin, representing himself as a friend and scout for John McGraw's Giants, and by Art Devlin, a former third baseman for the Giants and a Georgetown University graduate. Irwin promised Lou that he would come under the watchful eye of McGraw himself, who was reputed to possess rare instincts for assessing talent.

Keenly aware of his family's need for money, Lou was vulnerable to the scouts' sales pitch. Picking up extra money in the summer playing baseball sounded like a good proposition. To suggest that Lou was innocent and guileless may be stretching a point, but it's possible he had only sketchy familiarity with the rules of college athletic competition. In addition, both Irwin and

Devlin were older authority figures, and Lou was inclined to have respect for such people.

Gehrig always insisted that he had no idea he would be barred from Columbia's teams if he accepted the play-for-pay offer. He didn't know, for example, that Collins, prior to his senior year at Columbia, had played semi-pro ball in New England, plus some additional games for the Athletics in 1906, all under the name of "Sullivan." This indiscreet episode cost Collins his last year of baseball eligibility at Columbia.

Gehrig reported to the Polo Grounds for several days of workouts, believing he would receive a fair tryout under the imperious but discerning eye of McGraw. What he got, instead, was an old-fashioned brush-off from the man who had developed so many young players, including Freddy Lindstrom, who played third base for Lane Tech the day Lou hit his homer in the ninth.

Dragging a beat-up first baseman's glove to the Polo Grounds at eleven in the morning, Gehrig quickly realized that McGraw was in no mood to pay him much attention. Preoccupied with a temporary decline in his team's fortunes, McGraw ignored Devlin's entreaties, even after Lou belted a half-dozen pitches into the stands. When Lou let an easy roller sift through his legs at first base, McGraw had seen enough.

"Get this fellow out of here!" he barked. "I've got enough lousy players without another one showing up." He then delegated Fred Logan, the clubhouse manager, to inform Lou not to come back.

As a result of such peremptory treatment, Lou developed an understandable distaste for the man called the "Little Napoleon," a redundancy if there ever was one. And to the Little Napoleon's eternal discredit, he missed the boat on this budding star.

Refusing to accept the failure of a mission, Devlin told the disappointed Lou he might be able to arrange for him to go to Hartford in the Class A Eastern League, with whom the Giants had a working arrangement. When Lou at last inquired whether playing for Hartford might harm his chances of playing in college, the scout assured him it wouldn't mean a thing.

That settled it. Lou decided to go to Hartford, Connecticut's capital, some 130 miles from New York City. At the time, Hartford thrived as an insurance center and producer of Fuller brushes, Underwood typewriters, and horseshoe nails. He would play under the assumed name of "Lou Lewis," as Devlin suggested. With this nom de first baseman affixed, in a silly attempt to preserve his amateur status, shouldn't Lou have been suspicious that he was being led down the wrong path? Why didn't the alteration of his name, poorly camouflaged as it was, suggest to him that something was fishy?

On June 2, 1921, the local Hartford papers, the *Times* and the *Courant,* announced that a "hard-hitting semi-pro from Brooklyn [sic], Lefty Gehrig, had been signed to play first base for the Hartford Senators." From that time on no further mention was made of Gehrig's real name. He was referred to only as "Lewis" or "Lou Lewis."

On June 3, 1921, with "Lou Lewis" playing the entire game at first base, the Hartford Senators beat the Pittsfield Hillies, 2–1. In his first game, Lou failed to get a hit in three times at bat. In reporting on Lou's debut, the *Hartford Courant* said Gehrig "appeared a bit nervous. After he gets used to the surroundings, he may develop. They seldom fail to make the grade with Arthur Irwin teaching them the ways of baseball."

When Lou got two hits on June 5, as Hartford belted Albany 10–2, the local papers trotted out their comparisons to Ruth, just as the Chicago papers had when Lou hit his Wrigley Field blast.

On June 8, the *Hartford Times* raved about a two-base hit that Lou hit up against the Buick advertising sign on the right-field fence. "Gehrig may not get a Buick for his clout," said the paper, "but he may be riding one before the season runs its course."

After a contest on June 15, Gehrig's name—or Lefty Lewis's name—never appeared again that summer in the Hartford box scores. As Lou Lewis he played a dozen games for Hartford, batting .261 in forty-six times at bat, while going hitless in only three games. His twelve hits included two triples, one double, but no home runs. His fielding still left much to be desired, but it was clear he had the potential to be a powerful hitter.

During his dozen games, Hartford won eight out of thirteen,

with Lou sitting out one game. The club climbed into first place in the Eastern League, but after Lou departed, the Senators fell to fifth. In a strange footnote to Gehrig's inaugural summer, Irwin, who had been born in Toronto and played in the big leagues before coming to Hartford, fell or jumped from a steamer during a voyage from New York to Boston. He was never heard from again. On that same day, Gehrig left Hartford to return to Columbia.

Whether Gehrig quit Hartford because of homesickness for his mother's cooking or because of the prodding of Andy Coakley, the Columbia baseball coach, nobody will ever know for sure. But we do know that when Coach Coakley discovered that Lou Lewis of Hartford was Henry Louis Gehrig, his fine baseball prospect, he paid Lou a visit and Lou quickly returned home.

It remained for Lou to win back his good standing, not only with Columbia, but with the other colleges that had relationships with the Lions. Watt took up Lou's case, for he felt Gehrig had committed an innocent mistake that shouldn't deprive him of a role in Columbia's sports program. While recognizing that Lou should pay some price for his indiscretion, Watt believed making him permanently ineligible was too harsh a penalty. Accordingly, Watt wrote to the schools that competed against the Lions in football and baseball, explaining what Gehrig had done, and recommending that Lou should be barred from competition in his freshman year in football and from baseball in his sophomore year. It remained for those who played against Lou to call the turn.

They did exactly that, tempering their collective judgment with mercy. Columbia's athletic rivals, including Dartmouth, Cornell, Amherst, and Middlebury (there was no formal Ivy League at that time), indicated they would have no objections if Gehrig returned to regular football and baseball competition in 1922 and 1923.

Certainly, Lou wasn't made to suffer for the subterfuge at Hartford, but for the rest of his life he remained unrelenting in his belief that McGraw had misled him by trying to conceal his professionalism from the authorities. McGraw, however, bitterly contended that such a ruse was hardly unusual during that period. He never stopped asserting that Gehrig had walked out on him.

But if McGraw had wound up with Lou on first base, what in heaven's name would he have done with Bill Terry!

Off the Sundial

On the sidelines for a year, Gehrig practiced faithfully. He loved to punt footballs, spending hours on South Field as groups of students scrambled after the ball. There was only one thing he liked to do more than punt. That was to hit baseballs toward the gilded statue of Alma Mater on the library steps on the other side of 116th Street.

Buck O'Neil thought Gehrig would make a fine lineman, despite the fact that Lou had been named as a Metropolitan all-scholastic halfback while at Commerce. But O'Neil knew the boy could also run well with the football. So the two achieved a modus vivendi. Lou would play halfback, and occasionally switch to the line, where he could serve as a tackler because of his bulk.

As a halfback Lou teamed up with Columbia's captain, Wally Koppisch, a superb running back with all-American credentials. However, in the Columbia yearbook of 1923 there is a photograph of Lou with a caption that reads "Gehrig, Tackle." The yearbook's roster also created uncertainty about where Lou belonged, for he was listed as "guard."

In the opening game of 1922 Columbia walloped Ursinus, a school in Collegeville, Pennsylvania, with Koppisch romping for three touchdowns and "lineman" Lou running for two. Paul Gallico, then writing in Columbia's *Alumni News,* was ecstatic about Gehrig's abilities as a runner. "Gehrig is the beef expert," he wrote, "who has mastered the science of going where he is sent, for at least five yards. His plunges seemed to carry force."

Amherst, the next opponent, fell to the Lions by the lopsided score of 43–6, as Lou set up a touchdown for Koppisch with one of his typical line plunges from the ten-yard marker.

The Lions remained undefeated, licking Wesleyan 10–6, but Lou wasn't a headliner in that game. Then Columbia beat New York University, 6–2, although to this day NYU claims the victory, 7–6, on a disputed play.

Williams administered the first defeat to Columbia, 13–10, with Gallico noting that the Lions' "nearest approach to the enemy goal in the first half was when Gehrig made a perfect kick to the Williams five-yard line."

Columbia then traveled to Ithaca, New York, where "Gloomy Gil" Dobie's team pounced on the Lions, 56–0. Lou shifted to the line against unbeaten Cornell. In the opening period, when Cornell punted to Columbia's five-yard line, Gehrig received the ball and promptly booted it back toward the middle of the gridiron, a typical tactic of that time. Eddie Kaw, Cornell's captain, caught Lou's punt and ran it back for his team's first score.

The Lions rebounded against Middlebury, 17–6, the next week. But then they succumbed to Dartmouth, 28–7. Gehrig played his final game against Colgate, on November 30, 1922. Though the Lions were shellacked, 59–6, Lou registered "two" touchdowns. The first was disallowed when Koppisch ignored a fair catch by a Colgate back. Lou snatched the ball and ran for a touchdown—but it didn't count. The Columbia touchdown that did count was on a forty-yard pass to Lou before the first half ended.

If Lou needed an orientation course on how to accept defeat,

his indoctrination with Columbia's footballers was ideal. However, those who played with him insist he was not one to give up
easily. "He was a battler," says Robert Pulleyn, of Oldwick, New
Jersey, one of two surviving members of that 1922 squad. "On the
football field Lou worked with everything he had."

Lou was also quick to help his teammates. During a grueling
practice scrimmage one afternoon, one of tackle John Donaldson's fingers was suddenly pulled out of joint, causing him to
jump up and down in pain. Taking one look at the finger, Lou
informed Donaldson he knew exactly what to do. He then proceeded to yank the balky finger back into place.

The same difficulties that Lou had with his body at the turnvereins continued when he played football at Columbia. His
thighs and lower legs constantly needed to be rubbed down vigorously, with compresses often being applied by the team
trainer.

But it was the image of Lou the baseball player that generally
remained in the minds of those Columbians who had dormitory
rooms that faced South Field.

"I was sitting one afternoon, cramming for an exam in Hartley Hall," recalled Donaldson, "when I heard a bunch of students
down below give a big yell. I looked out of the window just in time
to see a ball bouncing off the top of the sundial, maybe some four
hundred fifty feet from home plate. And there was Lou standing
there, in his baggy knickers, grinning from ear to ear. You don't
forget things like that."

The two years at Columbia for Lou were not all line plunges,
sports-page hyperbole, and legendary home runs. Lou's mother
continued to work hard at the Sigma Nu fraternity house, and his
father was ill a good deal of the time. Lou tried to help when he
had time away from his books and athletics.

For over a half-century Gehrig has been proudly claimed by
many generations of Columbia alumni as one of their own. Yet
it's doubtful that he experienced full acceptance while he was at
Morningside. At Phi Delta Theta, where he was pledged, he
waited on tables and performed other tasks. Some fraternities
welcomed good students or prize athletes, while others preferred

clones of themselves, young men of similar social backgrounds, bank accounts, or religion. Gehrig's credentials in these departments were lacking, so he was forced to rely on athletic prowess to win approval. But his social background, his immigrant parents who spoke poor English, his clumsiness off the field, and his bulging physical dimensions (his "architectural amplitudes," as *Vanity Fair* put it) made him an easy target for ridicule.

Lou never forgot or forgave the snobbery he endured at Columbia. Years later he would confide to his wife about the arrogant, mean-spirited condescension of many of his more privileged classmates, whose food his mother had cooked and he had served along Fraternity Row. Even in his own frat house, instead of being accepted as a fraternity brother, he had been looked down on by many as a clumsy, poor boy who couldn't pay his debts (for years he owed a small amount of money to the fraternity, a debt he never did repay). Whenever Columbia came calling in the years of Lou's fame, he generally turned a deaf ear to their entreaties.

Gehrig had few contacts with Columbia after he left it. Coach Coakley, a man to whom he thought he owed much for his professional success, was one of those he saw as a friend. Thirteen years after his Columbia days, Lou wrote a typical, formal response to a Columbia questionnaire that was sent to him by the *Columbia Alumni News:*

> I have been in the employ of the New York Yankees owned by Colonel Jacob Ruppert since June, 1923.
> My recreations are almost every form of sport.
> My hobbies are good books and athletic contests.
> I married Miss Eleanor Twitchell on September 29, 1933. No children.
> Sorry that I cannot accomodate [sic] you with a recent picture.
> Cordially, Lou Gehrig.

Encouraged to dwell on his Columbia experience, Gehrig didn't choose to do so.

One Columbia social activity, though, that was pleasurable for Lou was the annual Frosh-Soph Rush, a traditional fall jamboree. Letting off steam has always been an acceptable, if antisocial, pastime at Columbia, as well as other colleges. In the twenties the Frosh-Soph Rush was a quasi-athletic ritual, an informal rugby scrum, with a heavy accent on swinging fists and kicking. More than one participant ended up with a bloody nose or broken finger.

The 1922 Rush had almost degenerated into a full-scale riot, with the frosh getting the better of it. Word went out from the sophs that reinforcements were badly needed. Lou, a soph, was in Hartley Hall, safely tucked away from the scene of the crime. He was hardly one to fear physical contact, but having always thought of himself as an underdog, he wasn't displeased that the frosh were winning. When several soph classmates pleaded with him to join their cause, Lou somewhat reluctantly dashed to South Field. In short order, "this genial, lumbering giant," as Charles A. Wagner, a Columbia student, reported at the time, "loomed over the seething bundles of turmoil as a kind of Paul Bunyan." Dropping his armful of books Gehrig pitched into the fray with what seemed great zest, laughing through it all. Even in a fight Lou was a friendly type.

Lou worked hard at his studies, compiling a modest scholastic record. Considering the time he spent on sports, his C's weren't all that lackluster.

John Erskine, a professor of literature, appears to have kindled Lou's dormant intellectual curiosity. Erskine was a witty lecturer and writer of satiric novels who appealed to aesthetic scholars as well as to those who spent more hours on South Field than with their books. He often had the entire class, including Lou, rolling in the aisles as his sonorous voice jibed at such figures as Shakespeare, Thomas Carlyle, Pepys, and Ben Johnson.

Vernon B. Hampton, a fellow student of Gehrig's in Erskine's class, recalled how "Lou loved breaking out that wonderful grin of his, hearing Erskine's juicy morsels of literary scandal." One day in Schermerhorn Hall, Hampton said, as the class was examining a prehistoric beast of gigantic proportions, Lou got caught trying to slide down the monster's neck.

But it was in Professor Robert L. Schuyler's American history class that Lou showed special insight and memory. "Lou's prominence caused Professor Schuyler to frequently look at him over the rim of his glasses, as he would ask some question such as 'Mr. Gehrig, please explain the philosophy of the American Revolution, from the colonial standpoint.' With Lou sitting next to me, because alphabetically we were often in proximity to each other, the questioning was getting rather close to me, so I would shrink slightly, being much smaller beside Gehrig's huge bulk and fearing I would be next in line," recalled Hampton. "But Lou always knew the answer—he was a student as well as an athlete—and Schuyler invariably veered away to ask the next question somewhere else in the classroom. I was always glad that Gehrig had done the studying, for all too often I didn't know the lesson myself."

When Lou reported to Coach Coakley for Columbia's spring practice in 1923, for his only baseball season with the Lions, the country had just completed two years with Warren Harding in the White House. In those early days of the Era of Wonderful Nonsense, people were humming "Yes, We Have No Bananas" or "Tea for Two," and two Yale men started a weekly newsmagazine named *Time*. (In the 1930s Gehrig's picture would appear on *Time*'s cover.)

The Yankees were on the road to their third straight American League pennant, and their first world championship, which they'd win against the hated Giants. That 1923 spring the Yankees were also a month away from settling into their new three-deck, reinforced-concrete palace in the Bronx at 161st Street and River Avenue, directly across the Harlem River from the Polo Grounds, where they had been unwelcome tenants for a decade.

On April 18, the same cool afternoon that Gehrig was pitching for Columbia at South Field against Williams and striking out a record seventeen batters, Yankee Stadium opened its gates. Appropriately, the Babe christened the edifice with its first home run and seventy-five thousand fans roared in approval.

At Columbia, Lou pitched and played first base and the outfield. In some games, such as the April 3 opener against NYU and the April 7 game with CCNY, he played first base and pitched. Coakley felt that by shuffling Lou around he could do the team the most good. Whenever he was asked about Gehrig after Lou became a star with the Yankees Coakley responded that he had been the most enthusiastic, hardest-working player he'd ever coached. He denied that Gehrig was a "made" player, pointing out that the only thing he could take credit for was teaching Lou how to hit curves. One day in the 1923 season Coakley overheard the coach of one of Columbia's rivals advising his starting pitcher to throw Lou "nothing but curves—that's his weakness." "I was happy to hear that," recalled Coakley. "I knew Lou would handle it."

Coakley once told columnist Frank Graham that by college standards "Lou was a fair outfielder, a first baseman without any glaring weaknesses, and a good pitcher. In the outfield he covered a lot of ground, got most of the drives hit his way, and got the ball away fast with his strong arm. As a pitcher, he didn't have much stuff but he did have a better fastball than most college pitchers. Some days no college team could beat him."

In emphasizing that Gehrig's natural position seemed to be first base, Coakley conceded that Lou still had a lot to learn there but he was convinced he would master the skills that would make him a great first baseman. So much for the theories, often spread at the time, that Lou was as awkward as a gorilla at the position.

Lou's 1923 season with the Lions consisted of nineteen games, from April 3 to June 9, when the Lions closed against Penn. In that contest Gehrig was the losing pitcher. He played ten games at first base, eleven as pitcher, and three as a combination pitcher and first baseman. In one game, against Rutgers, he played right field.

He batted .444, with an astounding slugging percentage of .937, including six doubles, two triples, seven home runs, and five stolen bases. He came to bat sixty-three times, scored twenty-four runs, and had twenty-eight hits. Unfortunately, Columbia's statisticians did not compile runs-batted-in.

As a pitcher, Gehrig won six games and lost four, with one no decision. In five of the eleven games Lou struck out ten or more batters, including his performance against Williams, a contest the Lions somehow managed to lose. (Gehrig's strikeout mark of seventeen stood as a Columbia standard, until Paul Brosnan equaled it against Rhode Island in 1968.)

On April 21, playing at Cornell's new diamond in Ithaca, New York, Lou connected for his first home run for Columbia. George T. Moeschen was the captain and second baseman of that Lion team. At the age of eighty-seven, Moeschen vividly recalled the Gehrig blow: "That right field at Cornell had a high fence, then there was a road back of it, then a forest. Lou lifted his home run into the forest. I looked over at Coach Coakley, sitting near me on the bench, and he was slapping his head in wonder."

After the game, the Cornell coach and Coakley walked off the field together. The main subject of the conversation was not the Columbia victory, which was credited to Lou (with ten strike-outs), but Lou's long homer. "That young fellow Gehrig doesn't leave anything up to the umps," Coakley said. To this day Cornellians insist nobody has ever hit a ball farther at Ithaca.

On April 26, playing at Rutgers, Lou covered right field the whole afternoon and blasted two home runs. Before the game, on the train, Coakley was joined by Yankee scout Paul Krichell, who was on one of his busman's holidays. Other local colleges such as NYU and Fordham weren't playing that day, so Krichell thought he'd hop over to Rutgers to see if there were any promising youngsters on the field. Krichell asked Coakley if Columbia had anyone worth watching. Yes, said Coakley, there's a left-handed kid who throws pretty good, and he hits, too. Krichell assumed Coakley would start this boy on the mound. Instead, Columbia used a right-hander. Coakley must have altered his plans, thought Krichell.

But Krichell soon discovered a square-shouldered kid playing right field for Columbia. Twice this boy came to the plate and smashed home runs that disappeared into the trees surrounding Rutgers' field. He also managed to grab a couple of fly balls without getting hit on the head. If the boy had not mastered the finer points of outfield play, he had certainly picked up a few precious details about slugging.

After the game, Krichell was curious about the disappearance of the left-handed pitcher. "He was that kid in right field," laughed Coakley.

"He can sure hit a baseball," said Krichell. "What's the boy's name?"

"Lou Gehrig," said Coakley. "When he isn't pitching, I play him at first base or in the outfield."

When Krichell returned to New York he practically flew into the office of Ed Barrow, the Yankees' general manager, who had been hired away from the Red Sox just as Ruth had been.

Krichell had been a reserve catcher with the St. Louis Browns for two years, 1911–1912. As someone with a healthy respect for home runs, Krichell had never hit a single homer in his own brief time in the majors. Despite this background, Krichell would become the most respected scout in baseball, perhaps Barrow's most important acquisition, outside of Ruth himself. In time, not only would Krichell bring Gehrig to the Yankees but he would end up having recruited three-fourths of the 1927 infield—Gehrig at first base, Mark Koenig at shortstop, and "Poosh 'Em Up Tony" Lazzeri at second base. Krichell came to know the frailties, idiosyncrasies, and strengths of every player Colonel Ruppert employed. His judgment was never influenced by the usual baseball stereotypes, for he'd travel for miles to scout a little guy as well as a big one.

When baseball scouts like Krichell spot talent like Gehrig it's hard for them to conceal their excitement. Even a cache of gold doesn't work up their adrenaline the way a Gehrig or a Bob Feller does.

"I think I've just seen another Babe Ruth" was Krichell's euphoric message to Barrow, who could not have been blamed if he considered Krichell slightly dotty. Ruths, he knew, didn't grow on trees, whether at Rutgers or Columbia. So Barrow advised Krichell to take another look. (Joe Judge, the Washington first baseman, and a Brooklyn native, had earlier been tipped off about Gehrig by Coakley. Judge informed Clark Griffith, the Washington owner, about the boy—but somehow Griffith's New York scout failed to follow up on the suggestion, a monumental mistake if there ever was one.)

When the Lions played their next game with NYU on April 28 at South Field, Krichell was there, along with a few hundred other souls. Coakley started Lou on the mound that day, but Krichell wasn't interested in Lou's pitching. The Yankees—with Waite Hoyt, Herb Pennock, Bob Shawkey, "Bullet Joe" Bush, "Sad Sam" Jones, and Carl Mays—had a surfeit of hurlers. It was Lou's hitting power he had come to see, and Lou didn't disappoint: He belted a nonstop home run all the way to 116th Street and Broadway, some 450 feet away. The blow has since been described as the second-longest home run in South Field history. The longest would be hit by Lou against Wesleyan on May 19. That one bounced high off the Journalism School steps.

Gehrig's performance against NYU also included a single, two walks, eight strikeouts, and only six hits allowed the opposition. Those accustomed to Columbia's less-than-hysterical attitude toward sports might be surprised how the events of that April afternoon were memorialized in the Columbian Room files:

> Columbians had followed the high school star, Lou Gehrig, and had cheered as he earned national fame during the first Columbia season. Now, in this climactic NYU game, he was good on the mound and sensational at the plate! . . . Several days later, "Columbia Lou" Gehrig signed his first major league contract.

5

Coming to the Yankees

The life of a baseball scout in the 1920s was a sweltering odyssey through anonymous cities and hamlets—a Snow-Shoe, Pennsylvania; an Ashflat, Arkansas; a Ninety-six, South Carolina; a Blessing, Texas—with cockroach-infested, airless hotel rooms more often than not the order of the day. Driving an old automobile from one port of call to another, a scout lived on short wages, stomach-grinding food, and sly tips and hints from winking know-it-alls who had seen a remarkable kid in this or that town or on this or that rutted sand lot.

A scout lived on hopes and hunches. Disconcerting false alarms added to his general fatigue and the club's gasoline bill. He had to be a hardened traveler, searching for some kid he'd never seen before and might never see again. A scout knew, and always insisted, that there would be another Cobb, another Matty—and maybe in some godforsaken village, another Ruth.

A scout like the bow-legged, chubby Krichell practiced an inexact science, to say the least. He could make practical judgments about batting eye, power, muscular coordination, and speed around the bases, but he could not assess to any degree of perfection a young prospect's visceral commitment, concentration, burning faith, or mental attitude.

Leo Durocher, the combative manager of successful teams in Brooklyn and New York, once summed up the qualities that make for a complete big leaguer: a fellow who can hit, hit with power, run, throw, and catch. However, there were traits Durocher didn't include: discipline, temperament, character, resolve, and work habits.

In today's market an insightful scout must also know something about a young man's companions, about how he sleeps (or doesn't) on airlines, and about how money (or lack of it) influences his efforts. In 1923 Krichell didn't have to analyze any of these factors. What he saw at Rutgers and at South Field was a bulky twenty-year-old with immense hitting power. From an admiring coach Krichell also learned that the boy had a domineering mother who would prefer that her son finish out his education at Columbia. If Krichell had prepared a written scouting report on his candidate, he might have penned a caustic memorandum: "Tough hitter, tougher mother."

So, after Gehrig hit his huge blast out to 116th Street and Broadway, Krichell pushed his way through a noisy pride of Lions to reach Gehrig in the dressing room of Furnald Hall, a dormitory facing Broadway and 115th Street. They talked amid the tumult. "I'm Paul Krichell. I scout for the Yankees," the stranger said, holding out his hand. If Lou figured it was a joke, he was quickly disabused of that notion when Krichell proposed that Lou come to the Yankee offices the next morning.

With Coach Coakley along for guidance, Lou arrived a few minutes late for the appointment, enough to make Krichell squirm. Ed Barrow and Krichell wasted little time telling Gehrig he had a promising future in the Yankee organization. They laid on the table an offer of $2,000 for the remaining four months of the season and $1,500 as a bonus for signing, a veritable Comstock lode to Lou and his family. With his mother down with pneumonia and his father constantly complaining about his health, Gehrig, in good conscience, couldn't resist.

Prior to making his final commitment to the Yankees, Gehrig sought the advice of Professor Archibald Stockder of Columbia's Business School, where Lou was taking an undergraduate course. Lou told Professor Stockder of the Yankee offer and added that he had to make an immediate decision. He also pointed out that his parents had their hearts set on his graduating from college and then pursuing a profession. A considerate, contemplative man, Stockder leaned back in his chair and looked squarely in Lou's eyes. "Lou," he said, without harshness, "you've been in my class for almost a year . . . I think you better play ball." When Lou completed his first season with the Yankees, Professor Stockder received a beautiful box of Corona Coronas from him, with a hand-written expression of gratitude.

"The financial inducement for me to leave Columbia was tremendous," Lou said years later in the *Sporting News.* "The money they put before me was enough to turn any kid's head. I was still not sure I wanted to go into baseball as a steady profession, but I decided to grab what I could of it. That's the wrong way to look at baseball and I soon changed my mind."

It was a frightened, unassertive young man who reported at Yankee Stadium to manager Miller Huggins on a bluebird-sky summer afternoon in 1923. Huggins was a gnomelike figure of five-four who looked as if he should have been riding horses at racetracks rather than riding herd on an irrepressible gang of Yankee players, but he had been a fine defensive second baseman in the National League, as well as a skilled leadoff batter. Soaking wet, he may have weighed 135 pounds but he was capable of handling men who were almost double his size. Oddly, Huggins had set out to be a lawyer until one of his professors, William Howard Taft, advised him to choose baseball. "You can become a pleader or a player," said Taft, "but not both. You seem to like baseball better."

Coming to the Yanks in 1918 as manager, after five years as manager of the Cards, Huggins was at first overshadowed by McGraw, the hotheaded genius across the river. By 1921, with Ruth, Bob Meusel, and Whitey Witt in the outfield, Wally Pipp at first base, Everett Scott at shortstop, Frank "Home Run" Baker at third base, Aaron Ward at second, and Wally Schang catching, the Yanks won the pennant. In 1922, they won again. Each time they lost to the Giants in the World Series.

It was not clear where the big kid from Morningside Heights would fit into this array of Yankee talent. Pipp, a Chicagoan, had been a fixture at first base for the Yankees since 1915. He was rated as one of the best clutch hitters on the club and was an excellent fielder. An aggressive man on an aggressive team, he had once knocked Ruth off his feet when the Babe criticized his defensive prowess. Just thirty years old in 1923, Pipp appeared a cinch to be Huggins's first baseman for several more years.

Huggins knew little about Gehrig when Lou first reported to the Yankees, other than the hearty endorsement from Krichell. Somehow, he thought the youngster might be Jewish. After all, Gehrig was a New York boy, New York had a large Jewish popula-tion—and just what kind of a name was Gehrig? For years McGraw had searched, without success, for a Jewish ball player to add to his Polo Grounds cast. The tyrannical Irishman was aware of the yearning of his sizable Jewish clientele for one of their own for whom they could cheer. If Gehrig disappointed Huggins by not being Jewish, his hitting made up for it.

The baseball world that Gehrig entered in 1923 was peopled mainly by southern boys off farms—but not, of course, southern black boys (they were barred and invisible, as they were in most working and social segments of American society). There were tough Irish, Germans, and Poles, too, many of them trading in their jobs in factories, mills, and mines to play baseball. College-bred ball players like Christy Mathewson, Frankie Frisch of Ford-ham, Bill Wambsganss of Concordia College (Fort Wayne, In-diana), Paul Waner of State Teacher's College (Ada, Oklahoma), George Sisler of Michigan, Eddie Collins of Columbia, Eddie Plank of Gettysburg College, Harry Hooper of St. Mary's, and Gehrig himself were a rarity.

Baseball's environmental pace at that time was slow, relaxed, even somnolent. There were no screeching scoreboards bombarding fans with highlights, commercials, and electronic games that noisily vied with the action on the field. There was no instant replay on TV to second-guess and harass umpires. In fact, there was no television to contribute to the destruction of a wide network of small-town minor league farm teams, from Triple A down to D classification. There was no unyielding AstroTurf to jeopardize the careers of the players.

Baseball was truly a leisurely pastime. For millions who crowded into America's urban neighborhoods, it was an ersatz pastoral experience. Games were played under sparkling blue skies, in glorious sweet-smelling daylight. Most players, if they had wives, usually got home for supper not long after six o'clock, and most of them lived near the ballpark. If they weren't out carousing or belting down the booze (as many of them did), they got eight or nine hours of sleep, then journeyed to the place of their employment. There would be batting and fielding practice in the early afternoon, mindless joking in the dugouts, and a chance to sit and talk baseball, endlessly.

Rogers Hornsby, the cold-eyed line-drive hitter who won six straight National League batting crowns from 1920 to 1925, with three marks over .400, would never think of discussing anything except hitting. He never went to the movies, fearing that the flickering black-and-white images would destroy his batting eye; the only things he ever read were the racetrack odds. "Baseball is my life," growled Hornsby; "it's the only thing I know and care about."

Not all ball players of the twenties shared Hornsby's monomania. But when they "hung around," as many of them did after ball games, they liked to talk about the game they played and loved, for they were not businessmen first and ball players second, as many are today.

The price of admission to ballparks was a few quarters. A hot

dog was a nickel, as was a bag of peanuts. There was time between innings to talk to your neighbor, for the noise level was
more salutary.

There were no 162-game schedules or TV-generated dual
climaxes of seven-game championship playoffs followed by the
traditional seven-game World Series, games that ultimately wear
pitching staffs to a frazzle.

The chief activity of ball players on the road in the musty,
non-air-conditioned hotels was skirt-chasing and lobby-sitting. A
man could furtively pick his teeth in comfort, scan his newspaper, or sign autographs for kids, who then as now always knew
where the ball players stopped when they came to town. Each
team had its "iron-ass," a man capable of sitting for interminable
hours in hotel lobbies without moving a muscle or blinking an
eye.

On stifling nights in hotel rooms some players would soak
their sheets under cold water and then wrap themselves up in the
hope they could buy a few hours of sleep. (Gehrig often did that,
winding up with aching joints from the chill.)

When teams traveled by rail from one city to another there
were endless card games of bridge, poker, gin rummy, and
hearts. Sometimes the stakes would get too high and tempers
would flare. But card-game relationships bred great camaraderie.
(Today many managers discourage card-playing in the clubhouse.) Writers traveling with the teams had more time to collect
anecdotes, rumors, and lies, while the more curious players
could watch America pass by outside their windows.

On Saturdays and Sundays, as fans walked on their hometown streets, they could hear radio accounts of ball games waft-
ing out of open windows. In the early evening in cities like New
York, tabloids would arrive at corner newsstands bearing the
hastily written reports as well as box scores of the afternoon's
ball games. Small clutches of people, who had already listened to
the game but sought reassurance about what they had just heard,
eagerly gobbled up the papers.

If there was a prickly negative in those supposedly best-of-times it was that ball players, the ignorant as well as the wise, were dreadfully underpaid. Picayune salaries went largely un-challenged by these athletes, many of whom might have played for nothing. Ruth, rescuer of baseball from the Black Sox quag-mire, was soundly despised by the owners for demanding as much money as he did. After all, they felt, that would give the others silly notions about their own worth.

The Babe's largest wage was in 1930, when he collected $80,000. The Yankees' stylish southpaw, Herb Pennock, was con-sidered highly paid at $20,000, while Gehrig rented out for his personal high of $39,500, after fourteen years of effort. In his entire career Gehrig received about $316,000, scarcely an over-payment for such diligence.

In 1921 Ty Cobb, certainly appreciative of his own value, made $35,000, which was reputed to be the largest sum paid to anyone in baseball, outside of John McGraw. In 1926, two years before his twenty-four-year career as a major leaguer ended, Cobb signed for $50,000, which until Ruth's $80,000 was the most ever given to a player. Hornsby, the right-handed equivalent of Cobb, never made more than $18,000.

If players chose, or even dared, to hold out for more money, they had scant chance of gaining anything for their stubborn-ness. Edd Roush, a graceful outfielder with a lifetime batting aver-age of .323, couldn't come to terms in early 1930 with McGraw, causing him to remain away for the entire season. Unlike Roush, Gehrig rarely objected to terms offered him by the Yankees. He invariably would sign and send Yankee contracts back immedi-ately for he always feared they might change their minds about him! "I always wondered every year," he once said, "whether the Yanks would sign me again."

So Lou Gehrig arrived for work at Yankee Stadium not in a fancy Pierce-Arrow car (which cost about $1,700 at the time) but via the subway (a nickel). Wrapped up in a newspaper were his spikes and his glove. Krichell was a one-man greeting committee.

Years later, Waite Hoyt, the Yankees' brilliant right-hander, who had developed his insights on the streets of Brooklyn, recalled Gehrig's initiation rites: "Two or three of the big hitters, who thought they needed extra work, were working out with the pitchers. The Babe was there, so was Everett Scott, Aaron Ward, and Wally Pipp. The group stood back of the batting cage, with their spikes resting on a bolster rod. From the direction of the bench, in marched two men, though marching is hardly the way to put it, for there was nothing military about the way they walked. The little guy, with spindly legs and toes turned outward, was Huggins. The guy with him was a smooth-faced Atlas, an all-American type, a typical first-boy-in-the-seat in Sunday school. He walked with an ungainly roll as he trailed after Huggins shyly, with his sloping shoulders and leg calves that bulged like balloons. This was my first look at the Yankees' child of destiny."

Hoyt could be florid in his reminiscences, but his memory was never challenged. He went on to relate that he and his buddies at the cage were impressed not so much with Lou's physical makeup as with his escort. Surely, he must be somebody to rate the manager as a chaperon.

Huggins stopped at the batting cage, where Pipp was taking his practice swings.

"Hey, Wally, let the kid hit a few, will ya," Huggins chirped in his high-pitched voice.

Gehrig hadn't brought along any favorite bat of his own, as many players do, but he picked one out from a bunch of bats that were resting against the back of the cage. He didn't know it, but the bat happened to be the Babe's favorite, and weighed in at forty-eight ounces, a lot of wood for any man to swing, even one as strong as Gehrig.

Only moments before, the Babe had been introduced to Gehrig in the Yankee clubhouse. Ruth had been tying his shoelaces when Doc Woods, the Yankee trainer whose forgeries appeared on many autographed baseballs when Ruth got tired of signing, tapped Babe on the shoulder.

"Babe, I want you to meet Lou Gehrig, from Columbia," said Woods.

Ruth looked up, grinned, and extended his meaty hand.

Never much on remembering names, he probably hadn't the faintest notion that Columbia was someplace in uptown Manhattan. But he was always a cordial man, using his booming voice to assert his friendliness.

"Hiya, keed," he said.

"Ordinarily," said Hoyt, "a batter prizes his bat more than he does his watch. In this instance, Ruth could have said, 'Oh, no, kid, that's my good one, grab yourself another stick.' But somehow the Babe didn't protest; it choked in his throat. He said nothing."

Lou took his place at the plate, as the early birds hung around to watch. He ground his left spiked shoe into the earth once or twice setting himself for the pitch, missed a couple, then hit a few dribblers to the infield. If he seemed nervous as the devil, it was certainly normal under the circumstances.

Then, from behind the box seats back of the Yankee bench, someone yelled, "Show that big guy, Lou. He's not the only one that can hit it out of the park." A small cheering section from Columbia had accompanied Lou to the Stadium.

After his unpromising start, Lou took heart. Gripping the handle of the big bat tightly, he took careful aim at the next delivery. This time when he swung the ball took off, higher and higher. It landed in the right-field bleachers, the private preserve of the Babe himself, where fans settled in the hope of picking off Babe's wallops.

The batting-practice pitcher, whose name has been lost to history, threw a few more fastballs straight down the middle, which is what such men are paid to do. Each time, Lou sent the ball zooming off into Ruthville.

When the fusillade stopped, the Yankees at the cage were quiet. One or two stole glances at each other. But Gehrig's personal claque could not restrain themselves. "Atta boy, Lou," they yelled, "Babe knows he's got company now!"

The loud supporters were an embarrassment to Lou. Head down, he grabbed his worn glove and headed for first base.

"What's this guy's name?" Whitey Witt asked Herb Pennock.

"Gehrig, I believe," said Pennock. "He comes from Columbia."

If Hoyt and his chums saw a potential star in Lou, they also perceived his rawness around the edges, his inexperience, his shyness. Some early observers even portrayed Lou as a clone of the hesitant, ungrammatical characters who filled the pages of writer Ring Lardner's pieces about ball players. In an article in the *New Yorker,* Niven Busch remarked that Gehrig "was one of the most bewildered recruits anyone had ever seen."

Slow-witted, Gehrig rarely had a comeback for the wisecracks directed at him. He never wore an overcoat, hat, or waistcoat. Leaving Yankee Stadium one raw day, a team executive stopped to offer him a hundred bucks, related Busch. "Go buy yourself a suit and some clothes," said the executive. "You can pay me back later." Lou refused, saying he saved his money and had plenty but never wore an overcoat or vest because they made him feel dressed up.

6

Seasoning at Hartford

There wasn't a place for Gehrig in the Yankee lineup of 1923. Led by the Babe's all-time-high Yankee batting average of .393, the New Yorkers waltzed to their third straight American League title. To top off a season that was surprisingly serene, the Yanks went on to defeat the Giants in the World Series, for the first time in the last three tries.

With Captain Tillinghast Huston relinquishing his half-interest in the Yanks, Colonel Ruppert was now sole owner of the club. Ruppert quickly got what he wanted—the world's best baseball team. Across the Harlem River that separated the Bronx from Manhattan, McGraw sulked in his tent, aware that his once-dominant role in New York baseball was coming to an end.

While these developments took place, the raw rookie Gehrig was relegated by Huggins to sit on the Yankee bench. Though Huggins was confident Gehrig had the credentials to become a fixture with the Yankees, he knew the time was not yet ripe.

When Lou's parents started to come to the ballpark, despite their reservations about baseball, they were puzzled because Lou didn't get to play, yet still received his wages.

"They pay you to be a bummer. You do nothing. What kind of a business is this?" asked Pop Gehrig of his son.

Gehrig reassured his folks that his manager wanted him to soak up the strategy of the game. There was much he could learn from watching this team from the bench, Gehrig said.

"Lou would have jumped through fire, or charged a runaway train, if Huggins ordered it," wrote journalist Fred Lieb. But Huggins was asking for no such trial by torture. He simply wanted Lou to sit there and absorb as much as he could from the veterans around him.

On June 16, Gehrig got into a Yankee game for the first time when Huggins sent him in to replace Pipp in the ninth inning, against the St. Louis Browns. But Huggins appreciated that Gehrig needed more action than such occasional appearances. So he sent him on option to Hartford, which now had a working agreement with the Yankees. The manager at Hartford was Paddy O'Connor, who had once coached under Huggins and had played one game as a catcher for the Yankees in 1918.

Returning to the scene of his earlier "crime," Gehrig did not achieve immediate success. He played poorly, both in the field and at bat in his first two weeks. "I thought I might quit," said Gehrig, when he was interviewed in his prime.

Again, the long arm of Krichell came to his aid. Although he was off on one of his scouting trips, this one to Spartanburg, South Carolina, Krichell was ordered by Ed Barrow to hustle up to Hartford to find out what was ailing his young discovery. Krichell first spoke to O'Connor, who thought that Lou's trouble might be that he'd gotten in with the wrong bunch on the ball club. Bad influences lead to bad play, insisted O'Connor. Krichell listened, then sat through Hartford's ball game as Lou "took the collar" in four times at bat.

As soon as the game was over, Krichell approached Gehrig. Lou was pleased to see him, though he was puzzled at this appearance in Hartford. Krichell explained that the Yankees were concerned about his performance. Gehrig didn't make excuses. He acknowledged things were going badly for him and told the scout how disappointed he was in himself and how he couldn't possibly live up to the advance notices he'd received in the Hartford papers.

Playing amateur psychologist, Krichell felt that Lou was running a fever called fear of failure, a baseball affliction not peculiar to Gehrig. Baseball can be the strangest of games. A hitter connects for only three hits in ten times at bat, yet reaches the coveted .300 level, a plateau of batting excellence to which all big leaguers aspire. But a ratio of three out of ten also means a hitter has failed seven times. Under ordinary circumstances, that's a mess of failure. A baseball team wins 91 games out of 154, as the Yankees of 1926 did, or 98 out of 154, as the 1923 Yankees did, and it wins a pennant. That's still a lot of losing, yet these teams were winners—just as .300 batters are considered winners.

Gehrig, under Krichell's prodding, tried to grasp this enigma. He mustn't expect to hit every time at the plate. Some days, Krichell informed him, you won't hit anything. Get used to it. Nobody in this game is perfect. You can strive for perfection, but that state of affairs is elusive. In baseball, a .400 batting average was something belonging only to superior men like Rogers Hornsby, Ty Cobb, or George Sisler; yet again, a man batting .400 failed six out of every ten times. This was a concept that Gehrig had to comprehend if he was to transcend the nagging fears that he would never succeed as a ball player.

The lesson that Krichell tried to impart to Lou had to be reinforced by O'Connor. Once he knew how much the Yankees believed in this youngster, O'Connor invited Gehrig to dinner. "You have a wonderful career ahead of you," O'Connor told Gehrig, "but you have to accept the good with the bad. Nothing can stop you, except Lou Gehrig. For another thing, that gang on this team that you're traveling with is poison. You can wind up a rich man from this game. Six months of work, six months of ease, all for two hours of hustle each afternoon for one hundred fifty-four games. Think it over."

Gehrig did think it over. He said goodbye to the players who were not helping his career. Soon after, hits began to fall. In a few days Gehrig was crushing the ball. Playing his home games in Hartford's Bulkeley Stadium, Gehrig soon became a hero to the fans.

True, he was playing in the Eastern League, where crowds were small, travel was in overheated buses, and hotel rooms rarely had working showers. But this, Krichell insisted, was Lou's necessary apprentice training.

Gehrig played in fifty-nine games for Hartford. After an unproductive start, his average wound up at a very respectable .304. But what was significant was that of his sixty-nine hits twenty-four were homers, thirteen were doubles, and eight were triples. In one remarkable stretch Lou hit seven homers in seven days. In another seven-day span he hit five home runs, one each against Bridgeport, Waterbury, and Pittsfield, and two against Albany. The newspapers speculated on how many home runs he might hit for Hartford in a season of 154 games. And Paddy O'Connor, once so glum about Gehrig, was telling everybody who would listen that he "always knew the kid had the makings of a powerful hitter."

Lou also exhibited his strength in other ways. One day a Hartford pitcher named "Zip" Sloan, who liked his beer, bought his little girl a rag-doll monkey. Roaming around the team's hotel, the monkey in hand, Zip entered Gehrig's room and, without warning, pounced on the sound-asleep Lou. The two men then got into an informal wrestling match, with Lou getting a scissors hold on Zip.

"Hey," yelled Harry Hesse, Lou's roommate, "let him go, you're gonna kill him. He's turning blue!"

When Lou released his grip on the frightened Sloan, there was nothing left of the monkey but sawdust.

"That incident taught me a lesson," said Lou. "I didn't know my own strength. I never cut loose after that."

Hesse, who never made it to the big leagues, was the first ball player ever to establish a close relationship with Gehrig. Normally a first baseman, Hesse had to shift to the outfield, but he never felt any animosity toward Lou because of the switch. Hesse roomed with Lou for several days before he realized Lou didn't have a dime. When Lou's father recovered from a serious operation, Lou sent his parents on the first vacation they'd ever had. He had stripped himself down to nothing except his ragged clothes to do it, but Lou's first concern continued to be his parents.

Reflecting on Gehrig's agonizing start with Hartford, which had sent his average down to .062, Hesse said he never saw anyone suffer so much: "He took everything to heart and was a guy who needed friends, but didn't know how to go about getting them. He'd get low, sitting there hunched over and miserable. It was pretty tough to pull him out of it."

When Gehrig began to terrorize the league's hurlers, his attitude changed almost overnight. For the first time he had a date with a young woman, who was introduced to him by Hesse. When the girl spoke to him he was uneasy and blushed, but Hesse was proud to have nudged his friend toward a new sociability.

When the Yankees clinched the American League pennant a few days before the Eastern League season ended, Huggins brought Gehrig up to the Yanks so he could play in a few end-of-season games. This way there'd be only slight pressure on the boy, for it didn't matter whether the Yankees won or lost.

The day after Lou arrived, Huggins called on him to pinch-hit against the Washington Senators. Lou struck out on three pitches against Bonnie Hollingsworth, a mediocre right-hander from Tennessee. The following game Gehrig tied the score with a double, after replacing Pipp at first base in the late innings.

Huggins now wanted to rest some of his regulars in order to get them in good physical shape for the upcoming World Series. Always a durable man, Pipp played in 153 games in 1920 and 1921, and 152 in 1922. In 1923 he played in 144 games and knocked in 108 runs. Huggins named Lou to start at first base instead of Pipp, in another game with Washington.

When Bullet Joe Bush, a hard-throwing right-hander with an explosive disposition, got wind of Huggins's plan, he registered strong disapproval. "Don't put that damn clown out there at first," growled Bush. "This game may not mean anything to the team, but it means a lot to me. That guy will gum it up." Bush was scheduled to go after his nineteenth victory that afternoon. He figured winning the game would then give him a chance at twenty wins, always an arbitrary mark of excellence for pitchers.

Huggins had had previous arguments with Bush, but this time he was in no mood to heed a rancorous outburst against Gehrig. When the game began, Huggins had Lou at first base.

Early on, as Gehrig misplayed a bunt off the bat of Joe Judge, holding on to the ball as a runner scooted home from third base, Bush seemed prophetic. In moments, he was also apoplectic. Stalking over to Gehrig, he yelled, "Ya stupid college punk. Where's your brains, dummy?" Almost everyone in the park could hear the abuse.

Lou kept looking at the ground, blinking in embarrassment. In the eighth inning, with two out, the Yankees mounted a rally. Two Yankees got on base, with the Babe due up. Washington's manager, Owen Bush, directed his pitcher to walk Ruth, loading the bases, with the score still 5–2 in the Senators' favor. Bush then pulled his right-handed pitcher, replacing him with Ray Francis, a big Texas lefty.

It was Gehrig's turn to bat, lefty against lefty, not an attractive percentage situation. Joe Bush expected that Huggins would send up a right-handed batter to pinch-hit for Lou. "I wanna win this one," Bush grumbled. "Don't send this kid up there!"

But Huggins refused to listen to Bush. He looked over at the nervous Gehrig. "Go on up there and hit that ball," said Huggins. Gehrig did exactly that, rocketing the first pitch off the right-field wall for a double, scoring all three runners and tying the game at 5-all. When a single followed, Gehrig scored the winning run. Never much at apologies, Bush sidled up to Gehrig in the dugout. "Look, kid," he mumbled, "you may not be so hot with the glove but you can pound that ball." (A year later, Bush was gone from the Yankees, swapped to St. Louis for pitcher Urban Shocker.)

When the Yankees traveled to Boston to conclude their season, Pipp injured his ankle when he stumbled getting off the train. That was sufficient reason to give Lou another opportunity to appear in the starting lineup. On the afternoon of September 27, 1923, facing "Wild Bill" Piercy, a righty from El Monte, California, Gehrig banged the first major league homer of his career.

That 1923 summer, the Kaiser returned to Germany from his exile in the Netherlands, Silent Cal Coolidge succeeded the ill-fated Warren Harding in the presidency, George Gershwin wrote his thrilling "Rhapsody in Blue," and Emile Coué came to the United States from France to spread his simplistic philosophy of autosuggestion: "Every day, in every way, I'm getting better and better."

As far as Gehrig was concerned, Couéism was working for him. His late-season sojourn with the Yankees yielded a hefty .423 average. So impressive had Gehrig been that Huggins went to Colonel Ruppert to attempt to get Lou declared eligible for the World Series, since Pipp was still nursing his ankle. Gehrig had not been with the Yankees long enough to qualify outright, having joined the club after the September 1 deadline. But Colonel Ruppert suspected that Commissioner Landis would be reasonable and give Lou an okay to play because substitutions for injured players had been granted in the past. The Yankee front office, though, didn't reckon with the long-simmering hostility McGraw, manager of their rivals for the World Series championship, harbored against the Yanks and Gehrig. When Landis approached McGraw, the manager was implacable. He wouldn't hear of Gehrig going on the active list. "If the Yanks have had an injury, it's their hard luck," he snapped.

Despite Ruppert's rage and Huggins's disappointment, the 1923 all–New York World Series had to do without Lou. Instead, Pipp played, his ankle wrapped in tape, and battled .250, and the Yankees beat the Giants anyway.

In 1924 Pipp was back as the regular Yankee first baseman, thus putting Lou's first-base career on hold.

7

It Could Have Been Harvard

In 1886 Albert Goodwill Spalding, the flamboyant owner of the Chicago White Stockings of the National League, was determined to get his players in shape for the season to come so he sent his club to Hot Springs, Arkansas, where they could purge themselves of a winter's accumulation of excess weight. Ultimately Chicago's manager, Cap Anson, became skeptical about the concept, reasoning that when players are returned to colder environments all the benefits of boiling out in a warm climate would be negated. But in 1894 Ned Hanlon of the Baltimore Orioles took his club to Macon, Georgia, for exposure to the warm rays of the South. There was considerable snickering about Hanlon's attention to the weather. But when the Orioles emerged as champions, other envious baseball people began to adopt the spring training ritual.

Spring training has since been dedicated to getting players

into prime mental and physical condition. A supplemental benefit for the owners has been the money reaped in those communi-
ties where camps have been located. Another benefit is the press
agentry gushing from the training sites, meant to excite fans who
have hibernated all winter in their Hot Stove Leagues.

Lyrical reports out of the camps, with the inevitable flummery about flowers that bloom in the spring, are designed to
send fans into a state of rising expectations. What baseball fan
hasn't been vulnerable to those pictures flowing out of Florida or
Arizona of pampered players breaking a sweat in neat, graceful
stadiums as children and old men squint from under oversized
baseball caps?

Gehrig's first spring training camp was in New Orleans in
1924. It was in this southern parish, known more perhaps for its
Bourbon Street, brothels, and gastronomic specialties than for
baseball, that Lou and his teammates got to know one another.

Not yet twenty-one years old, still not wise in the ways of the
world, Gehrig reported to the Louisiana camp with a modest
cardboard suitcase and $14 in his pocket, which his mother had
given him.

In the early twenties players did not receive a penny of salary until the season began, although expenses during spring
training were paid by the club (including laundry money). But
there were always tips and incidentals for which the club had no
responsibility.

Gehrig had not yet made any pals among the champion Yankees. In addition, rarely having extra pocket money, he was
forced to spend a good deal of time by himself. One day, while he
was wandering through the streets of New Orleans, he ran into
Dan Daniel, a New York baseball writer. Daniel took one look at
Lou's glum face and asked what was wrong.

"Things are pretty tough, Dan," Lou replied. "I can't seem to
find a job, not even washing dishes."

"What are you talking about?" asked Daniel, in his gruff
voice. "You're a Yankee, a player with the best team in baseball.
You're not supposed to go around searching for a job. If you're
broke, go see Huggins."

"I just can't do that," responded Gehrig.

Daniel knew Lou would never approach the manager, so he did it for him. When Daniel told Huggins he'd seen Gehrig roaming around looking for a job, Huggins immediately called Lou in for a chat.

"Here's one hundred dollars as an advance," Huggins said to Gehrig. "Now please stop looking for a job."

In short order Huggins also arranged for Gehrig to move into a New Orleans hotel with two other Yankee players, neither of whom appeared to be important components of the New York team. One of them was Hinkey Haines, a twenty-six-year-old outfielder from Sharon Hill, Pennsylvania, who had been a fill-in outfielder. The other roommate was Benny Bengough, a twenty-six-year-old catcher from Niagara, New York, whom the Yankees had bought from Buffalo in mid-season of 1923. Bengough was an upbeat, articulate man who had learned to handle pitchers with skill. Although he had joined the Yankees only the year before, he was a favorite of Babe Ruth. The Babe liked to warm up with Bengough before each day's game. When he couldn't locate Benny, the Babe would ask everybody, "Where's that Googles guy?" An expert at mangling names, Ruth had gotten "Googles" from a popular comic-strip character of the time named Barney Google. After all, "Googles" was close to Bengough, wasn't it?

The arrangement with Gehrig, Bengough, and Haines worked out quite satisfactorily, even if Lou was forced to sleep on a cot because there weren't any bigger rooms available. Haines was dropped after spring training, but Bengough became a stabilizing force for the pitchers, remaining with the Yankees through 1930.

Though Lou felt that his two roommates were considerate toward him, he wasn't able to share most of their after-dark experiences with them. They generally seemed to have a few dollars to spend and liked to go out on the town. When Haines and Bengough were around they liked to swap stories, putting Lou at a disadvantage. He would listen quietly, his mouth open and uncommunicative. Was there a mixture of resentment and envy in him? After all, almost every night they'd go somewhere for dinner or to a theater, while Lou fretfully tried to figure out how he could pay his tips the next day in the dining room.

"I was glad the team worked out every day from eleven to one," Lou once remarked, "so I could just skip lunch."

Many evenings Lou walked the hot streets of New Orleans by himself, feeling desperately homesick and wishing he was back in New York.

One night, after discovering to his surprise that Bengough had as little pocket money as he had, Lou suggested that the two of them get jobs waiting on tables at an expensive restaurant on Canal Street. Lou told Bengough that he had waited on tables at a Columbia fraternity house and thus could give him valuable pointers. When they arrived at the restaurant they realized, much to their embarrassment, that several Yankees, including Pennock, Hoyt, Joe Dugan, and Bob Meusel, were sitting at a table near the door, tussling with oversized lobsters. Since Bengough didn't think it was wise to let their teammates see them waiting on tables, the two of them left, reluctantly.

Gehrig constantly felt money and social pressures during that New Orleans spring. "Near the end of our stay in New Orleans," Gehrig said, "I left my last money as a tip in the dining room. Later that day I borrowed a couple of dollars against the day when we would break camp and all of us would get our meal money for the trip north. Boy, the day Mark Roth [the Yankees' traveling secretary] came around with our meal money was a red-letter day for me!"

Meal money came to some $70. After paying off all of his outstanding debts, Lou had a little bit left over. His first thought was to go out and have a good time, something he hadn't experienced during the entire doleful spring. "But then I thought about that fourteen dollars that I started out with and how hard it had been to string out that money," said Gehrig, "so I decided against spending any money foolishly."

Long after he had become a Yankee mainstay, Lou talked with a measure of bitterness about those introductory days in the Yankee world. "When I broke into this league," he recalled, "the

Yankees, mostly the oldsters, were clannish and sullen toward the rookies. They made it hard for us. You had to be one of the clan off the field, too. If you weren't, you didn't get a break on or off the field."

Rookies like the vulnerable Gehrig were often rudely crowded out of batting practice by spiteful veterans. It was commonplace for youngsters who wanted to get in their pre-game licks to be shoved around, and Lou was no exception. Carl Mays, the submarine-throwing right-hander who beaned Cleveland's Ray Chapman in 1920, resulting in Chapman's death (baseball's only on-field fatality), took sadistic delight in ragging Lou. One day Mays's baiting became so fierce and constant that Lou offered to fight him in the clubhouse. The invitation was declined.

"Sometimes when I wanted to take some batting practice," recalled Lou, "I found my favorite bat sawed in four parts, the kind of meanness that was hard to understand."

When Lou appealed to Huggins, the sympathetic manager would assign Charley O'Leary, a Yankee coach who was especially close to the manager, to journey to the ballpark at ten in the morning, with Lou, and throw to him in batting practice.

Despite such a hostile environment, Lou continued to show improvement. Huggins worked with him almost daily, trying to iron out Gehrig's stiffness on the field and any flaws in his batting style. In time, Huggins concluded, his pupil would be bound to get the hang of it.

If there were obstructionists in the cast, and the usual ill-wishers, there were also those who tended to be supportive. Ironically, one such player was Pipp, the long-time regular at first base. No man likes to concede that he is playing out his time in a twilight zone. Certainly Pipp did not believe his usefulness to the Yankees had come to an end. But he began to appreciate that Lou might have more of a future with New York than he did.

Pipp worked hard with Lou that spring. Instead of resenting his would-be successor, Pipp showed his better nature by instructing Gehrig in the artful tricks of effective first-basing— charging in for bunts; playing behind the runner; circling properly under pop flies, fair or foul; throwing to the correct base; playing on the line in late innings; touching the base with the right foot, etc. After the 1925 season Pipp would go on to finish his career in Cincinnati, where he spent three more years, two as a regular. Lou was forever grateful for the man's decency.

As Huggins brought his team back to the Bronx to start the 1924 campaign, President Calvin Coolidge was brushing up his oratory to run for another term; the sensational Chicago trial of the kidnappers Loeb and Leopold was beginning to dominate the front pages; Mussolini was a big winner in the Italian elections; and J. Edgar Hoover was made America's FBI chief. Still not certain where he would be playing in 1924, Gehrig heard disquieting rumors that various high-classification minor league teams such as Atlanta, Louisville, and St. Paul were interested in his services. He wanted to remain with the Yanks for the summer, yet suspected Hartford might get him for another year.

Huggins finally informed Lou that as much as he wanted to have him around, it was unfair to imprison him on the bench for much of the year. Therefore, he told Lou, "I'll keep you around for a while, send you down, then get you back in the fall, when you'll be here to stay." It was a downbeat message as far as Lou was concerned. But he trusted Huggins and was confident that he'd be back with the Yanks in the final days of the pennant race.

Lou played in a few games, mostly as pinch hitter and fill-in; he went to bat a dozen times and got six hits. He then packed his shabby suitcase and returned to Hartford.

By this time Mom and Pop Gehrig had gotten used to the baseball roller coaster. Since Hartford sounded like Harvard when it went trippingly off the tongue, how bad could it be! Also, money was coming in more regularly and people kept saying such nice things about Lou.

By June Lou was assaulting the fences in the Eastern League parks. He celebrated his twenty-first birthday on June 19 by hitting a homer, triple, and double in a 9–8 victory over Worcester. He did this despite the fact that Mom had written to him saying it "would be very nice" if he could come home to be with his parents for the occasion. When Lou approached his manager with his mother's proposal, O'Connor told him to take off if he wanted to. "But I'd prefer you stayed here," he said. "We're in a damned hot pennant race."

Lou stayed of course. Batting in the cleanup position and pounding the ball at a .383 pace, Lou accepted his role. His mother would have to wait for the next day, Monday, an open date for the Hartford club. So he traveled to New York to be with his mother a day after the fact.

The rest of the year at Hartford was nothing less than a dream. Playing in 134 games, he cracked out 37 home runs and 40 doubles, and accumulated 186 hits. He scored 111 runs and continued to show surprising speed on the bases with 13 triples. One cannot be a sloth moving the 360 feet from home to third base. In commenting on Gehrig's quickness, Ruth once said that Lou came to the Yankees "loaded to the decks with hog fat and we took it off him. He still has some of it above the neck. But he's workin' hard on that."

A premonitory sign that Lou might not be up to snuff in his fielding was his twenty-three errors at Hartford in 1924. But Huggins and his coaches were determined to work on Lou's defense. The *Hartford Courant* even ran an article hinting that O'Connor had thoughts about putting Gehrig in the outfield.

By early August the Yankees had come on strong; they walloped their nearest rivals, the Senators, five times in a row, and it appeared they might win the pennant again. But the Senators, sparked by their twenty-eight-year-old manager and second baseman, Bucky Harris, refused to buckle. They came storming back, with the help of pitcher Walter Johnson, who continued to win games in the fading days of his career. When the Senators captured two out of three from the Yankees in late August, they moved into first place. So when Lou returned to the Yankees in September he found a team engaged in a desperate bid to win its fourth straight American League flag. That the Yankees would fail was due in no small part to injuries to men like Earle Combs and Aaron Ward.

In a late-season series with Detroit, Lou suffered his first brutal jockeying since the days he was everybody's "Heinie." Ty
Cobb, who had taken a visceral dislike to Gehrig's straight-arrow
personality, stood in the third base coaching box one afternoon
spewing vile insults at Lou. Reacting hotly, Lou raced out of the
Yankee dugout, accompanied by Everett Scott, the Yankee shortstop.

Within moments Tommy Connolly, the dean of umps in the
American League, thumbed Lou and Scott out of the game, while
Cobb smirked with satisfaction. It was Lou's first ejection, and
one of only a handful in his career.

8

Gehrig for Pipp

n December 1924, Bozeman Bulger, writing in the *Evening World,* suggested the Yankees were about to obtain the veteran Urban Shocker. Shocker had won twenty games four times for the St. Louis Browns. He threw an effective spitball and was one of seventeen pitchers still permitted to use such a pitch in the big leagues.

The deal supposedly would send Gehrig to the Browns, along with Bullet Joe Bush, in return for Shocker. Bulger's hypothesis was rooted in the fact that the once-great first baseman George Sisler, who batted over .400 twice for the Browns in 1920 and 1922 but had slumped to .305 in 1924, was troubled by eye problems. Gehrig, said Bulger, could replace Sisler.

Shocker *did* come to the Yankees. But the trade as outlined by Bulger was never made. Gehrig was not part of the package, though Bush departed along with two other Yankees as Shocker returned to New York, where he'd played in 1916 and 1917. When Huggins was asked if he'd ever really contemplated trading Gehrig to the Browns—or shifting him to the outfield—he was adamant in his denial: "That's the silliest thing that was ever written. If I'd have traded Gehrig at that stage of his career, I should have been shot at sunrise."

In 1925, for the first time, the Yankees pitched their spring training camp in St. Petersburg, Florida. Lou was prepared to spend another year as understudy to Pipp, who in 1924 had batted .295 with 113 runs batted in, his personal all-time high. Few figured Pipp was in decline or that this would turn out to be the most dismal year of Huggins's reign. In truth, Huggins was already envisioning that Gehrig would someday neatly complement the Babe in the power department. "What I wouldn't give to be that kid right now," said the manager.

But the news percolating from the South, where the Yankees were sharpening their weapons to oust Washington, turned out to be catastrophically bad. While other assorted cultural phenomena—the Charleston craze; crossword puzzles; Charlie Chaplin in *The Gold Rush;* the Scopes Monkey Trial in Dayton, Tennessee; Harold Lloyd in *The Freshman;* and books like F. Scott Fitzgerald's *The Great Gatsby* and Theodore Dreiser's *An American Tragedy*—all reaped a share of attention, no event won more concern from the public than the sudden physical collapse of the Babe.

As the Yankees' train chugged northward on April 7 from its training headquarters, the Babe caved in from excruciating pains in his stomach, with a whole nation seemingly wired to his distress. Until that moment, Ruth had been having a spectacular spring. Now he was ailing, like no other human being had ailed before, or so it was said. He was delirious, feverish, and vomiting till he fainted. Speculation about his condition ranged from the suggestion that he had eaten his way through a mountain of hot dogs washed down by a waterfall of soft drinks (W. O. McGeehan said it was "the bellyache heard around the world") to the ill-spirited surmise that the great man had contracted a venereal disease.

Whatever it was, the newspapers made the Babe's illness a constant front-page item. In some stories he was near death; in others he had already expired. In truth, the bellyache was an intestinal abscess. Operated on in mid-April, the Babe remained in a New York hospital for weeks. It wasn't until May 26 that he rejoined his teammates. By June 1, with the Yankees floundering badly, Ruth finally got back into the lineup.

Since the spotlight was focused exclusively on the progress of the fabulous patient, hardly any note was paid on that same June 1 afternoon to a youth named Gehrig, some eighteen days short of his twenty-second birthday, as he pinch-hit for shortstop Peewee Wanninger. Wanninger had replaced Scott at shortstop on May 6, putting an end to Scott's all-time consecutive-game mark at 1,307. But in the month following that event, he hadn't been hitting much. Now, in the eighth inning against Washington, Huggins directed Gehrig to bat for Peewee.

Lou did not produce a hit. But the date would become a baseball landmark, for that afternoon Lou commenced the long string of games that would earn him his nickname "Iron Horse," as well as his remarkable reputation for durability.

In batting practice the following day, Pipp stepped in to take his cuts against a big, strong kid from Princeton named Charlie Caldwell, Jr. Batting-practice pitchers are supposed to be specialists in control. On this occasion Caldwell failed in his job, for he unleashed a toss that hit Pipp squarely on the head. Inadvertently, the Yankee career of Gehrig truly began.

"I just couldn't duck," Pipp recalled in 1953. "The ball hit me on the temple. Down I went. I was too far gone to bother reaching for any aspirin tablets, as the popular story goes." The story said that Huggins spied a headachy Pipp searching for aspirin tablets and decided, on the spot, to give Pipp a rest. There was no way Pipp could have reached for anything. He was groggy and semi-conscious and had to be carted away to the hospital for two weeks.

Gehrig started at first that June 2 day, Caldwell returned to Princeton, where he later became the school's football coach, and Pipp's Yankee career came to a halt.

Nobody could have anticipated the importance of Caldwell's faulty aim. However, in a supporting blurb to its June 3 story the *New York Times* proclaimed: "RADICAL SHIFT BY HUGGINS... Gehrig Supplants Pipp, Shanks Has Ward's Place and Bengough Does the Catching."

Facing Washington's left-hander George Mogridge, followed by relief pitcher Allan Russell, Gehrig batted three-for-five that afternoon, connecting for those three hits his first three times up, including a double. He batted sixth in the lineup, behind Meusel, with Ruth in the cleanup slot.

Gehrig often reflected on those few days that changed the shape of his life. "Before I went in for Pipp," said Lou, "I was so discouraged at my slim prospect for getting regular work at first that I asked Hug to try me in the outfield, which already had Ruth, Combs, and Meusel in it."

If Huggins didn't care to do that, Lou wanted to be sent out somewhere or do something that would get him off the bench. He felt that Huggins may already have had something in mind for him, although the manager never said anything about it to him at any time. He just kept telling Lou to be patient, that his chance was coming up soon. Lou was in the clubhouse before the game on June 2 when Huggins walked out of his office at the end of the dressing room and approached him. "You're my first baseman today," said Huggins, pointing his bony finger at Lou. "Today— and from now on."

When Huggins delivered this commitment to Gehrig, Lou didn't utter a word. He reached for his first baseman's mitt and quickly headed for the diamond.

"Now take it easy, boy," Huggins added. "Don't get rattled. If you muff a few, nobody's going to shoot you."

In a way, Gehrig was fortunate the Yankees were suffering through a season of turmoil. Otherwise, Huggins may not have been so quick to remove Pipp, who had served well for eleven years. But the team's precipitous plunge into the second division of the American League, with a seventh-place finish beckoning, hastened changes that Huggins ordinarily might have delayed.

The entire year was full of dark comedy. In August the Babe had been removed for pinch hitter Bobby Veach, who in his four-teen-year career amassed sixty-four homers, three more than Ruth would hit in 1927! It was the only time that Ruth, who had not been hitting, was so ingloriously jettisoned. On another occasion, the Tigers massacred the Yanks, 19–1, in the most one-sided defeat in the club's history.

Still another explosive moment remained for the Babe. Despite his springtime bellyache, the Babe had not been entirely chastened, for he continued to wolf enough hot dogs and swill enough booze and soda pop to sink the state of New York, not to mention his employers. To Huggins, who cherished the humility of a Gehrig, Ruth fitted into only one category, if he fitted into anything at all in those days: he was a man-child sorely in need of discipline. So one August day Huggins opened fire on Babe in the visitors' clubhouse at St. Louis's Sportsman's Park.

"Don't bother getting into uniform today," Huggins snapped, as the Babe continued to break all records for arriving late at the ballpark. "This is all I'm gonna take. You're fined five thousand and suspended."

"For two cents I'd smack you in the mush," roared the indignant Babe.

"If you didn't have ninety pounds on me," shot back Huggins, "I'd lick you right now. Get the hell outta here!"

This little vignette, staged in a locker room redolent of liniment, soiled socks, and a seventh-place ball club, evolved into a turning point in the Babe's turbulent life. With Colonel Ruppert backing up the authority of Huggins, the fine stuck. After a huddle a few days later with Colonel Ruppert, a contrite Babe apologized to Huggins. The suspension was lifted, and Ruth went back to playing ball. In the last weeks of a frustrating season the Babe raised his average from a puny .246 to .290. His batting binge, coming too late to boost the Yankees in the standings, served notice there were better days to come.

Playing in such a jarring environment, Lou remained in the background. He sat close to Huggins on the bench, at the risk of being dubbed "manager's pet," worked on his fielding almost daily, scarcely spoke to reporters, and came to work every day, much as a clerical worker would report to his office without fail or privilege.

Although built along the lines of a Percheron, Lou showed himself to be an agile base runner. On June 24, 1925, he got his first stolen base—he stole home. He may have been the first player ever to steal home on a first theft, a curious achievement.

At the end of the year Lou had 20 home runs and 68 RBIs, the only time he ever knocked in fewer than 100, until his last year in 1939. He had 23 doubles and 10 triples among his 129 hits, finishing with a batting average of .295. (In 1925 American League batting averages overall were .292, which meant that Lou's .295 was hardly anything to crow about. Detroit's Harry Heilmann topped the League in 1925 with .393.) Not until his .295 mark in 1938 would Lou's average ever again drop below .300. On July 23 Lou hit the first of his 23 professional grand slams, a mark that remains to this day. (The all-time runner-up to Lou in this department is the Giants' Willie McCovey, with 18.)

As reporters took notice of Lou's grim daily pursuit to improve his performance, Lou himself never perceived that such constant practice, especially in fielding, was a hardship. Even after doubleheaders, Lou delighted in playing in the streets with his neighbors' kids. He'd wear an old pair of pants and a sweatshirt and his baseball shoes, from which he'd removed the spikes.

Conceding Lou's conscientiousness, others remarked about his painful self-consciousness and penuriousness. While the Babe, extravagant and open-handed, was regarded with warmth by most men in the press box, Lou had difficulties dealing with them. He was not very articulate, and invariably left the waiters pennies for tips, while Ruth was throwing around five-dollar bills. Many of the writers, as well as Lou's case-hardened teammates, were put off by his personality. There was little appreciation by others in those beginning years of his dogged desire to improve and to make himself indispensable to his team.

Lou Gehrig in infancy.
(National Baseball Library,
Cooperstown, New York.)

Lou was graduated
from public school
in 1917, when he
was fourteen.
(National Baseball
Library,
Cooperstown,
New York.)

HIGH SCHOOL OF COMMERCE
1920 NATIONAL HIGH SCHOOL BASEBALL CHAMPIONS

Commerce High's baseball team. Lou is third from right, second row. (National Baseball Library, Cooperstown, New York.)

The Commerce football team was a cross section of New York City. Lou is in the top row, seventh from the left. The yearbook misspelled his name as "Gherig." (Commerce *Caravel* yearbook, 1920.)

THE FOOTBALL SQUAD, 1920. ..

Standing left to right: Wiener, Navarro, Kulick, Horvath, Levine (Captain-elect), Sternbach, Gherig, J. Atheneos, Iannitti, Manag
Rosen, Captain Wiedman, Miehoffer, Sesit, Ashley, Kaplan, Parker, Asst. Manager Guala, Wilson, Bunora, Yates, Solomo
Golden, B. Atheneos.

At Columbia in 1922 Lou (third from left, front row) played on the line and in the backfield. (National Baseball Library, Cooperstown, New York.)

On South Field Lou hit near-mythic homers for Columbia that made him a campus hero. (*Columbia* magazine.)

Mom and Pop
Gehrig.

Lou and his mother.

Never exactly balletic at first base, Lou made this out on the Browns' Gene Robertson in a 1928 game. (National Baseball Library, Cooperstown, New York.)

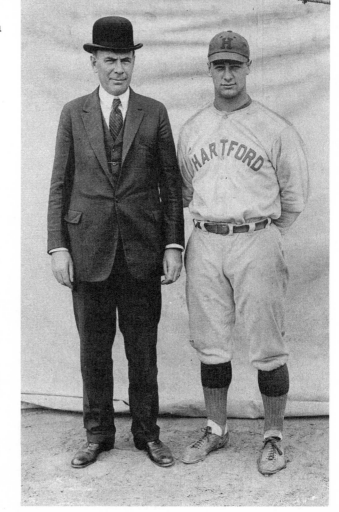

Paddy O'Connor, an ex-Yankees' coach, was Lou's manager at Hartford. (National Baseball Library, Cooperstown, New York.)

Spring training, sometime in the late 1920s. (National
Baseball Library, Cooperstown, New York.)

A formidable Roaring Twenties triumvirate: Lou, Notre Dame
football coach Knute Rockne, and the Babe. (National
Baseball Library, Cooperstown, New York.)

Even when Babe and Lou went fishing, Ruth somehow wound up ahead of his teammate. (National Baseball Library, Cooperstown, New York.)

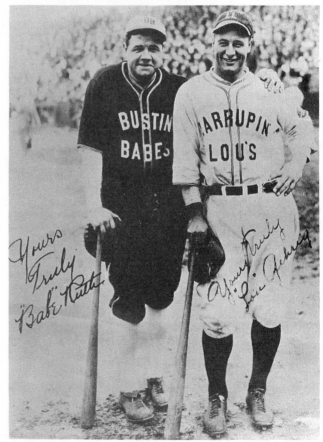

On the barnstorming circuit the two Yank sluggers attracted thousands who had never seen a major league game.

Rogers Hornsby, one
of the National
League's premier
hitters, swapped
batting tips with Lou
in 1928. (National
Baseball Library,
Cooperstown,
New York.)

Lou signing one of
his many autographs.

After the "called-shot" home run against the Cubs in the 1932 World Series. (AP.)

Lou and Babe. (National Baseball Library, Cooperstown, New York.)

Lou and Eleanor on their wedding day, September 29, 1933. A few moments later he was off to the ballpark. (Wide World Photos.)

Lou and Eleanor on holiday.

Eleanor and Fred Fisher, Lou's pal, collaborated on this song, which didn't turn out as popular as "Take Me Out to the Ball Game."

Sometimes to ingratiate himself with others, he'd bring to the Yankee clubhouse a package of goodies that his mother wanted him to share with his friends. Wouldn't everyone love his mom's pickled eels! Well, there were those who didn't, and some scoffed at the youth who offered them.

Eventually, as Lou matured, and as his teammates watched him grow up, he did win the affection of most of those who came in contact with him. In the end, perhaps, it was only waiters and taxi drivers who didn't react smilingly to Lou's characteristically small tips.

"In the beginning, I used to make one terrible play a game," Lou said to magazine writer Quentin Reynolds. "Then it was one bad play a week, then finally I'd pull a bad one once a month." Though he may have viewed his fielding in such a light, Gehrig never fared that badly. In time he became as adept at guarding first base as anyone in his generation of first basemen, with the possible exception of Bill Terry. Of the other American League first basemen, only Joe Judge of Washington, George Burns of Cleveland, and Lu Blue of Detroit rivaled him in the field.

For a while, Lou was particularly inept on cutoff plays, often forgetting what he was supposed to do with balls thrown back to the infield after hits to right field and center field. In a game with Detroit, a runner on second for the Tigers made a dash for home on a single to right by Cobb. Meusel, in right field, threw to the plate in an effort to head off the run—and to show off one of the superior throwing arms of all time. Everyone in the park knew Meusel didn't have a chance. Gehrig should have known, too, for on such a play it was his duty to cut off the throw to prevent Cobb from going to second base. Instead, Lou let the throw go through to the catcher. The run scored and Cobb seized the opportunity to advance to second, from which he scored the winning run a moment later.

After the game, Huggins, usually so patient with his pupil, turned on Gehrig. "What's'a matter with you, Lou," he barked. "Can't you learn to make that cutoff play? After this, it'll cost you."

Gehrig was silent. He said nothing. A few minutes later, as he left the ballpark with several teammates, Gehrig brought up the reprimand from Huggins.

"I know you'll think I'm dumb," he said, "but what the hell was Hug talking about?"

The players weren't certain they'd heard him right. But one of them tried to explain it. "I don't think Lou was ever caught that way again," remembered Waite Hoyt.

Lou also had to learn how to respond to pitchers who threw close to his head. An early embarrassment occurred in 1925, when the Yankees were facing Detroit at Yankee Stadium. Earl Whitehill, a southpaw with a wide, sweeping curve and a crossfire fastball, was protecting a sizable lead.

Even at that point, Gehrig had earned a reputation as a hitter with startling power. Whether he liked it or not, he was already fair game for the intimidating brushback pitch, a weapon many pitchers had at their disposal even if they didn't choose to use it. Sluggers had to expect such treatment; it is a truism of the game that pitchers must pitch inside to be effective.

When Whitehill threw a sidearm pitch that almost grazed Lou's jaw, it was assumed the pitcher had not thrown with any intent to hit Gehrig. However, Lou was convinced otherwise.

Hitting the ground as if he'd been bludgeoned, he leaped to his feet in blind rage, then took a few steps toward the mound. Only five-nine and weighing 170 pounds, but with a reputation for pugnacity, Whitehill wasn't about to ignore the challenge. He moved to meet Lou. But the umpires intervened. Continuing to jabber at the pitcher, Gehrig hollered: "Come on, if ya wanna fight, knock the chip off my shoulder." Whitehill responded promptly: "Wait for me under the stand." Gehrig said: "I'll be there."

After the game, Whitehill had to pass through the Yankee bench to get to the Detroit clubhouse. Lou rushed down the steps and waited for Whitehill, assuming a wrestler's position, his feet spread wide, his arms akimbo. Whitehill made a wild rush at him, joined by others in the narrow passageway.

Traditionally, ball-player fights are as perilous as pillow fights between five-year-olds. This was no exception. However, with such indiscriminate flailing going on, Gehrig lost his footing. As he went down, he banged his head on a concrete stanchion. While on the ground, Lou's old tormentor, Cobb, aimed a couple of unheroic kicks at him. Spying this, the Babe, who had joined in the donnybrook, threw a haymaker at Cobb. Harry Heilmann grabbed the protesting Whitehill, preventing him from doing any further damage. Meusel helped the groggy Gehrig to his feet, practically carrying him to the Yankee dressing room.

When Lou regained full consciousness, he asked his team-mates, "Who won?" Not being very sympathetic with Lou's role in the brawl, his buddies abruptly turned their backs on him and walked off in a huff. Lou had totally misread the situation, for most of the Yankees were not convinced that Whitehill had purposely tried to hit him with a pitch. It seemed to them as if Lou had overreacted.

In 1925 Gehrig was still something of an oversized babe (small "b") in the woods, one who had a considerable amount to learn about the motivations of opponents who could be expected to play as hard against him as he played against them.

Lou and the Yanks
Come of Age

Few predicted in 1926 that the Yankees would be in strong contention. However, they failed to reckon with Huggins's sorcery, plus an infusion of new blood.

After his initiation at first base in 1925, Lou was counted on heavily by his manager in an infield that included only one veteran, Joe Dugan at third base. At shortstop was Mark Koenig, who had come up to the Yankees from St. Paul at the end of the 1925 season. The new second baseman was Anthony Michael Lazzeri, a lean, close-mouthed graduate of the San Francisco sandlots. Much was made of the fact that "Poosh 'Em Up Tony," as he was called by his Italian-American supporters, had never seen a big league game before he arrived with the Yankees. Yet here he was, along with the question-mark Koenig at short, helping to anchor the club's inner defense.

Playing on the right side of the Yankee infield with Gehrig,

Lazzeri became an instant favorite. Like Gehrig, Lazzeri was so uncommunicative that it was said interviewing him was "like trying to mine coal with a nail file and a pair of scissors."

Lou, at twenty-three, already lent an aura of dignity and high resolve to the Yankee team. By his actions, not his words, Lou made it clear that he was dedicated to winning. More than anything else, he was a team player.

When the Yankees broke camp to head North, Huggins spoke glowingly of Gehrig. "Lou has become an influence to the entire team," said Huggins. "You get a player with that kind of spirit and it spreads like a contagion to the other players. He has come much faster than I dared to expect."

This was an astonishing endorsement from his manager, for Gehrig was still being formed as a man and as an athlete. Often his persona grated on his mates, for he was too perfect, a living monument to rectitude. Yet he was earning respect for his quiet demeanor, his humility compared to Ruth's diverting worship of himself, and his willingness to listen to advice.

Perhaps one of the strangest examples of Gehrig's behavior occurred as the 1926 pennant race came down to its finish. After eight victories in a row at the opening of the season the Yankees had moved into first place. Despite a strong late-season bid by Cleveland under Tris Speaker, in his last hurrah as the team's manager and center fielder, the Yankees stayed in front of the pack, with the Athletics coming in third.

Toward the end of this three-way struggle, Lou revealed he might still be fighting his way out of adolescence. In the eighth inning of a game against the White Sox, the Yankees put two men on base with Lou coming up to bat. A hit could have given the Yankees a tie; a long hit would have meant victory. Lou took a hard swipe at the first pitch, lifting a pop fly above the catcher's head. It was turned into an easy out, causing Lou to shuffle slowly back to the Yankee bench. Despite this misadventure, the Yanks rallied.

Through the noise on the bench that celebrated the Yankee comeback, Gehrig's anguished sobbing could be heard. He was crying uncontrollably, unable to curb tears of disappointment. Huggins studied Lou for a moment, then in tones not meant to be harsh, said, "C'mon, Lou, c'mon, Lou."

Few of the hardened Yankees had ever been exposed to such a reaction. They felt Lou was still a mewling baby in a man's world. One of those sharing the bench with Gehrig was Waite Hoyt, who volunteered that Lou was crying because of an imagined failure in the clutch. "The others," said Hoyt, "would take refuge in gobs of cynical, muddied profanity."

Lou was determined to repay those who had helped him; he felt duty bound to prove to Huggins, Krichell, Colonel Ruppert, and Ed Barrow that their investment of time and energy in him was worthwhile. When he thought he had failed, he became distraught.

His earlier bout with Whitehill notwithstanding, Lou was rarely bellicose. With his weight and strength, he might have been an intimidating man. But he never chose to fling his physical presence around. An amusing encounter Lou had with Francis "Blackie" O'Rourke, a Detroit infielder who was five-ten and weighed only 165 pounds, points up that there was nothing of the bully about him.

O'Rourke was covering second base when Lou came barreling into him. Pivoting on the throw to first, trying for a double play on Lazzeri, O'Rourke was upended by Lou. "I thought a truck hit me," said O'Rourke.

Umpire Billy Evans, judging Lou's slide to be interference, ruled Lazzeri was also out at first base. As Gehrig trotted off the field, O'Rourke picked himself off the turf and yelled several unprintable names at him.

Gehrig started after O'Rourke, then stopped when a Tiger teammate shouldered Gehrig away from the second baseman. The next day, during infield practice, O'Rourke noticed that Lou was standing a few yards away at first base, his arms folded.

"He was looking as if he was going to bore a hole right through me," O'Rourke said. "Since our bench was on the first-base side, I'd have to pass Gehrig to get to it."

After taking more grounders than he cared to, in the hope that Gehrig would disappear, O'Rourke set out for the Detroit bench. Gehrig slowly advanced toward him, leading O'Rourke to think about a safe refuge.

"Suddenly Lou put out his hand to me and said, 'Frank, I'm sorry I went into you so hard yesterday. I shouldn't have done it.' I shook his hand as warmly as if he had been the president," recalled O'Rourke. "Then I said, 'Forget those names I called you, young fellow.' Lou smiled at me. We were always firm friends after that."

Gehrig's 1926 season, with his .313 batting average, 107 RBIs, 135 runs scored, 47 doubles, and 20 triples, lived up to Huggins's expectations. But there was one flaw to his overall performance: He hit only 16 home runs in 155 games.

Through most of the season, Lou mysteriously hit almost everything thrown at him to left field. Since he was thoroughly capable of hitting balls to right field, even when pitched to the outside of the plate, Huggins couldn't figure what Lou was up to. After all, with the many inviting short right-field fences in American League parks, Lou wasn't taking full advantage of his natural inclination to go to right field. Many of his hardest blows wound up in outfielders' gloves in center and left center.

When Lou told Huggins late in the year that he thought he'd achieve the best results by going to the opposite field, since most pitchers were throwing to him outside, Huggins stayed calm. But he reminded Lou that he could "pull" any pitcher in the world. All he had to do was set his mind to it. Gehrig never forgot the lecture.

Huggins continued to be critical of Lou's work in the field. He encouraged Lou to play farther off first base. "Then see if you can still stop them on your left," he said. "You're still weak on your bare-hand side. Try to break this weakness. Another thing, you don't come in well on bunts. You never know when to come in or when to stay back and let the pitcher handle the bunt. Work on it every day."

What Gehrig didn't need to take instruction for was base

stealing. Early in the season, still batting third in front of Ruth, he was on the front end, at home plate, of two double steals engineered with the Babe. One took place in a 12–11 Yankee victory in Boston in the year's opener.

Lou's career mark of fifteen steals of home, always on the run-scoring end of a double steal, rates as one of the more serendipitous statistics in the books. Who ever would have expected "Piano Legs" to navigate the bases with such adroitness! True, Gehrig had competent base-stealing partners like Lazzeri, who worked the double steal with Lou four times, and Ben Chapman, who combined with Lou on three. One was pulled off with his loyal roomie, Dickey. But when one considers that the aggressive Cobb stole home only thirty-five times, Gehrig's achievement becomes more remarkable. Consider, too, that Lou Brock never stole home a single time in his entire career, while Jackie Robinson worked it only nineteen times. The Babe, surprisingly, managed to steal home ten times. But that was one department in which Lou was able to surpass him.

In recent years stealing home has become less frequent in baseball, even though base stealing has proliferated through the ranks. But that seems due to the overall strategy of the game and not to any lack of aggressiveness on the part of the players.

Days before the Yankees clinched the 1926 American League pennant, the country was saturated with news of the Big Fight between Gene Tunney and Jack Dempsey. Tunney, a former Marine, took the heavyweight championship away from Dempsey in a bloody bout on September 23 in Philadelphia's Sesquicentennial Stadium. Over 135,000 people looked on, the most ever assembled for a sporting event. Sportswriters couldn't resist the temptation to drag Jack and Gene into every paragraph they typed. For example, the *New York Post*'s Walter Trumbull wrote: "The Yanks, with Ruth and Gehrig, carry a wallop which makes Dempsey's left hook and Tunney's right to the body look like a gentle pat." So it went. Dempsey, Tunney, and the Yankees were metaphors for bruising power, at least until Tunney administered a slick boxing lesson to the Manassa Mauler.

In the National League the St. Louis Cardinals edged out Cincinnati and Pittsburgh to snare their first pennant. The Cards, under Rogers Hornsby, rang up an embarrassing winning percentage of .576, the lowest ever for a winner in their circuit. With the aid of a supporting cast that included "Sunny" Jim Bottomley, the man who owned the all-time record of 12 RBIs in a single game, at first base and a pitching staff of Jesse Haines, Flint Rhem, and Willie Sherdel, the Cards were primed to surprise a lot of people.

Although Lou had batted cleanup in many games during the 1926 campaign, Huggins placed him in the fifth slot for the Series, which turned out to be an unforgettable seven-game thriller. Lou couldn't rival Ruth's four home runs, but he finished with a .348 average on eight hits in twenty-three times at bat. He had three runs batted in, cracked two doubles, and scored one run.

The Yankees began with a 2–1 victory behind Pennock, as Gehrig drove in both runs. In the second game Lou went hitless against the old workhorse Grover Cleveland Alexander, as the Cards won 6–2.

When the Series went to St. Louis, Haines, a thirty-three-year-old right-hander, stymied the New Yorkers on five hits as he coasted to a 5–0 victory. Gehrig had two hits, the only Yankee to have more than one.

Promising that he'd hit two home runs in the fourth game, the Babe fell down on his prediction. He connected *three* times, two off the Cards' starter Rhem and one off relief pitcher Herman Bell. In the 10–5 Yank win, tying the Series at two games each, Lou had two hits, including a double.

During the season Lou had gotten into the habit of cheering on his pitcher as he returned the baseball to the mound. "That's the old fight, stick in there," he'd say encouragingly. But Hoyt, the winning pitcher in the fourth game, didn't care for such verbal support. "Let me provide my own inspiration," he'd growl at Gehrig. However, as the years went by, Hoyt learned to appreciate Lou's unaffected enthusiasm, openly praising him for it.

Pennock, the southpaw stylist, put the Yanks ahead with a

fifth-game 3–2 victory in ten innings. In the tenth, Sherdel gave up a single to Koenig, who went to second on a wild pitch. The Babe was intentionally walked. Meusel moved up both runners with a sacrifice, causing Sherdel to walk Gehrig purposely to fill the bases. The strategy failed when Lazzeri hit a long fly to score Koenig with the winning run.

The sixth game was played on a cold, blustery day at Yankee Stadium. With Alexander again asserting his mastery, the Cards pounced on several Yank hurlers for a one-sided 10–2 victory.

The seventh and decisive game also began under bleak circumstances, with twenty-five thousand seats vacant. The contest started in a cold drizzle, with Hoyt pitching for the Yanks and Haines for the Cards.

In the seventh inning, with the Cards ahead 3–2, the Yankees almost—but not quite—pulled out the Series.

Fighting a blistered finger, Haines walked Combs to start the inning. Koenig sacrificed Combs to second. The Babe was walked intentionally. Meusel forced Ruth, Combs moving to third. With runners on first and third, manager Hornsby utilized the intentional walk, this time to Gehrig, thus loading the bases. Throughout their careers Babe and Lou were often intentionally walked, probably the most effective weapon that could be employed against them. However, when Lou batted immediately behind the Babe, it became a dubious proposition to reward Ruth with first base.

At this moment, Hornsby called on Alexander to relieve Haines. The oft-told tale insists the Card manager peered into Alex's world-weary eyes and concluded that the thirty-nine-year-old hurler, who had pitched and won a complete game the day before, hadn't been out on the town whooping it up. Alex lost no time getting the count even at one ball and one strike against Tony Lazzeri. On the next pitch, Lazzeri drove a shot to left field, just on the wrong side of the foul pole. That ball has come closer to going fair in the constant retelling of the episode. If it had, the Yanks probably would have won the Series.

On the fourth pitch, Alex burned one in over the plate, Lazzeri swung and missed, and three runners were stranded. The Yanks still had two innings to get Alex. But they never did. The strikeout remains one of the most celebrated in the game's annals and, for years after, old Alex, down on his luck, recited the details of his confrontation with Lazzeri at sleazy flea circuses.

It was a painful loss for the Yanks. Colonel Ruppert, who hated to lose, was more than disappointed. Huggins was bitter. Yet one had to keep the season in perspective. The Yanks had come all the way from a miserable seventh-place finish in 1925. They had seen the quick development of Gehrig and had watched a reformed Ruth bat .372 with forty-seven home runs, the most he'd hit since 1921.

10

An Incredible Year

The decade of the 1920s was dizzying, with ballyhooed personalities and events flooding the American imagination. In that ten-year span called the Roaring Twenties there was no more quintessential year than 1927.

Gehrig, now twenty-four years old, came of age in that year—but unlike other celebrated figures in the worlds of sport, politics, society, entertainment, and crime, he entered the public consciousness, if at all, almost as an afterthought. Despite a monumental season with the Yankees, he continued to be cast as an epigone, a supporting member in a dazzling cast.

So much happened in 1927, as the Yankees graduated from being the American League's best team to becoming unarguably the Greatest Team of All Time, that Gehrig curiously was only a footnote in his own tight little society. The year even started with rumors that Huggins was searching for a right-handed first baseman. During spring training Huggins got around to denying such stories, but only after Lou angrily said he didn't know what such talk was all about.

"It can't be that anyone who can field any better than I do is needed," said Gehrig. "If there's some mysterious guy who is being considered because he's supposed to be more effective in hitting left-handed pitching, that's a laugh. I can hit lefties as well as right-handers, and just as far."

Lou proved his point during the 1927 campaign. His home-run production, impartial to right-handers and left-handers alike, swelled to forty-seven. Only the Babe had ever done any better. Lou's RBIs went to 175, a new mark at the time, even more impressive when it's considered that he came to the plate sixty times after Ruth had cleared the bases with his home runs.

Gehrig batted .373 and had a league-leading 52 doubles, 18 triples, and 149 runs scored. (Heilmann of Detroit led American League hitters with .398.) Of Lou's total of 218 hits, 117 were for extra bases, a remarkable demonstration of power. In his second full season as a Yankee, Lou was voted his league's most valuable player.

From the moment the Babe crushed his first homer against Philadelphia's Howard Ehmke on April 16, Ruth and Gehrig, batting back-to-back, staged a personal home-run duel that enthralled the fans. Lou followed two days later with his first two homers against the Red Sox. The battle royal was on in earnest.

Typically, when Ruth hit his second homer of the year and Lou followed with his third, the *Herald-Tribune* noted that "the fans applauded Ruth's home run. That's his business. Not so Gehrig's. He's just a first baseman."

As late in the season as July 5, when Gehrig had twenty-eight homers and Ruth had twenty-five, the *New York Telegram* ran a headline saying "The Odds Favor Gehrig to Beat Out Ruth in Home Run Derby." If the Babe got stronger as the year ran out, nobody argued against the point that Gehrig had put on a wonderful show against his teammate.

Ruth himself, after connecting for his sixtieth homer, wasn't reluctant to praise his home-run twin. "I don't know," he said, "if anyone will ever break my record. I don't know and I don't care.

But if I don't, I know who will. Wait till that bozo over there [he shoved a finger in the direction of Lou] wades into them again and they may forget that a guy named Ruth ever lived."

With 110 victories in 154 games, the Yankees finished nineteen games ahead of Philadelphia. In third place, twenty-five games behind the Yanks, was Washington. The Red Sox, last in an eight-team field, were fifty-nine games behind New York, certainly an exercise in futility.

All by himself Ruth out-homered every other team in the league. As a club, the Yanks battered 158 homers, a new record. The A's were a pallid second, with 56. Together, the Babe and Lou had 107 homers, unheard of in those raucous times. Those '27 Yankees stood for "mountaintop greatness playing with a ferocity that was unprecedented," as Donald Honig has written.

"I'll lay five bucks against one thin dime," wrote the poetic John Kieran in the *New York Times,* "there was never a team came crashing through, like Ruth and the rest of the Yankee crew, like Combs, Lazzeri and Buster Lou."

The Yankees' scenario played out against a background of frenetic events that competed with the bombardiers in the Bronx. Even the playboy mayor of New York, Jimmy Walker, the Beau Brummell of shabby politics, spent much of his time applauding the Yankees at the ballpark.

On the mid-May afternoon that Charles Lindbergh flew alone across the Atlantic to Paris in his *Spirit of St. Louis,* the Yankees dropped a game to Cleveland, a loss almost as rare that year as Lindbergh's own passage. In winning ten games from the Yanks in '27, the Indians managed to win more games from them than any other team. Another club, the St. Louis Browns, lost to the New Yorkers twenty-one times in twenty-two tries!

When another more inglorious Ruth of '27—Ruth Snyder, the frosty-eyed blond—was sentenced to death on Friday, May 13, for the brutal murder of her art editor husband, the Babe and Lou were in the second month of their home-run competition. Ruth had eight at that stage, Lou seven.

On August 23, when shoemaker Sacco and fish-peddler Vanzetti defiantly went to their deaths in Massachusetts by electric chair, after years of controversy, the Yanks embraced a fifteen-game lead, Ruth had just etched his fortieth homer, and Lou trailed at thirty-nine. On September 6, the two men were tied at forty-four homers each. After that, it was all Ruth.

In the hours before Tunney retained his heavyweight title on September 22, by decisioning Dempsey in Chicago's Battle of the Long Count, the Babe banged his fifty-sixth home run. (Both Babe and Lou, being partial to sluggers, had picked Dempsey to win.) Babe's September song of seventeen homers was capped by his sixtieth home run off Tom Zachary of Washington on the next to the last day of the season. The following afternoon, in the Yankees' finale, Gehrig blasted his forty-seventh homer to beat the Senators, 4–3.

As the 1927 season unfolded, with Gehrig becoming a believable competitor of Ruth in the home-run department, the cognoscenti often remarked on their respective batting styles.

Not one to deprecate the latent talents of Gehrig, Huggins still felt he "lacked the grace of the Babe at bat." Ruth was a much more mobile hitter than Lou, he said, for the Babe was always on his toes. "The Babe swings with a free motion of his wrists," pointed out Huggins, "and the swing comes right out of his powerful shoulders. Lou, on the other hand, hits with a rigid wrist. Since he's somewhat flat-footed at the plate, he's in a position to get more direct power from his drives—and to get more hits off good balls. Lou's stance is less flexible than Babe's, it's more dug in."

Lou would stand at attention, his weight resting on his left foot. As the pitch was thrown, his weight shifted accordingly in a short stride. He was more inclined to hit to all fields with his blacksmith arms. When Lou swung, he never corkscrewed, as the Babe did with such inimitable flair. Many of Lou's batted balls were low line drives that rose swiftly.

Not yet the fat man of legend in '27, the Babe rested his weight on his right foot and more often than not pulled balls to right field in an arc precariously close to the clouds. Today commentators would call Gehrig's drives "ropes."

One of the more amusing results of the destruction wrought on enemy pitching by the Yanks' Murderers' Row was the anguished cry that arose to "Break Up the Yankees!" The phrase, half-hysterical, half-serious, served only to further mythologize Colonel Ruppert's window-breakers. Nothing could have been more flattering for the Colonel than to hear these bleats. The notion of dissolving his predators was about as far from Ruppert's intentions as trading Gehrig to John McGraw.

Dan Howley, the Browns' manager, suggested one day when his forlorn team visited Yankee Stadium that each Yankee hitter should be penalized one strike before coming to bat. Howley also thought Ruth might be slightly easier to face in a crucial series than Gehrig. "You can usually figure what the Babe might do," he said, "but you can *never* tell about Gehrig. Lou is likely to hit any kind of ball to any field."

Shortly before the 1927 World Series began, Mom Gehrig became seriously ill, requiring immediate surgery. Lou was so disturbed that he threatened to stay at her bedside until she recovered, which meant he would miss the entire Series. "She means more to me," he said, "than any ball game ever invented, even a World Series."

Faced with the prospect of Babe without Lou, Huggins diplomatically intervened. The manager informed Lou that Mom was in good hands and that she could get along without his physical presence. Reluctantly, Lou agreed to play, although not without a measure of guilt.

Facing the Yanks in the Series were the Pittsburgh Pirates, who had defeated Washington in the 1925 Series. There were two important additions to the Pirates' cast: the outfielding brothers Paul and Lloyd Waner.

Paul, or "Big Poison," was born in Harrah, Oklahoma, the same year Gehrig was born. Paul hit .380 in 1927 and won his league's Most Valuable Player Award. Of slight build, Paul, if called upon, could outdrink Ruth himself. Lloyd, or "Little Poison," the Pirates' leadoff man, was a fraction of an inch taller (five-nine), five pounds less than his brother, and three years younger. They weighed less than 300 pounds between them and cracked out a remarkable total of 460 hits.

Against bulkier types such as the Babe and Lou, the Waners and fellow Pittsburghers were given little chance to win. Exploiting this expectation, Huggins wisely decided to stage a bit of business that would have done honor to Hollywood producer Cecil B. DeMille.

On October 4, the day before the Series was to start at Pittsburgh's Forbes Field, Huggins planned for his charges to take a prolonged batting practice. He knew that the Waners, Harold "Pie" Traynor, Clyde Barnhart, Glenn Wright, and company would be scrutinizing the workout from the stands in their civilian clothes.

"I can still see that bunch of murderers stepping up there to take their cuts at the ball," reminisced Bengough, the peppery catcher on the '27 Yankees. "One after the other they came—Combs, Koenig, the Babe, Lou, Meusel, Tony. There wasn't a one of 'em, with the possible exception of myself, who couldn't send that ball winging out of the park. And bang 'em out of sight they did. Over the fences, against the fences, into the seats. It was unforgettable.

"All the while the Pirates stood by, open-mouthed, watching the demonstration. Now they knew that all the things the writers kept saying about these guys were true. But what they didn't appreciate was that Huggins, who probably had a deeper understanding of ball players than any other manager, had pulled off a classic gag. Hug simply had instructed Hoyt to lay the ball in there for each batter. 'Let 'em hit it, Waite,' he instructed—and Waite obliged. No pitcher ever followed a manager's instructions better than Hoyt did that day."

During this exercise the Babe and Lou hit at least a dozen balls into the double-decker bleachers that curved around right field. Most of the Pirates were familiar with the Babe but few had ever seen Lou hit before. They were in for a royal treat, for Lou propelled one of his drives far over the center-field fence, something that had never been done by any National Leaguer, even in practice. Taking in the foreboding scene, Little Poison whispered to Big Poison, "Jesus, they're sure big guys. Do they always hit like that?"

Manager Donie Bush of the Pirates tried to minimize the impact of the demonstration. "The hell with that stuff," he said, projecting a brave front. "Let's show 'em we've got a few hitters ourselves."

But Ring Lardner, reporting on the Series for the *Evening World,* figured that the Pirates-Yankee matchup was patently unfair. "I don't mean to imply that the Pirates are scared," he wrote, "but if they ain't nervous, they ain't human."

The first game was won by the Yanks, 5–4. Gehrig was now in the cleanup slot behind the Babe. In the first inning, with Ruth on base, Lou got a triple when Big Poison missed a shoestring catch on Lou's drive to right field.

While making an impression with his bat, Lou also drew raves for his budding defensive prowess. Joe Vila, the *New York Sun* columnist, couldn't get over how "George Grantham was deprived of a double in the fourth inning, when Lou made a running pickup near the foul line back of first base." In the eighth, Lou again robbed Grantham on a seething grounder.

Even before the Series began, Lou spent considerable time pacing off the distance from first base to the new field boxes that had been installed by the Pittsburgh owner, Barney Dreyfus. With such attention to detail, Lou was fixing in his mind how far he could scramble into foul territory for vagrant Pirate pop flies. Lou had come a long way in erasing his image as an artless baby hippo.

"There has never been a good player who was dumb. Beef and bulk and mere endurance count for little, judgment and daring for much," Jacques Barzun, the Columbia historian, once wrote.

Everyone knew Lou could hit. Now it also became a pleasure to watch him field. One witness to his improvement, writer Adie Suehsdorf, retained a glowing image of Lou making the first base to shortstop to first base (3–6–3) double play. "Lou could dig the ball out of the dirt, as well as Terry, maybe better," says Suehs-dorf. "I'll always remember him in the last round of infield practice. The third baseman has made the play home and left the field, likewise the shortstop and second baseman. Now the ball is thrown to Lou, who gathers it in and fires home. The catcher comes up the line a few feet and slams it back to Lou. Lou comes in a few feet, one-hands it, wheels, and fires. So it goes, once or twice more, until the two are throwing bullets to each other from only twenty-five to forty feet apart. Lou then breaks off with a wide grin and lumbers to the dugout. He experienced sheer joy in the whole ritual."

In the second game at Pittsburgh, the Yanks won again, 6–2. Lou doubled during a three-run third inning and also batted in a run during a three-run eighth.

For days there were dire predictions that the Pirates would feast on the left-handed Pennock. It was pointed out that the Pirates had beaten up on National League southpaws all season. These theories didn't deter Huggins from starting Pennock in the third game.

In the first inning Combs and Koenig singled. Then Lou hit an enormous drive to deepest center field that scored both Combs and Koenig. Trying to convert the triple into an inside-the-park homer, Lou was thrown out at home on an excellent relay from Little Poison to shortstop Wright to catcher Gooch. "That was the most thunderous hit of the Series," said the *World.*

Pennock, meanwhile, retired twenty-one men in a row. In the eighth the spell was finally broken, when Traynor singled. Lou had another good afternoon, going two for three, as the Yanks won, 8–1.

The next day the Yankees made it four straight, winning 4–3. Ruth hit a homer, his tenth in Series play, but Lou was blanked in five tries. Having made a shambles of the American League race, the Yankees had become the first American League team to register a four-game sweep in the Series.

Each Yankee received a Series share of $5,592, which almost equaled Lou's 1927 salary of $8,000, little more than a day's pay

at that time for the average Wall Street plunger. The Babe was up
to $70,000 per year, Combs earned $10,500, Meusel pocketed
$13,000, and the popular Lazzeri matched Lou's $8,000. The me-
dian Yankee salary was $7,000, the average about $10,000. One
almost has to refrain from gasping at these figures.

With the record-shattering season at an end, Ruth and Gehrig were the most popular tandem in American sports, surpassing
those other twins of demolition, Dempsey and Tunney. The Yankee stablemates were in great public demand, particularly in
those sections west of the Mississippi where major league baseball entered the consciousness only through newspaper stories
and silent newsreels.

The practice of putting famous athletes on display, whether
on stage, screen, or cross-country tour, originated with the bois-
terous heavyweight champion John L. Sullivan in the late 1890s.
After "Gentleman Jim" Corbett upended Sullivan, Corbett emu-
lated his predecessor in several stage appearances.

In 1926 tennis's Suzanne Lenglen, a chic Frenchwoman, went
on tour. In just four months Lenglen brought in an astonishing
$250,000. Another tennis titan, the stage-struck Bill Tilden, ap-
peared as Dracula in an embarrassing New York production.

Publicist Christy Walsh, who was also Ruth's business manager, took note of such artistic precedents. Hired to keep the
Babe from falling into bankruptcy, Walsh decided a nationwide
tour for both Ruth and Gehrig was just the thing to add cash to
Ruth's bank account while also affording people in the remotest
boondocks an opportunity to get a look at the two home-run
icons. Through Walsh, Babe made Lou an offer that provided Lou
with more money for a month than he got for the whole season.
At least that was what Ruth told people.

On October 11, three days after the Yanks nailed down the
Pirates, the twosome departed from Pennsylvania Station in New
York on a three-week barnstorming itinerary. Amid much
hoopla, the movable home-run feast wended its way through the
middle American Bible Belt, then on out to the Pacific coast,
where it would be another thirty years before big league base-

ball arrived. Day after day, Babe and Lou played in sold-out ballparks before crowds of the idol-worshiping curious, many of whom had never seen a big league game. More than a quarter of a million fans in eighteen states paid their way in to watch Ruth's "Bustin' Babes" confront Gehrig's "Larrupin' Lous," the two teams being composed of local players from each town on the agenda.

In San Francisco on October 22, thirteen thousand fans cheered for their two favorites and Lou came through with a home run. On this occasion, Ruth failed to produce.

In San Francisco's Recreation Park on October 24, Ruth delivered by hitting two home runs that set off a tumult.

When the barnstormers reached San Jose, all of the city's twelve schools as well as most of the industry in the town of sixty thousand closed down. It was like the Fourth of July or a circus in town, without the elephants and clowns. Sodality Park was packed with over three thousand fans, each paying about $1.50, a large sum in 1927.

From San Jose the tour rolled on to Fresno, Santa Barbara, and San Diego. On October 29, thirty thousand fans assembled in Los Angeles's Wrigley Field, where the state's lieutenant governor, Buron Fitts, tossed out the first ball.

Over the tour Babe connected for twenty homers and had a .616 batting average. Lou trailed with thirteen homers, while his average nipped the Babe's at .618.

Often Babe would emerge from the back platform of his railroad car to bestow his papal blessing on the crowds, for he always enjoyed such exchanges with the public. But Lou didn't care for it. Invariably, he would hide away in the interior of the car while the Babe would encourage him to get out there and say hello to the folks.

"C'mon, keed, they want to see you, too," the Babe would say. As Ruth dispensed autographs wherever he went, he never failed to pull Lou over to join him. Lou was always obliging, but didn't revel in it the way the Babe did.

As the ultimate sports hero of his time, Ruth was always "on" for his admirers, even at the risk of occasionally acting like a buffoon. Gehrig, on the other hand, was remote. However, it took the two of them to brighten up the lives of their countrywide constituency.

11

The Odd Couple

After several years playing alongside the Babe, plus the tumultuous weeks on the road after the 1927 Series, Lou should have grown closer to his larger-than-life teammate. Sharing confidences and quarters, eating together, receiving selfless hitting tips from the great man, playing cards, and receiving invitations (which he supposedly refused) to join Babe in hotel orgies with pickups, Lou assuredly had to be regarded as a friend. However, questions always remained about the exact texture of the relationship.

Sometimes, the purported closeness between celebrated duos isn't quite what press agents tell us. An amusing case, for instance, was the relationship between Bing Crosby and Bob Hope, who made many popular "road" movies in the 1930s and 1940s. In truth, when the two weren't cavorting on the screen together, they had little to do with each other. Word finally leaked that Crosby never so much as invited his comic sidekick to his home for a cup of coffee.

Though Lou and the Babe shared many moments together, on and off the field, they were complete opposites. Yes, they enjoyed fishing together and the Babe liked nothing better than to indulge in Mom Gehrig's home-cooked meals. But there was too much difference in temperament and character for a firm bond of friendship to have formed.

It was common for sportswriters to suggest that Lou had a genuine admiration for the Babe and was content to live in the Babe's shadow. Much of that may have been wishful thinking, an oversimplification. As time went on, nobody could be certain that Lou freely accepted his role, with its eternal billing as second banana. As a lesser plant trying to blossom in full, Lou may have been secretly resentful of his spear-carrying assignment. How could a man relish constantly being eclipsed by a mighty oak?

Lou couldn't have been blamed for private reservations about one who lived such an undisciplined, tempestuous existence, always in the headlines, yet rarely being forced to pay for his derelictions. With each act of hell-raising and uninhibited carousing Ruth curiously won increasing plaudits, while Lou, "unvarying and ongoing as a railroad track," in writer Donald Honig's words, received only a measure of admiration for his steadfastness.

When the *New York Times* published an article in 1927 about an exhibition game that the Yankees played in St. Paul, Minnesota, the headline read "FANS WORSHIP RUTH BUT FORGET GEHRIG." At the time Lou was one home run ahead of the Babe in their personal home-run duel, yet the article went on to describe Lou as little more than a "pretender." During the game, "Ruth was kept busy signing baseballs and otherwise being tormented by his worshippers. One youth rushed out on the diamond to present a bottle of pop to the Babe, while Gehrig was practically in seclusion." It isn't difficult to fathom how Lou must have reacted to that story. Even if this was a fair account of how the Babe was loved and Lou was ignored, Gehrig wouldn't have been human if he didn't nurse a burning distaste for such a public depiction of their differences.

Yet, in spite of such dismissal, Lou remained publicly laudatory about the Babe. When the two barnstormed again after the 1929 season, Lou was generous in praise for his road companion. "Babe sure knows how to live," he remarked. "It was the most wonderful education I've ever been given. I don't mean in books. I mean in getting the most out of life, in learning how to meet people and having a good time and really seeing all there is to see."

Lou continued in this view as if he was trying to be supportive of the view others had of him. "I'm just the guy on the Yankees who's in there every day," he'd say. "I'm the fellow who follows the Babe in the batting order. If I stood on my head, nobody would pay any attention."

But even for a man of Lou's modesty, such a posture had its limits. Did one ever detect any undertone of envy in Lou's words, any giveaway body language that exposed his innermost feelings?

When Leo Durocher was a cocky rookie infielder with the Yanks in 1927, he observed that the only time he ever heard the Babe utter a word to Lou was to tell him that when the season was over "you'll be behind me in homers!" Durocher thought the relationship between the two was scarcely friendly, though he didn't think that they disliked each other.

The truth may never be known. But a revealing story was told by the late Bob Shawkey, a pitcher who served as the Yankees' manager in 1930. During spring training the two sluggers always elicited many gasps of approval from spectators as they sent repeated blasts into the cloudless Florida skies. On one of these days, Lou, who followed the Babe into the batter's box, waited on the bench to hit. His eyes concentrated on each Ruthian swing, on the heavenly flight of each ball, as if he were observing such artistry for the first time. His face never changed expression. He was utterly fascinated by the Babe's performance.

Even if he watched with a mixture of awe and envy, he just couldn't take his eyes off the figure at home plate.

As Lou kept watching Ruth, Shawkey, standing off to the side, kept watching Lou. For an instant, Lou's eyes moved from Ruth to Shawkey and he became aware that Shawkey was staring at him. He turned quickly away from his Babe-watching. Was he embarrassed to be caught thinking something he didn't want anybody to know about? Shawkey thought that to be the case.

At the start of his career Lou was desperately insecure. When his high school baseball coach expressed disapproval for his failing to appear on time for practice one afternoon, Lou could offer only a lame excuse. Evasively, he told the coach he was doing something else, but he was too fearful to point out that he'd been anxiously walking outside of the field to steel himself for the occasion.

After he became a celebrated Yankee, Lou continued to experience difficulties handling questions from the press. He was constantly concerned that he wouldn't comport himself intelligently. "When these writers would ask me questions," he said, "they'd often think I was rude if I didn't answer right away. They didn't know I was so scared I was almost shitting in my pants."

There was at least one moment, however, when Lou lashed out in uncontrolled anger at writers. One day in the Yankee locker room, where snacks were available to players and press, a baseball writer devoured a hot dog that produced a startling result. Within moments, the man became miserably ill. After the writer's needs were tended to, he was removed from the premises. Gehrig, who had been out on the field, was informed about the little drama that had just taken place. Without hesitation, he snapped: "A writer? Good, they should have given the guy rat poison!"

Lou's difficulty with the press stemmed from his inability to master the art of small talk. Not adept at ornamental language or rhetorical flourishes, Lou had a tendency to speak in flat, undramatic sentences, much to the chagrin of reporters who wrote about the Yankees.

The intemperate attack on the writer, as unexpected as it was out of character, remains a mystery, for Lou was constantly held up as an exemplar of virtue. The writer probably never had composed an uncomplimentary paragraph about the man.

Another incident with the media, an incident more amusing than upsetting, evolved out of Lou's appearance on Robert L. Ripley's "Believe It or Not" coast-to-coast radio show. At the time Lou was being paid $1,000 for his endorsement of Huskies, a breakfast cereal manufactured by Quaker Oats. During the course of the broadcast Ripley asked Lou what he ate for breakfast every morning. What helped him hit all those homers? Lou, in his nervousness, promptly responded: "A heaping bowlful of Wheaties!" Wheaties was a product of General Mills, a rival company of Quaker Oats.

Lou's verbal foul ball caused considerable embarrassment. But when he tried to set things right with Quaker Oats by returning the $1,000, the company wouldn't hear of it. They reasoned that the gaffe had earned them ten times more publicity than if Lou had managed to get his lines straight.

To make amends, Lou was invited back on Ripley's show. This time, when asked the same question about his breakfast habits, he hit it right out of the ballpark. "My favorite is Huskies, and I've tried them all," he said breezily. Millions cheered quietly in their living rooms for the poor guy, while Quaker Oats was strongly supported in its contention that every ball player was entitled to at least one mistake.

In only one reported instance did Lou ever publicly excoriate a teammate. That turned out to be Babe himself.

Lou enjoyed playing bridge and hearts with people like the Babe, Earle Combs, Bill Dickey, and Robert "Red" Rolfe. From time to time sportswriters such as Grantland Rice, Stanley Frank, and Richards Vidmer also sat in. These games were often marked by Babe's explosions and friendly insults. But one evening as the train chugged through the night to St. Louis, he became especially rancorous over a bridge hand that he felt he had "loused up."

"Hey," boomed the Babe, "I butchered that one just like McCarthy handles the goddamn pitchers!"

Hearing this, Lou's face flushed with anger. After a few painful seconds of silence, he accused the Babe of having a big, loose mouth. The others at the table, unused to this side of Lou, offered no rebuttals.

The next day, presumably after he'd had time to cool off, Lou was still aggrieved. He told Frank that Ruth popped off too "damn much" about a lot of things. Frank reminded Lou that the Babe, always a wild bidder, especially when he was nursing a bottle of prohibition scotch, really didn't mean to say what he did. But Lou was unrelenting. He believed that anyone who would demean baseball should be censured. He thought, as he told Frank, that Ruth had a special obligation as the game's prime celebrity to behave himself.

"For Lou," said Frank, "the game was almost holy, a religion." It had raised him from a grubby lower-middle-class environment to national fame and he felt he had a special obligation to it.

Everyone on the Yankees was aware of Ruth's feelings toward Joe McCarthy, the former Cubs manager who was hired to pilot the Yanks in 1931. It was no secret that the Babe wanted the Yankee job and hoped that Colonel Ruppert would tap him for the assignment. But even if Lou had rooted for the Babe to get the post (there is no record of his ever expressing himself in this way), he didn't think it was proper for Ruth, in front of reporters, to discuss his resentments. One has to wonder, too, if Lou's outburst against the Babe wasn't an expression of a hidden antagonism usually well concealed.

Pennant-winning players have never failed to be assertive at contract-signing time. This was true even sixty years ago, when baseball owners acted like patroons, exploiting the one-sided reserve clause that gave ball players little room for bargaining.

After the 1928 season, Colonel Ruppert and Ed Barrow faced more than the usual resistance from their troops. Amusingly, Ruppert pleaded that he wasn't worth as many millions as his players thought he was.

While some players threatened to hold out for more money, the only one who achieved any success in this sparring was the Babe. Not only did Ruth have the batting numbers going for him, but wherever he went around the American League he was an enormous drawing card. The Yankees even paid large premiums to insure the Babe's life.

Ruth's annual salary confrontation with the Yankees was always headline stuff. The Babe's biographer, Robert Creamer, wrote that the "formal signing of Ruth's contract each year was covered like a Presidential press conference. . . . No one really noticed when Gehrig signed." Prior to going to the mat with Ruppert in 1928, the Babe extracted a promise from Lou that Gehrig would turn down anything less than $30,000 a year. For all of his good-natured braggadocio, the Babe wasn't so preoccupied with himself that he ignored the skills of his teammates.

"You go in there and ask for what you're worth," he advised Lou. "I broke the home-run record, you knocked in all those darn runs. We've got them where we want them. If I hold out, and you do, too, I'll bet you can get ten thousand more than you expect."

But the Babe was no psychologist. He failed to reckon with Lou's free-floating insecurity and overlooked Lou's exaggerated respect for authority. Lou, indeed, promised Ruth he'd ask for $30,000. However, once he got into a salary discussion with Barrow, his demands melted like ice cubes in the Sahara.

After an hour of talk with Barrow, Lou emerged with his typical grin. He had a contract for two years for $50,000, $5,000 less per year than he'd promised the Babe he would ask for.

When the news broke in the newspapers, Ruth called Lou. "Why didn't you keep your promise?" he asked. Lou had no satisfactory response.

"I didn't give a damn really," the Babe said, "but I was mad at him for not letting me know. I thought the guy was seriously listening to me." It may have been the start of the Babe's indifference to Lou's fortunes.

Lou just did not have the stomach to fight the Yankee front office. He'd leave it to Ruth to raise salary standards for himself and others.

The most intense competitors often tend to be unassertive once away from the playing field. Driven to excel, many are inept and awkward in their day-to-day social environments. Gehrig appeared to fit that mold exactly.

12

A Series Hero

Whether the frivolous rich, the bootleggers, the booboisie, or the silk-shirted stockbrokers knew it or not, 1928 would turn out to be the apogee of the Roaring Twenties.

With Calvin Coolidge announcing "I do not choose to run," the way was then paved for Herbert Hoover to defeat Al Smith of New York for the presidency. Hoover also got his chance to utter one of the least redeemable political promises in history: "Two cars in every garage, two chickens in every pot."

In six years of Coolidge's White House such brazen crime lords as Al Capone, Bugs Moran, Legs Diamond, Waxey Gordon, and Owney Madden racked up unimaginable profits as they littered the landscape with corpses. Madden, a former Hell's Kitchen roughneck who schemed his way to the top of the illicit booze business, employed Mom Gehrig at one time to clean his house when he lived on Manhattan's West Side.

While such shenanigans were taking place, the Yankees went about proving that 1927 was no aberration. Oddly, they managed this despite a profusion of injuries to some of their key men. The Babe spent much of his time nursing charley horses, Combs was taped up like a mummy, Lazzeri had a bad shoulder, Pennock's left arm went limp, and even Lou complained of a pain or two. Of course, such trivial wounds didn't prevent him from playing every game of the schedule for the third straight year.

During a series with Washington, Bucky Harris, a feisty little infielder, tried to intimidate Lou. With the score tied in the eighth inning, and a Senator on third, Harris bunted down the first-base line. When Lou fielded the ball cleanly and tried to beat Harris to the bag, Bucky pounced hard on Lou's big toe. As the player on third started for home, Gehrig threw the ball a half-mile over the catcher's head and the winning run scored.

"I've never seen a man look so surprised and hurt," Harris recalled, as he discussed Lou's reaction to being purposely spiked. "But he never uttered a word of complaint."

For the rest of the year, Bucky expected Lou would try to square accounts with him. The idea frightened him, for Lou had sixty pounds on him.

"But Lou never did a thing," said Harris. "Every time after that when I got to first, he just gazed at me as though to ask me how I could do such a thing. I got feeling so ashamed of myself for what I'd done that I finally apologized to him. You should have seen the poor guy light up!"

By the middle of the 1928 season the Yanks were seventeen games in front of the Athletics, threatening to break open the race the way the 1927 club did (the '27 Yankees were twelve ahead on July 4, the largest margin by that date in American League history). Inexorably, though, the injuries took a toll. By early September when the Athletics crept briefly into first place, other events occurred that created ripples in the Yankee clubhouse. Cobb, with the Athletics in his sunset days, glumly announced he was retiring. Though Lou rarely wished another man ill, there were no discernible tears on his cheeks. But tears did

flow, for Lou and other Yankees, when the sad news arrived that
Urban Shocker, their dependable pitcher in 1926 and 1927, died
of heart disease in Denver on September 9, at the age of thirty-
eight. (Shocker was the first of the '27 team to die. As the years
went by, a number of players on that club, including Lou and the
Babe, died tragically early in life in a chilling mockery of the
actuarial tables.)

Despite their misfortunes, the Yankees rallied their forces to
win. They did it the hard way, too, beating the Athletics in a
crucial September 9 doubleheader. Both the Babe and Lou again
had spectacular seasons. The Babe banged fifty-four home runs,
off a bit from the sacrosanct sixty of '27, while Lou hit twenty-
seven homers, but Lou had 142 RBIs, which led the league for the
second straight year, and he batted .374.

The rivals in the 1928 World Series were the Cardinals, who
had drubbed the Yanks in 1926, but this was a different Card club
than the one that had faced the Yanks two years before. Second
baseman Frankie Frisch, a New York boy like Lou, had attended
Fordham in the Bronx. The irrepressible Walter "Rabbit" Maranville was at shortstop, playing in his first Series since 1914, and Bill
McKechnie had replaced Hornsby as manager.

At thirty-three, Babe was eight years older than Lou. If he
was hurting and complaining, that was scant reason for Card
pitchers to take solace, for the Babe always seemed to rise to the
occasion.

There was evidence, too, that Lou had matured. His handsome, dimpled face, with its strong chin, had lost some of its baby
fat, giving him the stereotypical all-American good looks that he'd
carry the rest of his life. If his early shyness had diminished, he
was still a man not totally at ease with himself or his surroundings. Peculiarly, he still did things in innocence that could raise
the few hairs on Ed Barrow's balding head.

One day word reached Barrow's office that Lou had been
engaging in twilight games of stickball with the gang from his old
home neighborhood. To put it mildly, Barrow looked askance at
this practice, since there was always the chance that Lou would

suffer an injury in this street game, which was played with broom handles instead of bats and hard rubber balls instead of base-balls.

What further angered Barrow was that one of the players, perhaps even Lou, had knocked a ball into the window of a local butcher, spreading splinters of glass into the chopped steak. As a result, the kids were hauled off to the nearest police precinct, where Lou "confessed" to the sergeant behind the desk.

"My name is Gehrig," he said. "Wait till Mr. Barrow finds out about this!"

The sergeant, reputedly a Yankee fan, didn't press charges. But when Barrow heard about it, he threw a small fit. If Barrow had never been sympathetic to Babe's style, he regarded Lou, in his own icy way, as an adopted son.

"This silliness must stop, Lou," Barrow said. "It's just stupid to play another game after you've already played all day." That was the last Lou ever heard on the subject from Barrow.

The Cards were favored by the odds-makers, who may have been influenced by the fact that prior to the Series the Babe was still limping around, while the Iron Horse's lip was swollen, the result of his having stopped a sharp grounder with his face in September.

With Hoyt on the mound in the first game, the Yankees de-feated the Cards, 4–1, on a warm, sunny day. While a fifty-strong contingent of Hartford fans provided him with a personal cheer-ing section, Lou came through with a double and a single, driving in two runs.

The next day the Yankees also won, 9–3, with Lou again sounding the clarion call with a first-inning, first-pitch home run into the right-field bleachers, scoring two men ahead of him. Sadly, Lou's blow came off Alexander, the hero of '26, but now a harmless forty-two-year-old pitcher with a dinky curve.

Alex tried to be philosophical. "The ball Gehrig hit was the same kind I fed him all through the 1926 Series, when he never hit a hard one off me," he said. "This time I gave him a screwball on the outside, and look what he did to me. Goodnight!" Apparently,

Lou had gotten much better and, alas, Alex had passed his prime.

Ahead in the Series two games to none, the Yanks confidently traveled west on their October 6 day off. Around midnight Lou got up from a bridge game with the Babe, part-time infielder Mike Gazella, and one of the reporters and returned with an armful of fried chicken, thanks to Mom Gehrig, who had brought the delicacies along for the Yankee troupe. It was not unusual for Lou's mother to accompany him on many Yankee road trips.

She also made it her business to visit the Yankee training camp each spring, and tried to be a daily spectator when the Yanks were at home. For much of 1927 she had been ill and so couldn't be on hand to watch her son. However, in 1928 she was again a presence. Mom Gehrig had been a constant goad in her son's life, encouraging him when he was distressed and nursing him when he needed her homemade remedies to heal the broken bones, bruises, and "strawberries" that were the inevitable price he paid for playing the game unyieldingly.

Her presence wasn't resented by either Lou or his teammates, especially when she provided such delectable food for all the hungry young men. At this time Mom Gehrig was still getting along marvelously well with Ruth, fondly calling him "Judge" (a corruption of George, the Babe's real first name).

Though Lou's baseball salary helped the Gehrigs forget their early life of deprivation in Yorkville, they were still rather miserly with money. But that didn't prevent Mom Gehrig from setting a table, on the road or at her New Rochelle house, that would have drawn envious stares from the maître d' at Lüchow's, on 14th Street, which was then the most popular German-American restaurant in Manhattan.

In the third game on October 7 at Sportsman's Park in St. Louis, Lou hit two homers to knock in three runs, as the Yanks won, 7–3.

Lou's first homer was an orthodox affair, off the roof of the right-field bleachers. But the second, in the fourth inning, was a line drive that center fielder Taylor Douthit unwisely attempted to corral for a shoestring catch. Instead, the ball rolled all the way to the flagpole, as Lou pounded around the bases on the Babe's heels, for an inside-the-park home run.

After Gehrig dominated the Series for three games, the Babe resumed his kingpin role in the fourth game. He hit three home runs, the second time he'd accomplished that feat in a Series. Lou also hit one, his fourth, as the Yanks won, 7–3, to pick up their second consecutive world championship. Lou's homer put the Yanks ahead to stay in the seventh inning, but Ruth wound up winning most of the applause. The two Yankees had attained near batting perfection in baseball's showcase event, yet, again, Babe drew the notices. The *New York Times* underlined the paradox: "Gehrig tied Ruth's record of four home runs in a Series, yet few knew he played." The Babe remained incorrigible and charismatic, a much more compelling, unambiguous hero than Gehrig.

The World Series of 1928 could have been described as *nolo contendere,* though the Cards did show up. In the Yanks' four-game sweep, Ruth hit .625, on ten hits, the highest average ever compiled by a player in a four-game Series. Lou was right behind Babe, at .545 on six hits. He drove in nine runs and scored five, while Babe batted in four runs and scored nine.

There was irony in the way the Cards pitchers dealt with the two sluggers. In 1926 against the Cards, Babe walked twelve times in seven games, mostly on instructions from the ever-vigilant Hornsby. In 1928 Babe walked only once, while Lou drew six passes. Within two years it seemed that Gehrig's appearances at the plate had become more ominous than Babe's.

Whatever the relative qualities of the two sluggers, at this stage it was obvious that they had put on the greatest demonstration of two-man power that any World Series had ever seen.

The Yanks wasted no time whooping it up on the Yankee Special returning to New York. Ruth was joined by other celebrants, including Gehrig, as they tried to dispossess everyone of their shirts. Partial to such humor, Lou got together with the Babe to break into Colonel Ruppert's stateroom, where the owner and his friend Colonel Fred Wattenberg were trying to rest for the night.

Ruppert was hardly surprised to find the Babe engaging in such rowdy behavior. But he was mystified by Lou's presence. The Babe emerged proudly holding Ruppert's pajama top for all to see, while Lou seized a piece of Wattenberg's sleeping attire. Someone else made off with Huggins's false teeth. The chief suspect was Durocher, the former pool hall hustler from West Springfield, Massachusetts, who, like Gehrig, needed no boozy stimulation to participate in such hijinks.

When the Yanks arrived at New York's Grand Central Terminal an hour late on the night of October 10, thousands were still gathered there to cheer for them. To the victors belongs the noise. When Lou and Hoyt preceded Babe out of the train, there was dutiful applause. But when the Babe finally appeared, the applause was deafening. Lou had to settle for a small share of the triumphant moment.

13

Things Come Loose

In 1929, there was no reason to suspect all hell would soon break loose. America was still perceived as the Rock of Gibraltar of the world economy. Didn't the stock market quotations that competed for front-page space with the late baseball scores prove that?

From the fat cats to the friendly florist, from the shoeshine boy to the sales clerk, from the chorus girls with their bee-sting lips to, yes, the men who played big league baseball, almost everyone was up to his neck in the soaring stock market. (Oddly, only the veteran speculator Bernard Baruch had stopped speculating. Instead, he was investing in bonds.)

But the tide turned swiftly. "It was difficult for those born late," wrote author Edmund Wilson, "to believe it really occurred, that between 1929 and 1933, the whole structure of American society seemed to be going to pieces."

In the world of baseball, the three-year Yankee dynasty ripped apart at the seams just as unceremoniously.

The Yankees had started fast and with considerable style. (The club became the first in the big leagues to feature numbers on the backs of its players, in accordance with their respective batting-order positions. Thus, the Babe was number 3 and Lou was 4.) In May Gehrig hit three consecutive homers in one game. In June and July the Yanks appeared to be in a position to retain their laurels. In August the Babe hit his 500th home run.

But in three days of impotence in August the Yanks were shut out three straight times by the Browns, the fourth-place team. From there on, it was all downhill. The Athletics won the American League flag by eighteen games over the Yanks, just a few weeks before the bottom fell out of the country.

"Everything nailed down is coming loose," said Gabriel to De Lawd in *Green Pastures.* Communist dictator Joseph Stalin laughed scornfully at America's distress; John D. Rockefeller started rationing his dimes to the public; people who softly hummed "Button Up Your Overcoat" in 1928 didn't have an overcoat to button up in 1929.

For the dethroned Yankees it was a time of turmoil and disappointment. In a year of periodic slumps, Lou saw his batting average dive seventy-four points to .300. The Babe, whose estranged wife, thirty-one-year-old Helen, died in January during a fire that swept her house in Watertown, Massachusetts, went from fifty-four homers in 1928 to forty-six in 1929. The taciturn Meusel, a lifetime .311 hitter, sunk to .261 and played his last game in the Yankee outfield. Hoyt and Pennock won nineteen games between them, down from forty the previous season. In May two fans died in a mad rush for the exit at Yankee Stadium during a sudden squall.

How ironic it all was! When the 1929 season started, the anguished cries of "Break Up the Yankees" had again emerged. Rumors again also circulated that the Yanks were about to trade Lou, the reasoning being that Babe and Lou shouldn't be permitted to wreck the balance of competition in their league. It was never explained how Ruppert would masochistically engage in such an act of equity. Huggins reassured the panic-mongers there was no need to break up the Yankees. "The time will come," he said, with baffling prescience, "when this team will crash."

Today, it makes a sprightly exercise to speculate on how much Gehrig might have brought if Ruppert had dangled him in front of his competitors. When Ruth became a Yankee in 1920, the Red Sox received in return $125,000, plus a $300,000 loan against a mortgage on Fenway Park. What would Lou have been worth almost a decade later, in the Era of Wonderful Nonsense?

But nobody had to break up the Yankees. Connie Mack's A's simply did the job on the battlefield. Mack, a former catcher, took over as pilot of the A's in 1901. He had already run through two cycles of glory in 1902–1905 and 1910–1914. Now, in 1929, he embarked on the third cycle.

Meanwhile, Huggins's spirit and body sagged. He couldn't sleep and his appetite was gone, as the Yankees crumbled. One day toward the end of the season, he said to Ruppert that he didn't "think the Yankees could make it this time." Ruppert was unbelieving, for he thought the Yankees could recover and go on to win. How could a team with Babe and Lou lose!

"This team is just tired," said Huggins, who could have been talking about himself. On September 20, Huggins arrived late at the Stadium. He felt so weak he could hardly climb into his uniform. His coaches, Charlie O'Leary, with Huggins since 1921, and Art Fletcher, were alarmed when they noticed an angry red carbuncle on the side of Huggins's face. Huggins insisted on taking his place in the dugout when the game with the Red Sox started. But he wasn't around after the third inning, for a doctor was summoned to examine him and he was ordered immediately to St. Vincent's Hospital.

"See if you can do any better with this team than I have," whispered Huggins to Fletcher. Those were the last command words he'd ever utter. On September 25, despite four blood transfusions, Huggins died of erysipelas, an infectious disease of the skin. He was just fifty.

As hard-boiled as most of that swaggering Yankee crew were, many of them cried when they heard that their little manager was dead. There were also a few who reacted with tight-lipped silence, for some had resented Huggins and chafed under his leadership. Surprisingly, that did not include Ruth, even if he had instigated several minor wars with Huggins.

"He was my friend, a great little guy," said Ruth. "I got a big kick out of doing things that would help him."

Of all the Yankees, perhaps the one who reacted to Huggins's death with the most sorrow was Lou. From the beginning, Huggins had been his support, his mentor. It was always clear that Lou had not come to the major leagues as a born player. He was not a "natural" in any true sense of the word. Only grim determination to succeed, plus his magnificent physique and stamina, had enabled him to make his way with the Yankees. Huggins was the other necessary component, for he had worked assiduously to drill baseball savvy into his earnest pupil.

"Only Lou's willingness and lack of conceit," said Huggins, "will make him into a complete ball player. That and those muscles are all he has."

With Huggins's death, Lou felt a great personal deprivation. "I guess I'll miss him more than anyone else. Next to my mother and father, he was the best friend a boy could have," he said. "When I first came up he told me I was the rawest, most awkward rookie he'd ever seen or come across in baseball. He taught me everything I know. He gave me my job and advised me on salary matters. He taught me how to invest my money. Because of him I had everything a man could ask for in a material way. There was never a more patient or pleasant man to work for. I can't believe he'll never join us again."

14

The Home Run that Didn't Count

J ust when the Athletics seemed on the verge of winning their third straight world title in 1931, an unshaven Oklahoman named John Leonard "Pepper" Martin of the St. Louis Cardinals ran himself into a household word.

In the Indian summer days of early October, Martin emerged as America's depression-time hero, literally stealing the World Series from under the proud noses of the Athletics. Not since Ruth became the nation's undisputed sports idol had anyone threatened his majesty.

Before Martin seized the stage, the Yanks had finished second in 1929, then third under one-term manager Shawkey in 1930. In Joe McCarthy's first year at the helm in 1931, the Yankees ended in second place.

When McCarthy, the National League manager, came to the American League and New York, he was a complete stranger to the Yankees. At forty-four, McCarthy was a rarity at the time—a man who had become a major league manager for the Cubs without a day of playing experience in the big leagues.

In his first spring training with the Yanks, McCarthy realized that many of the players regarded him with suspicion and a measure of contempt. But he won Gehrig's friendship and most of the others fell into line. In an exhibition game against Milwaukee, of the American Association, the Yanks unloaded a positively scary offense, winning by 19–1. Jimmy Reese, the skinny infielder from the Pacific Coast League, was so excited that he squeaked to McCarthy, "Well, how did you like that! Some score!"

McCarthy could give away his feelings by the look on his face. "Against that kind of a team, nineteen runs is nothing," he growled. "We should have scored thirty!"

Reese was flabbergasted. But two others who overheard it, Lou and his roommate, Dickey, were pleased.

"You know, Bill, I think this man is going to be all right. I like him. I like his attitude," said Lou.

"So do I," said Bill, who rarely disagreed with Lou about baseball matters. "He's our kind of guy."

Gaining Gehrig's respect, McCarthy, in return, admired Lou for those qualities that Huggins also had respected. More of a disciplinarian than Huggins, McCarthy was never content to let things slide. Although he became known, somewhat disparagingly, as the "push-button manager," he was a man who hated to lose and refused to coddle his athletes. That was precisely the kind of manager Gehrig appreciated, for he shared McCarthy's intense desire to win.

McCarthy invoked a rigid dress code—jackets and ties for players in the dining room—and demanded that players take each game seriously and be well conditioned. Lou agreed with McCarthy's decrees and McCarthy knew it. The two men were a perfect baseball marriage. Childless, as Huggins had been, McCarthy was attracted to Lou immediately. It was inevitable that McCarthy would come to regard Lou as the son he'd never had. The only facet of Lou's behavior that McCarthy, who was a heavy drinker, deplored was Lou's pipe smoking. Whenever the manager was around him, Lou hid the pipe from view.

Gehrig may have had a sweet smile, but he possessed a tough interior rarely on view. Playing with great intensity, he refused to accept defeat equably. After a losing effort by the Yankees, a reporter had to be a fool to confront him. Generally, it took Lou an hour to cool down and purge himself of the vile mood that would often engulf him.

Lou was not averse to chastising players if he suspected they were loafing or acting in ways that discredited the team. But he was careful not to make public inquisitions out of such outbursts. He confined his attacks to the clubhouse, invariably on a one-on-one basis and never with outsiders present to spread tales about dissension.

Lou took defeat out on himself, more than on others. After particularly wrenching losses, he could be seen on occasion sitting next to his locker sobbing and disconsolate. In 1930, after a 1–0 defeat, manager Shawkey gently reprimanded Lou for removing his foot from first base too cavalierly on a close play, thus costing a run and, as it turned out, the game. Gehrig's response was a quiet flow of tears and a promise that he had learned his lesson.

Even before McCarthy was hired in 1931, the Yankees were not exactly comatose. Fresh faces had arrived, including Dickey, the tall catcher from Bastrop, Louisiana, who would become a Hall of Famer, and Charles "Red" Ruffing, a right-hander who had lost twenty-five games in 1928 and twenty-two in 1929 with the Red Sox, testimony to his grit. Outfielder-infielder Ben Chapman, up from St. Paul, brought base stealing back to Yankee Stadium, as well as a violent temper. A slightly built southpaw from Rodeo, California, Vernon "Lefty" Gomez, joined the Yanks and won favor with his facile quips. In no time at all, Gomez replaced Pennock as the league's premier left-hander. Gomez attributed his pitching success to "clean living, a fast outfield, and that big fellow Gehrig at first base."

As a disciple of McCarthy's dead-serious approach, Lou usually did not care to lend himself to stunts dreamed up by publicists. But in spring training of 1931, he consented to bat against a young Georgia girl named Verne "Jackie" Mitchell, who reputedly threw a baseball with sufficient skill to be regarded as an equal of big leaguers. Lou and Ruth were enlisted to buttress Mitchell's reputation.

While a sizable crowd cheered, Mitchell, wearing the uniform of the Chattanooga Lookouts, faced the two famous sluggers in succession, striking them out on six pitches. Despite this display, Mitchell never made it to the "show." In fact, she was never heard from again, though Lou and the Babe both expressed amazement at her prowess. Until the day she died in 1987, Jackie Mitchell denied the exhibition was a prearranged joke.

In the three years that the Yankees failed to win the pennant, it was primarily Philadelphia pitching that did them in. Lefty Grove of the Athletics threw with such blistering speed that rival players swore that home-plate umpires couldn't see his pitches well enough to call them. "That third strike *sounded* high," whined his victims.

Grove insisted that he had mastered the trick of pitching to Gehrig, who already had hit three home runs in a game three times by mid-1930.

"I'd never think of throwing at Gehrig," acknowledged Grove, a man known to be as mean-spirited as a cornered rattlesnake. "You never want to get that fellow stirred up. There's just something about him that tells you to lay off him—or you'll get killed with a line drive."

Between them, from 1929 to 1931, Lou and Babe crammed more runs across the plate than any other duo in history. Lou had 35, 41, and 46 homers, respectively, for a total of 122. The Babe hit 46, 49, and 46 for a total of 141. Their cumulative home-run production added up to 263, enough to give most managers cardiac arrest. In those three years Lou batted across 484 runs, and Babe had 470. Lou's 184 RBIs in 1931 is still the all-time high for any American Leaguer and 29 runs more than the 155 games he played in that year.

Five times in his career Gehrig's RBIs would exceed the number of games he appeared in, a remarkable level of productivity. Only Ruth, who did it six times, is ahead of him in this bracket. Putting the achievement into perspective, Joe DiMaggio knocked in more runs than games played four times, as did Hank Greenberg, Jimmie Foxx, and Al Simmons. The major league high for most RBIs in a season over number of games played belongs to that fireplug Hack Wilson of the Cubs, who in 1930 batted in 190 runs in 155 games, for a differential of 35.

With all of his power—he hit three grand-slam home runs within four days in 1931—Lou never managed to top Ruth in home runs in any single season. The closest he came was in 1931, with the ignominious "home run that didn't count." Lyn Lary had been sold to the Yankees in 1928 by Oakland of the Pacific Coast League, along with infielder Jimmy Reese, for $150,000, a veritable king's ransom in those years. Lary, known as a flashy dresser, thus accounting for his nickname of "Broadway," considered the Babe a good enough friend to name him godfather to his son. In 1931, Lary became a shortstop capable of knocking in 107 runs.

But he won his chief renown that year due to some mindless base running in Washington. The misadventure cost Gehrig the home-run crown. (Gehrig, indeed, led the league in home runs twice, but only after the Babe had departed from Yankee Stadium.) Lary had reached first base, with two out, when Lou hit a tremendous shot into the center-field bleachers. The ball hit the bleacher seats and bounced back into the hands of center fielder Harry Rice. Lary looked over his shoulder as he rounded second base and spied Rice catching the rebound. Concluding that Rice had caught the ball on the fly for the third out, Lary reached third base and then trotted for the Yankee dugout, some thirty feet away, oblivious to the screams of his teammates, who pointed at him to return to the field.

Meanwhile, Gehrig, his head down, trotted around the bases. Apparently he never saw Lary depart the field. As he went around third base, he was called out by the umpire, for he had passed Lary on the basepaths. There went his home run. In the record book it wound up as a triple. When the year ended he had forty-six home runs, the same as Ruth. But Lou was never heard to utter a word of complaint about Lary.

Joe Cronin, playing shortstop that afternoon for Washington, remarked: "It was simply not Lou's nature to complain about this misfortune, or any other." A couple of years later, after Cronin had been traded by Washington to the Red Sox for Lary (who had been traded by the Yankees in 1934), Lary botched a perfect double-play ball while the Senators were playing his old team. When he threw home to cut off a potential winning run for the Yankees, the hurried toss was wide and the runner was safe.

That night, while waiting to board a home-bound train to New York, the Yankees were harsh on their former teammate. "Same old Broadway Lary," a couple of them chorussed. "The guy's still got rocks in his head." Even manager McCarthy was sarcastic about Lary's miscue. Lou, taking it all in, quickly came to Lary's defense. "A dozen mistakes are made in every game," he said, quietly. "Anybody can pull a boner. I've been around ten years, but I still get brainstorms. Look at the stupid play I pulled a couple of weeks ago."

Lou was referring to an incident that occurred when the Yanks were ahead by one run. He had a habit of rolling the ball back to the pitcher after taking a throw at first base for the last out in an inning. With one out and a runner on second, Lou made a putout at first. But thinking it was the last out, he dribbled the ball to the mound in his customary fashion, as the runner rounded third. Realizing his mental lapse, Lou pounced on the loose ball before the runner could make a break for the plate. No damage was done; the mental mistake did not cost the Yankees.

Nevertheless, Lou was willing to indict himself in order to curtail criticism of Lary. He didn't like to hear players gratuitously blasting other players. It was the same reaction he had shown toward Ruth when the Babe had popped off against McCarthy.

15

The Human Side

Gehrig's refusal to blame others, as he markedly demonstrated with Lary, was not just window dressing. This quality endeared him to such diverse personalities in the Yankee hierarchy as the unsentimental Barrow, the insightful Huggins, and the tough-minded McCarthy. It also won him the admiration of most of his teammates. Even little boys like Frank Graham, Jr., who got to hang around with the Yankees because his columnist father covered the ball club, came to worship Lou because "he never acquired the cockiness that often accompanies athletic success."

Gehrig's relationship, for example, with Pete Sheehy, the Yankees' faithful clubhouse attendant for almost sixty years and the last link to the dynastic teams of the 1920s and 1930s (he died in 1985), confirms the general impression that Lou never developed a head too big for his dark blue Yankee cap.

Often driven home after games by Gehrig, Sheehy had the responsibility for calling Lou's mother to inform her whether the game was over or whether it had been canceled because of rain. Sheehy once volunteered that of all the players who ever came under his wing, Lou was the one he most admired, for he felt Lou was truly a modest and humble hero.

As dominant a hitter as he was, Lou always welcomed advice. More often than not, he actively sought it. It was Gehrig's constant fear that his ability to hit a baseball would suddenly desert him that impelled him to seek help from others; he was plagued throughout his career by this strange sense of imminent failure.

Like everybody else who has ever played the game, Gehrig suffered periodic batting slumps. Despite his incredible consistency, a day or two of hitless performances could send Lou, in sweating desperation, to the nearest teammate for counsel. How am I gripping the bat? How am I addressing the ball? How am I hunkering my shoulders? How am I moving my wrists? Is my stance too open or too closed? Am I taking my eye off the ball? Is my stride too long? Am I lunging at the ball? How is my timing?

In 1931, a year in which Lou's average dipped to .341 from a lifetime high of .379 in 1930 and in which, ironically, he batted in 184 runs (Lou averaged over his career almost one run batted in per game, a mark that only a handful of batters have come close to emulating), Lou begged Pennock to tell him why he wasn't hitting well. Pennock was a pitcher of sophistication and intelligence, but as a batter he hit only four home runs in twenty-two years of major league play. No rational man went to Pennock for hitting pointers.

"I'm doing nothing but popping up and striking out," complained Lou. "What am I doing wrong?"

Pennock was seeing at first hand the puzzling panic of a man who by any measurement was one of the great hitters of all time. He stared unbelievingly at Lou.

"I don't have any idea what you're doing wrong," Pennock responded.

Such answers, of course, afforded little satisfaction to Lou. He wanted someone, anyone, to tell him what was wrong, when in reality there was little wrong other than his temperament and his insecurity. Sooner or later, he'd emerge from his slump, as he always did, and it wouldn't be with confusing, disconcerting advice, if Pennock had his way.

The Gehrig anxiety syndrome is not unusual among athletes—and actors. The late Laurence Olivier, perhaps the most eminent actor of his era, acknowledged that after years as a performer he was still haunted by a grinding stage fright and a fear of forgetting all of his lines. The basketball star Bill Russell once described how he used to throw up before many games that had no importance.

If neither the Pennocks nor the batboys could help him, Gehrig would seek out others. Once he went to Jimmy Reese, whose chief claim to fame was that he occasionally roomed with Ruth— or at least with the Babe's traveling bag. After going two games without a hit, Lou asked Reese to come home with him to Larchmont. The two talked for hours about Lou's supposed hitting flaws. The next morning, right after dawn, they went to Yankee Stadium where Reese, an infielder, pitched batting practice to Lou until his arm almost fell off. Jimmy threw high, low, inside, outside, slow, fast—and Lou kept batting away in his own persistent way. In that afternoon's game, Lou banged out four straight hits.

"I guess it worked," said the suddenly revived Gehrig to Reese after the game.

As he grew older, Lou became compatible with all types on his team. After an inauspicious beginning as a rookie, when he was ridiculed as a puerile adolescent, Lou developed a quiet personality that demanded and gave respect. Hoyt, with a penchant for Broadway's bright lights, and a man who was as glib as Gehrig was tongue-tied in the presence of the press, enjoyed spending time with Lou, despite their disparate interests. When Hoyt had problems with his weight, owing to his large appetite for eating and drinking, Lou encouraged him to take up speed skating on ice, a pastime Lou adored. Hoyt thought of skating as a physical conditioner and as a way to shed pounds; Lou engaged in it in the off-season because he was convinced it would strengthen his heavy calves and thighs while exposing him to the invigorating cold air of the New York winter.

"Lou was great company out there on the ice," said Hoyt. "He was the most pleasant part of the whole program. Fitness was almost a religion with him. Those guys who thought Lou had the mind of a teenager didn't know what they were talking about." If he had had a son, added Hoyt, he would have wanted him to be just like Gehrig.

Lou was also friendly with Ben Chapman, the explosive Tennessean. (In the late forties Chapman became manager of the Philadelphia Phillies, where he achieved negative renown as one of the loudest baiters of the black newcomer to baseball, Jackie Robinson.)

On the Yanks, Chapman was a fine player with great speed, which he employed to work double steals with Gehrig. But the red-necked Chapman was frequently a storm center. Recognizing the contributions Chapman could make to the club, Lou sought to help him, though there is no evidence that he sympathized with Chapman's social attitudes. During a period in which baseball assiduously ignored the talents of a wondrous pool of black players, Lou was firm in his feelings about the rights of these men. He had played against blacks in post-season exhibitions and thus was familiar with their level of skill. "I have seen many Negro players who belong in the big leagues," he once said. "I don't believe there's any room in baseball for discrimination. It's our true national pastime and a game for all."

When Chapman reported to the Yanks in 1930, manager Shawkey tried him at third base. The young Southerner worked hard to master the position, but he couldn't handle satisfactorily the heart of that position's defense—the long throw to first base. Gehrig volunteered to aid Chapman. He spent many pre-game sessions with him, showing near-saintly patience and reinforcing Chapman's view that Lou was more than a congenial partner in the clubhouse hearts game.

One day, after a workout under a broiling July sun, Chapman

walked back to the bench with Lou. He was disconsolate because many of his throws had pulled Lou off the base or had tunneled into the dirt.

"Hell, I'll never be a third baseman," said Chapman. "I'm a lousy fielder with a lousy arm."

When Chapman walked over to the water cooler he noticed Lou was holding the thumb on his left hand. "I think it's broken," Gehrig said. Trying to come up with an errant throw, Gehrig had jammed the thumb into the ground. But the next day he was in the lineup as usual.

"You didn't hear a peep out of Lou," said Chapman. "Never a word of complaint about my rotten throw and what it did to his finger."

On July 4, 1932, Lou's best pal, catcher Bill Dickey, delivered a crunching punch to Carl Reynolds's face after a jarring collision at home plate. Reynolds was out of action for six weeks with a broken jaw, while Dickey suffered a fine and suspension for his blindside attack on the Washington outfielder.

The incident left the Senators vengeful. The next year, in the opening series at Washington, Buddy Myer, the Senators' tough second baseman, came down hard on Gehrig's heel with his spikes in a close play at first base. Bouncing off Lou was tantamount to challenging King Kong's territorial rights, and Myer almost wound up in the Senators' dugout.

Several days later, driven by fierce loyalty to Lou and perhaps by the fact that Myer was a Mississippi Jew, Chapman charged into him at second to break up a double play. With Chapman's spikes implanted in his thigh, Myer started kicking back at him.

Fans poured out of the stands, arms punched the air, bodies rolled in the dust (with Myer and Chapman on the bottom of the pack), and guards had to be called in to settle the boys down. Amusingly, Lou and the Babe remained on the sidelines throughout the proceedings, as they watched the bloody noses mount. When order was restored, Chapman insisted McCarthy had encouraged him "to take a shot at Myer." After all, it was Buddy who had committed the most unpardonable deed a man could perpetrate on a ball field: He had tried to inflict injury on McCarthy's favorite Yankee. Chapman and McCarthy were convinced that Myer had set out to spike Lou.

"We played for keeps in those days," said Chapman, "not for money. Lou was the most wonderful guy I ever knew in baseball and I just had to do something for him."

If Chapman's disposition was incendiary, shortstop Frank Crosetti, who came to the Yankees from San Francisco, had the opposite temperament. Like Lou, he conducted himself in an exemplary manner: early to bed, early to rise, never talk out of turn. Gehrig and Crosetti liked each other immediately.

"Lou believed in keeping himself in condition, but, it's funny, I never saw him on a scale," said Crosetti. "Players in those days rarely weighed themselves."

When the "Crow," as Crosetti was dubbed, became ill in his first year with the Yanks, he feared telling McCarthy. The team had an exhibition game scheduled against Yale in New Haven and McCarthy didn't take kindly to players who ducked such commitments. But Gehrig noticed the rookie looked white as a tablecloth, so he asked Crosetti what was ailing him.

"I've got an awful cold," said Crosetti.

Lou approached McCarthy, informed him of Crosetti's problem, and suggested he drive "the kid" home with him to New Rochelle, where the Crow would be ministered to properly by his mother.

Indeed, he was. Mom Gehrig fluttered around the player like a protective mother hen, presented him with a large glass of hot wine, then put him to bed in a room usually reserved for her son. Lou slept on the couch. "I am Italian, but I never had had hot wine in my life," Crosetti recalled.

The next day, after Crosetti made a miraculous recovery, Lou drove his young pal to the ballpark. Crosetti could never get over how this "really humble star" willingly played chauffeur for him and paid such attention to his needs.

"I think one of the things Lou liked about me," said Crosetti, "was that I wasn't a pop-off. He sorta looked after me all the time we were with the Yanks."

The two men also engaged in an effective conspiracy on the field. One of the most adept sign stealers in the game, Crosetti also qualified as a master of the hidden-ball trick. Usually, such a ruse required close cooperation between pitcher and shortstop; Crosetti also had Gehrig play a role.

With the ball buried in his glove, Crosetti would try to distract a runner perched on second base. Meanwhile, the pitcher would stare sternly at the batter, pretending the ball was nestled in his own glove. Lou was never sure whether the ball was in the Crow's glove or in the pitcher's glove. His assignment was to look away from Crosetti. Often, Lou would yell deceptive encouragement to the pitcher. It was all part of the fabric of the game, a spicy ingredient that Crosetti had mastered.

When the trick worked, Lou would get an enormous kick out of it. He'd roar with delight and march off the field—if it was the third out—with his muscular arm around Crosetti's skinny neck.

Hustle is an overused cliché in baseball. But with Lou it was the ultimate truth, deeply ingrained in his psyche. He lived by it and wanted others to do the same.

Billy Werber, an aggressive Yankee infielder in the thirties, who had been educated at Duke and Georgetown Law School, marveled at Lou's pride and his willingness to play with pain. Werber was almost suffocatingly proud of his college background, which may have accounted for his being partial to Lou, the ex-Columbian. But, as a fellow bridge player, he also got to know "loner" Lou better than other Yankees did.

"I can remember when Lou had a broken middle finger on his right hand," said Werber. "Every time he batted a ball it hurt him. And he almost got sick to his stomach when he caught the ball. You could see him wince. But he always stayed in the game."

Gehrig paid close attention to little details of the game, said Werber. Lou noticed, for example, that in right field the wall slanted off to the right, so that when balls caromed off at its base, runners could try to advance to second base or third, depending on Ruth's alacrity. While the Babe made his moves on these balls, Gehrig would cross the middle of the diamond and back up third base. It's pro forma for catchers to back up first base and for pitchers to back up third or home plate, but it was rare for a first baseman to provide defense at third. But that's what Gehrig did.

"Lou didn't mix too well," said Werber, "and he didn't like to be ribbed much. He was aloof and introverted—something like DiMaggio was. But he always gave his all for the team and believed in team effort. Woe to the guy on the Yankees who didn't hustle!"

Lou was rarely indifferent to young people, even if his shyness caused him at times to appear cold. Stories of his kindness to boys and girls are legion. Many youngsters in the twenties and thirties claimed him as a role model. One such person was Jack Orr, who later became a sportswriter. After emigrating from Scotland, Orr grew up in Bristol, Pennsylvania, a mill town up the Delaware River from Shibe Park, where the Athletics played in the thirties. Orr, a fourteen-year-old in 1932, hitchhiked regularly to watch the Yankees, and to see his particular hero, Gehrig. One day, following a Yankees-A's doubleheader, Orr went to the North Philadelphia Pennsy stop for a train back to Bristol. The Yanks were there, too, waiting for the New York train. Orr clutched his hardbound scorebook as the Babe and his entourage arrived. The Babe, wearing his familiar cap and camel's hair topcoat, was smoking a huge cigar. But Orr lost his nerve and held back, so he never got an autograph from Ruth.

Suddenly Orr spotted Gehrig, standing alone, reading a folded copy of the *Philadelphia Bulletin,* which included the first-game box score. Orr approached him and timidly extended his scorebook.

"Mr. Gehrig," Orr stammered.

"Sure, kid," he said, and he signed.

But Lou did much more. He put away the newspaper, took Orr's book, and walked over to a long bench where other Yankees were seated.

"Sign and pass it on," Lou said.

That's how Orr got the autographs of Earle Combs, Red Ruffing, Herb Pennock, and Tony Lazzeri, along with such spear-carriers as Lyn Lary, Danny MacFayden, Arndt Jorgens, George Pipgras, and Johnny Allen. Orr treasured that book for years, even after he went into the army.

Lou was particularly fond of Pipgras's daughter, LeMorn, whom he called his "little sweetheart." LeMorn's birthday was March 12. Every year on that date, when the Yanks were in spring training in St. Petersburg, Lou would personally deliver a box of candy to LeMorn. During the regular season LeMorn was also a frequent visitor at Mom and Pop Gehrig's house in New Rochelle, where two dogs, a chihuahua and a prize-winning German shepherd, would obediently respond to Lou's commands, always given in German.

Whenever Gehrig visited Chicago to play the White Sox, he took special aim at a billboard in Comiskey Park. A local jewelry store had advertised that it would reward any player, friend or foe, with a watch if he hit a ball over the billboard. One summer Lou hit two mammoth clouts precisely over that billboard. Much to LeMorn's delight, and also for the benefit of Earle Combs, Jr., the outfielder's tiny son, Lou presented each of them with a watch.

On those occasions when Lou's mother set table for her son and other Yankees at her New Rochelle home, Dorothy Ruth, the Babe's daughter, was usually there, too. When Dorothy was twelve years old, she developed a crush on Lou. She went for walks with him, joined Lou in playing with the dogs, and for a while had a room all to herself in the Gehrig home, which might lead one to conjecture that life with the Gehrigs was preferable to life with the Ruths. On many mornings Dorothy would sit in the bathroom doorway and watch Lou shave before he set out for Yankee Stadium. The Gehrigs were her second family and Lou was first in her affections.

"What young girl," she said, "wouldn't have had a crush on New York's most eligible bachelor?"

As sweet-dispositioned as Lou could be with young people,

he refused to put up with much nonsense from his teammates, especially when he thought they were strictly out of line. One year when the Yanks trained in St. Petersburg, an obnoxious alligator kept frightening children at Crescent Lake, which was not far from Miller Huggins Field.

George Selkirk, Ruth's successor in right field, and Jack Saltzgaver, an also-ran infielder, had noticed that Zip, a feisty water spaniel, also cavorted in the area under the restraint of a ten-foot leash. If Zip was unchained, the players thought, he'd provide a perfect lure to coax the reptile into the open, where they could then shoot him.

When Lou got wind of the plot, he tried to talk the players out of it. Believing in a proper public image for all Yankees, Gehrig was opposed to such behavior. Incivility or rowdyism was bound to win a frown or a private rebuke from him.

"It's not the right thing to do," he said, in his best straight-arrow fashion. "Some little kid loves that dog."

Despite Lou's entreaties, the two Yankees went ahead, unleashed Zip, then shot holes in the alligator. For their efforts they were summoned into court by the local law enforcement officers and fined.

"I told you guys to listen to me," Lou said with annoyance.

For those not close to him, Lou could behave enigmatically. Luke Appling, a Hall of Fame shortstop with the Chicago White Sox, once remarked that he'd played against Gehrig for over a decade but didn't recall exchanging ten words with him. Another Hall of Famer, Detroit's Charlie Gehringer, had a similar recollection of Lou. Gehringer himself had a reputation for being singularly quiet. He'd say "hello" when he showed up at spring training and "goodbye" at the end of the season, so teammates laughingly said about him. But even the taciturn Gehringer was surprised at how uncommunicative Gehrig could be. When Lou went to Japan with Gehringer in 1934, he said very little and didn't socialize much with people he didn't know very well.

Some Yankee teammates were resentful of Lou's long silences and inability to communicate. "Gehrig was a hard man to know," said Charlie Devens, a right-hander bred at Harvard and a Yankee pitcher from 1932 to 1934. "To me, he was without a light touch, a remote and inward-looking fellow. If he was in a slump, he was especially gruff and unfriendly. I actually recall him talking to me only once or twice. One time he said something to me about what a good football coach Percy Haughton had been at Harvard. [Haughton also coached briefly at Columbia, which might explain Lou's reference.] He never had much to do with young players like myself. During the World Series of 1932, when I went out to warm up in the bullpen next to Pennock, I was literally scared to death that McCarthy might call on me to pitch. But Gehrig never thought of saying a word to me to ease things."

Spurgeon "Spud" Chandler, a more successful pitcher than Devens and an American League Most Valuable Player after Gehrig was gone, echoed Devens's complaint. "For two years he didn't say a single word to me. Even with his best friend, Dickey, he didn't seem to talk much."

To a remarkable degree, Lou remained insecure in his relationships with most grown-ups. Kids and animals, now they were another matter; he usually warmed up to them immediately. But the shyness that carried over from his youth made him hesitate to enter new social situations with adults.

By nature Lou was a serious person, quite caught up in his self-designated role as loyal son, loyal team player, loyal citizen, loyal employee. Such an unquestioning commitment placed a heavy burden on him. Sometimes it cost him dearly in terms of his human relationships. For example, he seemed to assign himself the role of preserving, certifying, and codifying all rules of Yankee behavior. As well, he was the protector of what he perceived should be the Yankee image. On the other hand, Ruth was *sui generis,* a man who could play by his own renegade rules, thumb his nose at the world, leap out of bounds, defy custom, all without penalty or public scorn. Ruth was Ruth.

But for mere mortals, such as himself, Gehrig thought the rules had to be strictly obeyed; a man was not entitled to breathe too freely. He adhered to a moral code loftier, certainly, than the

Babe's, risking accusations from some that he was rigid, stuffy, and self-righteous. In his own self-abnegating way, he was a believer in dignified behavior. He was convinced others should share his sense of pride in being a New York Yankee. Lou took seriously the maxim, originally attributed to Hoyt, that "it's great to be young and to be a Yankee."

Lou was known, for instance, for rarely wearing an overcoat on winter's most frigid days. But in public restaurants and hotel lobbies, he was never seen without a sport jacket and tie. No matter how scalding the weather was, he always dressed properly. Those were the years before air conditioning, but sloppy sports shirts were not Lou's style. If his teammates chose to dress that way they risked a reprimand from him. If they behaved badly in public, it was Gehrig they'd have to answer to, but always privately.

To some outsiders, this rigidity, plus the Yanks' constant appearance in the winner's circle, tended to give the team a witheringly cold, impersonal image. Rooting for the New Yorkers, so said the growing legion of Yankee-haters, was like rooting for United States Steel. But Lou was content to ignore such reactions, for he had early set his course of stolidity and self-effacement.

Sophisticated banter could throw him off stride, even if he was better read than most players of his era. Those who were close to him appreciated that he was more articulate than he was given credit for, but there were writers and players who judged that Lou's photogenic smile, which he wore like a shield, hid gnawing feelings of insecurity.

An episode with Hank Greenberg, eight years younger than Lou and a competitor in the American League for first base honors, further pointed up Lou's basic diffidence. Before signing with Detroit, Greenberg had been pursued by Krichell, the discoverer of Gehrig. But Hank, in his wisdom, chose to play for the Tigers, figuring it would be years before anyone could replace Lou.

When Greenberg won the Tigers' first base job over Harry "Stinky" Davis in 1933, he made his first casual acquaintance with Lou. Between innings they'd exchange places at first base, like two large tankers, each in turn casually tossing his glove near the coach's box before descending into the dugout.

Greenberg would always say hello to Gehrig. Lou, in turn, would stare blindly back at Greenberg, without so much as acknowledging him. This went on for several games, until one afternoon Greenberg decided to drop his "hello" because he believed Gehrig just didn't like him—"the hell with him!" was Greenberg's attitude.

When the Yankees' turn at bat was concluded, Gehrig emerged from the dugout and approached Greenberg, who was trotting off the field. "How come you stopped saying hello to me?" Lou asked, in a subdued voice.

Pleased that Gehrig finally was acknowledging him, Greenberg smiled at him. "Oh, hello," he said. Then he disappeared into the Tigers' dugout. After that, whenever the Yankees played the Tigers, Greenberg never failed to greet Lou as they changed positions at first base.

"Maybe it was only a small thing," said Greenberg years later, "but it told me something about him. Lou seemed to be one of those guys who wanted people to like him, but he wasn't sure how to go about it."

Lou was moved when people, such as Greenberg, showed a fondness for him. A private, armored man in a public environment, he respected the privacy of others, just as he wanted his own privacy to be respected. For years, for example, he generally chose to park his car several blocks from Yankee Stadium, avoiding a worshipful public if he could.

One place in which Lou could be assured privacy was in the darkness of movie theaters. In the 1930s he'd frequently visit the Loew's Paradise, an ornate neighborhood moviehouse on the Grand Concourse near Fordham Road, in the Bronx. Lou would always wait in his car, parked up the street, until the theater lights dimmed and everyone was seated. Then he'd buy his ticket and, unnoticed, slide into a seat near the rear of the theater.

He thought people might recognize him and cause a disturbance, as well as a delay of the movie.

16

Four Quiet Four-Baggers

In the early years of the Great Depression, lyrics of popular songs reflected the nation's mood more accurately than any soggy predictions from economic clairvoyants. One couldn't miss the messages of "I Can't Give You Anything But Love, Baby," "Brother, Can You Spare a Dime," and "Boulevard of Broken Dreams."

Money got so tight in the big leagues that several owners proposed that baseballs (worth $1.25) hit into the stands should be returned, which would have violated a tradition adopted a decade before. However, team accountants lost this unholy cause because clearly such a policy would have been bad for goodwill.

Salaries for major leaguers dwindled to the neighborhood of $6,000, slightly more than the average American family managed to get along on in those tight times. The Babe, now a bloated caricature of himself, worked his way down to $35,000 in 1934, from a lofty high of $80,000 in 1930.

In 1933 and 1934, Gehrig, with 81 homers over two years and an average of 152 runs batted in, was obliged to settle for a $2,000 depression cut to $23,000, after having been at the $25,000 level from 1928 through 1932. However, while most people during this time of unparalleled economic poverty didn't have the cash to travel twenty-five miles from their homes, Lou became a world traveler.

In 1931, and again in 1934, Gehrig journeyed by boat to Japan, a land caught up in a mass love affair with America's national pastime. As traveling deities, Lou and the Babe joined an outstanding group of players in '31, including Frankie Frisch, Lefty Grove, Rabbit Maranville, Al Simmons, and Mickey Cochrane. In '34 the troupe was composed entirely of American League stars and was chaperoned by the avuncular Mr. Mack, who made sure to bring along some of his own players—Jimmie Foxx, Bing Miller, Harold "Rabbit" Warstler, Eric McNair, and Frank Hayes.

Serving as interpreter for the group was Moe Berg, a cerebral catcher who had prepared for his second-string role with the White Sox, Washington, Cleveland, and the Red Sox by studying at Princeton, Columbia Law School, and the Sorbonne in Paris. Mr. Mack had asked Berg to come along because of his facility in Japanese. "I spent years attempting to master foreign languages, including Japanese," Berg once said. "So what happens! I turn out to be a catcher, reduced to sign language on the ball field."

When exultant crowds gathered around Lou and the Babe at Tokyo Station and other points screaming "Banzai, Babe Ruth!" or "Banzai, Lou Gehrig!" Berg reminded them that this was a tender expression meaning "May you live ten thousand years!"

Lou spoke German at home and a pretty basic New Yorkese, but not a whisper of Japanese. But Berg was a competent instructor. In due course, Lou learned to say "Hello" *(Konnichi wa)*, "Thank you" *(Arigato)*, "Please" *(Dozo)*, "Goodnight" *(Komban Wa)*, and "Goodbye" *(Sayonara)*. More important, Lou learned that "Homu Runu" was what he and the Babe did best. One of

Lou's "homu runus" won the only 1–0 game on the entire '34 tour.

When Berg was invited to speak before university students in Tokyo, Gehrig, decked out in his baggy plus-fours, knitted sweater, and argyle socks, went along. One day, with both Lou and Jimmie Foxx sitting on the stage, Berg stated that these two men were the greatest American players alive. No, he hadn't forgotten the Babe. "He's in a class by himself," assured Berg.

So baseball-wise were the Japanese that some even commented on their distress over Lyn Lary's mistake that had deprived Lou of a home-run title. Wherever the Babe and Lou went in Japan, photographer's flashbulbs popped incessantly while smiling people hemmed them in and the wives of players kept receiving floral bouquets from officials. A meeting was arranged with Japan's emperor Hirohito (only slightly older than Gehrig) and his empress at the Imperial Palace.

The reception in Tokyo for the American invaders even exceeded the welcome extended to that other American hero Colonel Charles Lindbergh, who had visited Japan shortly before the ball players got there in 1931. Gehrig was overwhelmed by the Japanese greeting. He estimated that every one of Tokyo's two million citizens were in the streets to show their affection. "I'll remember this reception to my dying day," Lou said. "I've seen some excited crowds in baseball, but nothing like this. I don't know of anything in my entire career that's touched me as much as this welcome. My first thought was that I could only wish that my mom and pop in New Rochelle could have been in Japan to see it. It's difficult to give an accurate description of all this to the fans back home in America."

The Japanese were seeing Lou at the very peak of his career—or, as it turned out, his mid-career—for it was in that period that he reached his homeric height in a 1932 game. As the Yankees returned to the top in 1932, winning the American League flag by thirteen games over the Athletics, Gehrig accomplished something with a bat that even the Babe never had: He cracked four home runs in a single game.

In 1894 Bobby Lowe, an infielder with only seventy lifetime

homers, hit four homers for the Boston Braves one day, while Ed Delahanty of the Phillies matched that output in 1896. After those two performed the feat, nobody in the twentieth century had been able to duplicate it, despite increased emphasis on the long ball and the suspicion that a rabbit had, from time to time, inhabited the horsehide.

Shibe Park, home to the Athletics since 1909, had outfield dimensions at the corners that were modest compared to other American League parks. A ball hit to right field had to travel 331 feet to become a home run; a ball hit to left had to fly 334 feet. To dead center it was 450 feet for descent into home-run territory. Yankee Stadium alone had cheaper home-run routes. In Babe's right-field mecca a ball wound up a homer at 295 feet; in left, the home-run distance was 301 feet. Only in vast, unexplored center field did the Stadium's dimensions dwarf others.

This is not to imply that Lou was favored by Shibe's architecture, or that the Babe needed a short right-field porch in New York. Rather, it is to show that despite such pocket-size figures, others still failed to take advantage of these inviting targets. It was in Shibe that Lou hit his jackpot on June 3, 1932. It was no slouch of a pitcher that he picked on, either, for the Athletics' right-hander George "Moose" Earnshaw had won sixty-eight games in the three preceding years, plus four World Series victories. He may have been the best right-hander in his league.

In the first inning at Shibe Park Lou connected for a homer to right field. In the fourth, he connected again, also to right field. In the fifth, his third straight home run soared high over the right-field barrier. Each time the beleaguered Earnshaw was the victim. With those three blasts Gehrig took possession of another record, though he was unaware of it at the time: It was the first time anyone had hit three homers in a game four times.

After the third homer, Mr. Mack, who had been patiently watching the slaughter, his stiff collar wilting under the hot sun, decided Earnshaw had experienced enough embarrassment. The old man, then seventy, waved to the bullpen for relief pitcher Leroy Mahaffey, another right-hander. Turning to the distraught Earnshaw, Mr. Mack tried to counsel him.

"Sit here for a few minutes, son," he said. "I want you to see how Mahaffey does it. You've been pitching entirely wrong to Gehrig."

In the seventh inning Mahaffey, in the midst of the pitching lesson for Earnshaw, threw a fast ball that Gehrig instantly hit for his fourth consecutive home run. This one disappeared over the left-field wall.

Earnshaw had learned his lesson: "I understand now, Mr. Mack," he said. "Mahaffey made Lou change his direction. Can I shower now?"

Since the game was a rout, with the Yanks amassing twenty runs on twenty-three hits, Gehrig had chances in the eighth and ninth innings to add a fifth home run. (In baseball's long history no player has ever done that, though since Gehrig's feat others have hit four in one game.) Lou grounded out in the eighth. In the ninth, with Eddie Rommel, another right-hander, on the mound, Gehrig blasted a tremendous shot to the farthest part of center field. "A little variance to either side of its actual line of flight would have sent the ball over the fence or into the stands," wrote William Brandt in the *New York Times*. Instead, Al Simmons made a desperate dash to the center-field wall and, leaping high at the last split second, grabbed the ball before it could sail over.

Prior to the ninth inning, Mr. Mack had removed his regular center fielder, Doc Cramer, for a pinch hitter. Simmons was then switched to center from his normal left-field position. Cramer, known as "Flit" for his quickness, was a better defensive out-fielder than Simmons, yet it was Simmons who deprived Lou of a fifth home run. Would Cramer have gotten to the ball? One will never know. Years later, puzzling over his fate on that June after-noon, Lou said: "The last ball I hit was the hardest one I'd hit all day. But Simmons caught up with it. How do you figure it?"

Another dose of irony was still to come. Some 125 miles away in New York City, where the Giants were scheduled to meet the Phillies, it started to rain. The game was cancelled. John McGraw, Lou's tormentor, stayed at home, sulking. His Giants team had been floundering, his body ached, his spirits, at the age of fifty-nine, were flagging. He hadn't won a National League pen-

nant since 1924. Meanwhile, his despised Yankee rivals had won
pennants in 1926, 1927, and 1928, plus world championships in
1927 and 1928, each time with Gehrig in the lineup, a star second
only to Ruth.

It was enough to make a man sick, which is exactly how
McGraw felt. The previous day McGraw had summoned Bill
Terry, the Giants' first baseman, into his office. McGraw and Terry
were almost as icily remote from each other as were Gehrig and
McGraw. As Terry stood stone-faced in front of his manager,
McGraw grumbled a shocking proposal. Would Terry like to take
over as manager of the Giants?

In a state of disbelief, Terry said yes, he would, but only if
he'd really be the boss. He wasn't going to be anyone's pawn or
front man, least of all McGraw's.

So, on June 3, while Gehrig was pounding Earnshaw and
Mahaffey to pieces, McGraw's announcement of resignation was
distributed to the press. Terry, at thirty-three, next to Gehrig the
best first baseman in baseball, would inherit the job.

After thirty years and ten pennants, the competitive ferocity
had burned out of McGraw. For one more day he was the biggest
news all over America. On Saturday, June 4, 1932, the *New York
Times* featured McGraw on its front page, second column to the
left. A reader would have to turn to the sports pages to discover a
banner across page ten that announced: "GEHRIG TIES ALL-
TIME RECORD WITH FOUR STRAIGHT HOME RUNS AS YANKEES
WIN." That was scarcely underplaying Lou's feat. But it was
McGraw's resignation that dominated the newspaper and radio
accounts that bubbled across the country.

Only forty-eight hours after Lou's feat, not a single word appeared about it in the Sunday *Times,* not even a sentence in the
account of a doubleheader victory by the Yanks over the A's.
John Kieran, normally an avid admirer of Lou, devoted his entire
weekend column to "Memories of McGraw."

A few days later, with the Yankees playing the Red Sox in
Boston, Lou was asked to pose for a picture with a slightly built,
sixty-five-year-old man. He obliged, never even bothering to ask

the man's name. The photograph appeared in that evening's Boston newspaper, although Lou didn't happen to see it.

The next day when a writer admonished Lou for not telling him Bobby Lowe was in town, Lou said he didn't have the slightest idea what the fellow was talking about.

"Who's Lowe?" Lou asked.

"He's the guy who hit four home runs in a game damn near forty years ago," said the writer, surprised at Gehrig's ignorance, feigned or otherwise.

"I didn't realize that's who that old gentleman was," said Lou, chuckling at his own lack of awareness.

In the World Series that fall against Chicago, the Babe fortified his legend with his "called-shot" home run. When Lou followed with his own largely unremarked-upon homer, his year of well-forgotten homers completed its cycle.

It remained for Lou to try to put such treatment into perspective. The editors of *Liberty,* a popular five-cent weekly magazine, cajoled him into bylining an article—with assistance from a ghostwriter—which was entitled "Am I Jealous of Babe Ruth?" Playing his role of humble man (nobody else would have had equal credibility, under the circumstances), Lou acknowledged that after the Babe hit his finger-pointing homer, nobody could have been expected to pay much heed to his own home run.

"I'm glad it was so," wrote Lou, "for I wasn't trying to imitate Babe, but merely to hit the ball, to get one safe. I was secretly pleased when the reporters missed the remarkable coincidence of those two home runs. I have no trace of the inferiority complex towards Ruth that writers love to talk about . . . there's only one Ruth, so why argue with the facts!"

So the season of 1932, which could have belonged to Gehrig, belonged instead to a fatigued McGraw and the Babe, again at his theatrical best.

17

The Streak

As Gehrig's consecutive-game streak rolled along, little attention was paid to it. Of course, from time to time there were clinical assessments of Lou's physique. But durability has never been the most applause-winning ingredient in sports. Fans have usually been more taken with colorful performances than with doggedness, though a Boston Marathoner like Clarence DeMar or a Gertrude Ederle paddling across the English Channel did win some regard in Gehrig's time. However, writers were more inclined to exclaim about the Babe's feats than they were to write glowingly about Lou's resolve to play every day.

Behind the introverted Gehrig facade flamed an intense spirit that pushed him to meet the daily demands of his chosen trade. True, some of his own teammates, as well as rivals, sometimes questioned this grim commitment. Even Gehrig himself, on occasion, hinted there might be other reasons for prolonging the streak.

"I think it's a real stunt," he told Dan Daniel, when Daniel asked him why he persisted. "I don't think anybody else will try it again; they won't be that crazy. I am interested in it, the fans seem to be, and Colonel Ruppert mentions it often enough to make me believe I ought to go as far as I can with it."

With chilling foresight, Ruth said he thought Lou might be hurting himself by forcing his body into Yankee pinstripes day after day. When he chose to respond to such suggestions, Lou would offer the rebuttal that ball players ordinarily got time off when it rained or on off-days, so what was the fuss about? If some felt his never-ending streak was damnfoolery, so be it.

Since he was not insensitive to what was going on around him, he was aware that he'd played in an "awful lot" of games. He also knew that on many of those days he'd felt bad—his stomach ached, his back hurt, his arm was sore, his broken fingers tingled with pain. What he didn't know was the exact number of games he had played in since that June day in 1925 when Wally Pipp went searching for other employment.

It was a question from Daniel, the veteran sportswriter for New York's *World Telegram,* that led to Lou's knowledge that he was encroaching on baseball's consecutive-game record, held by Everett Scott, a shortstop for the Red Sox and the Yankees. Midway through the 1933 season, when it became apparent that the Yankees were not destined to repeat their 1932 triumph, Daniel's mind turned to other matters. Since he was a reporter with a Euclidean bent, Daniel was searching for a numbers angle—and he got one relating to Gehrig.

"Do you have any idea how many games in a row you've played in?" Daniel asked Lou, as they chatted after breakfast in a Washington hotel lobby.

"No, I don't," Lou said, in all sincerity. "I do know that I started in 1925, and this is 1933. So I guess I've played somewhere in the hundreds."

"It's much more than that," suggested Daniel.

"You'd think I'd know," said Gehrig. "Maybe I'm stupid or something, but I don't."

Daniel assured Lou that he wasn't stupid at all. He also promised to check out the precise figure. The next day, with the assurance of a CPA, Daniel informed Lou that at the close of the 1932 season he had played in 1,197 games in a row. Now, he said, the number had reached 1,250 games. That would put him some fifty or so games away from breaking Scott's eight-year-old record, set from June 1916 to May 1925, when Huggins finally benched Scott for not hitting.

"The lively ball ended my string, not bad legs," admitted Scott, whose slender frame belied his reputation for toughness. When Scott's streak was halted, it was thought he would retire the record permanently, for nobody envisioned that ball players would ever again be as durable. A hangnail, it was said nastily, would keep most of them from playing. (Times haven't changed. Today's players are also considered spoiled and pampered.)

Due to Daniel's detective work, the subject of Lou's durability at last became public property. The papers weren't overloaded with details about it, but attention was now being paid. However, Lou couldn't quite fathom what all the hullabaloo was about. If a man earned his wages for playing first base, that's where he was supposed to be, wasn't he? "I belong on the ball field," was Gehrig's explanation.

Playing against the Browns at St. Louis on August 16, 1933, Gehrig tied Scott's mark at 1,307. For Lou it was just another day at the office, as he got two hits in three times at bat. Since the Yankees lost, Lou felt relatively little joy in his personal accomplishment.

The next afternoon, as the Yanks lost again to the Browns, Gehrig played in his 1,308th straight contest. Again, he got two hits and, again, his joy was diminished by his team's defeat. However, he had become baseball's most dependable student, the man who refused to play hooky.

When the first inning was completed, Lou was invited to home plate, where a silver statuette was presented to him by Will

Harridge, the American League's president. Surrounded by his fellow Yanks and the rival Browns, Lou stood close to little Joey Sewell, the Yankee third baseman who, with 1,103 straight games, was once considered the most likely recordsetter.

That evening Lou received a telegram from Colonel Ruppert, who had recently taken to calling Gehrig "Louis" (previously, he had been careful to address him properly as "Mr. Gehrig"). "Accept my heartiest congratulations upon the splendid record of continuous service and accomplishment which you have just completed," wired the Yankee owner. "My best wishes are with you for many additional years of success."

Scott, who had become the proprietor of a bowling alley in Fort Wayne, Indiana, expressed his pleasure that if anyone had to break the record, it was Lou.

With such fanfare focused on his stamina, Gehrig insisted he was more concerned about his hitting. During this period he was experiencing some futile moments at the plate, causing him to become blue and disillusioned. When he finally hit two home runs in a doubleheader against the White Sox on August 20, it marked the first homers Lou had hit in a month. He ended the year batting .334, but for the second straight season his home-run output, at thirty-two, was below forty. With 139 RBIs he had respectable figures, but not enough to head pennant-winning Washington off at the pass.

The regular-season streak was, indeed, remarkable. But Lou had also participated in every exhibition game and World Series game since June 1925. That meant that nineteen Series games, plus over two hundred exhibitions, should also have been added to the total.

Those who expressed appreciation for Lou's refusal to step aside usually did not take into account that playing in so many consecutive games did not necessarily mean he was playing each game to its conclusion. Neither did it mean that he was never removed from a game for a pinch runner, a substitute, or a pinch hitter—or due to a sudden loss of temper or outrage at an umpire's judgment.

Nobody, least of all Lou himself, ever proclaimed that his streak was one hundred percent "pure," or totally free of minor subterfuge. For example, Ed Barrow was reported to have actually called off a ball game in the thirties on the pretext of rain so that an ailing Lou could have another day of rest. It is said that there wasn't a cloud in the sky above Yankee Stadium when Barrow issued his ruling.

Gehrig failed to play *complete* games forty-two times before August 17, 1933. A good many of these instances, seventeen to be exact, involved his being replaced in September games by Lyn Lary, Harry Rice, Cedric Durst, or Myril Hoag. On such occasions the move was made because a pennant had already been clinched or, as in the case of six September substitutions in 1930, the Yankees were out of the running either in the pennant race or in the ball game involved.

In one game in May 1926 when Lou was injured going for a pop fly, the Babe switched to first base, a position he enjoyed playing. The next month, when Lou suffered his first ejection from a game while playing against the Athletics, Ruth again took over first base.

Though Gehrig was not the most argumentative man in a baseball uniform, he shed his reluctance to assert himself as he grew older. He could make an intimidating figure putting his case to an umpire. Although big league umpires have rarely been small or vulnerable men, Lou was huskier and heavier than most of them. Arguing a point with an umpire, his wide shoulders could dwarf an umpire in the view of fans sitting in the stand.

Gehrig was not a screamer or a cap-kicker, and he would never threaten anyone with physical punishment. However, he was sufficiently volatile on a half-dozen occasions to get himself ejected from the game. Such contests, of course, were included in his streak, without any asterisks.

In the two months that preceded Lou's passing Scott in the record book, he was thumbed out of two games, oddly by the same umpire. On June 14, 1933, in Boston's Fenway Park, manager McCarthy's blood pressure was raised to an unhealthy level by a decision in the seventh inning. The fact that the Yanks trailed by eight runs, and had lost six of their last eight games, also contributed to McCarthy's dissatisfaction. But what marked the occasion was that Lou was ejected by umpire Bill Summers for disputing a call. That fact, wrote John Drebinger of the *New York Times,* "indicated clearly the unusual character of the game." Before withdrawing, Lou unloaded a few choice remarks at Summers.

A month later, on July 26, in a repeat performance at Fenway Park, Lou was evicted from the second game of a doubleheader by Summers, after protesting a close play at first base. Lyn Lary came in to relieve him, as he had also done on June 14. Summers was a newcomer to the American League umpiring staff, with experience as an amateur boxer; he worked with fellow ump Bill McGowan (in those years only two umpires presided over ball games).

Lou was never thrown out of another game by an umpire, which possibly meant he never again had to face the wrath of Summers. Nevertheless, even a total of six ejections over fifteen summers may come as a surprise.

Frequently medical explanations were sought regarding Lou's durability. Was he, in fact, so different from other players of his era, as sportswriters suggested? In terms of Gehrig's physique and attitude, many of these observers believed Gehrig was no ordinary man. They continued to seek medical support for their feelings and to fill out their pieces on Lou.

It was pointed out that most streaks in batting, pitching, and fielding required rare talent, while an unbroken string of ball games only signified a determination to play with pain and injury. "He stayed in many games, grinning crazily like a macabre dancer in a gruelling marathon," Jack Sher once wrote. Sher was underlining that it was Gehrig's obsessive nature, rather than any specific skill, that accounted for the streak's continuation.

Lou himself would casually dismiss most theories relating to his devotion to duty. "I have the will to play," he said. "Baseball is hard work and the strain is tremendous. Sure, it's pleasurable, but it's tough." He seemed to be deflecting those who tried to pry into his motivation. Such cursory explanations were as good as any, since they came from a man who was possibly the only big leaguer who actually looked forward to doubleheaders because they'd give him twice as many chances for base hits.

When Gehrig chose to be more expansive about himself, he would talk about his personal environment. He lived, he would say, in an "old-fashioned way," going to bed before midnight and drinking only a beer or two during the course of a week. He got along on a light breakfast, no lunch, and a big dinner, with an emphasis on fruit, lots of green vegetables, steak, and salads. Fruit juices were his favorites and he always went light on the sweets. (Such a regimen would be almost impossible today, for night baseball generally precludes eating big dinners before games.)

Such was Lou's prescription for clean living. That he failed to comment on his cigarette- and pipe-smoking habits was due to the fact that the medical world had not yet linked smoking to cancer and heart disease.

There were times when Lou talked about his powerful legs. "Ball players can last just as long as their legs last," he'd say, "and my legs are as strong as they ever were." There was little reason to dispute this, for he was deceptively fast on the bases and in the field, even as he carried around a body built along the lines of a railroad locomotive.

But if Lou continued to offer only simple answers to the curious, there were doctors who willingly served as amici curiae and, prodded by the press, developed something of a preoccupation with Lou's body structure, his cardiovascular system, and what appeared to be his astonishing threshold for pain.

One such analysis, undertaken by Dr. Joseph Eidelsberg and Dr. Augustine McKelvery of Columbia's Medical College, revealed that Gehrig had a small heart—there was no evidence of athlete's heart—with an ideal blood pressure of 126 over 82. His heart rate was timed at 72 beats a minute. After violent exercise, it would return to normal in 90 seconds. The only negative aspect of the report was the not unsurprising discovery that every one of Lou's fingers had been broken at one time or another. Another medical report on Lou showed, through X rays, that he had suffered 17 assorted fractures of his hands, all of which had healed by themselves.

As Lou turned the corner in 1933 on Scott's mark, another streak also began for him. That year he played in the first interleague All-Star Game as the American League's first baseman. For the next five All-Star Games, through 1938, he represented the league as its starting first baseman.

Arch Ward, the sports editor of the *Chicago Tribune,* conceived of the All-Star Game as a supportive promotion to Chicago's Century of Progress Exposition. The idea caught on, and became irresistible to the game's leaders. Commissioner Landis sensed that the nation's depression-time heartbeat thumped loud and clear in favor of adopting the All-Star Game on a yearly basis. Player selection by popular vote of the fans also appealed to the owners, who saw major league baseball as the quintessential product of a democratic society.

In the first election for the 1933 game, with the polling conducted by the *Chicago Tribune,* Lou was voted in overwhelmingly at first base for the American League. He led Jimmie Foxx of the Athletics, a respected rival, by 312,680 votes to Foxx's 127,104. Joe Kuhel of the Senators finished far behind in third place, with 4,836 votes.

In the 1934 balloting, when enthusiasm for exercising their voting rights appeared to diminish, Lou attracted 33,890 votes from the fans, while Foxx trailed badly with 2,151 votes.

But an event of more importance in Lou's life than the All-Star Game and the streak now loomed on the horizon. He had met and was wooing the first real girlfriend he had ever had—a young woman from Chicago named Eleanor Grace Twitchell.

18

Love Match

Athletes and ball players, in particular, have long had a penchant for dating and marrying attractive young women. Jack Dempsey collected two handsome show-business wives, Estelle Taylor and Hannah Williams. Many Yankee players possessed roving eyes for stagestruck women, mostly preferring blonds. If the blonds boasted a connection, however tenuous, with the glittery Broadway theater or the burgeoning movie industry, so much the better.

Ruth's second wife, Claire Hodgson, fit the stereotype, despite her russet hair. A sultry southern beauty with pearly white skin, she had come from Athens, Georgia, to conquer the big city and wound up as an artist's model. Along the way, she also added a minor stint in the glamorous Ziegfeld Follies, plus reviews she wouldn't care to post on her kitchen bulletin board.

Claire married the Babe in 1929. She had also been courted

by Ty Cobb, thus qualifying her for the distinction of dating two of the first handful of Hall of Famers. Claire met the Babe six years before their marriage. For most of the next half-dozen years she was Babe's girl—one of them, at any rate—during a period when the Babe was estranged from his first wife.

Lefty Gomez, the witty southpaw, had a highly publicized romance with a Broadway showgirl named June O'Dea, married her, and lived happily ever after. His teammate, Joe DiMaggio, married the ill-fated, self-destructive movie goddess Marilyn Monroe, in a match made in tabloid heaven. What people may not recall is that DiMaggio's first wife, Dorothy Arnold, was also a jazzy blond actress, with talents that may have slightly exceeded Claire Hodgson's.

The woman destined to marry Lou in 1933 was Eleanor Twitchell, a notable exception to the showgirl rule. Eleanor could have stepped out of a John Held, Jr., drawing of a flapper dancing the Charleston, with bracelets clanking, legs kicking at wildly crazy angles, and ropes of beads swinging uncontrollably. Auburn-haired, brown-eyed, vivacious, and urbane, Eleanor had a turned-up nose, high forehead, and a round-faced sweetness belying an often tart tongue. Her hair was cut in a Dutch-boy bob, in the manner of the popular twenties' movie star Colleen Moore, and she applied lipstick and rouge faithfully. From a good Catholic family, she practiced the minor heresy of smoking. Unfailingly stylish in her cloche hats, fur-collared coats, short chemise dresses, and long gloves, Eleanor had broader social horizons than other girls who dated ball players.

In the mob-dominated Chicago of the twenties, Eleanor grew up on the South Side of the city. She came into her adolescence during the jazz age, learning to drink early and often, mostly bathtub gin and prohibition scotch.

Her family was modestly well off, since her father, Frank Twitchell, was a supplier of food to restaurants and also handled concessions for food in parks on the South Side. Over the years, Twitchell, a man who loved travel, betting on the horses, fast talk, and fast-disappearing money, had dealings with a virtual army of

Chicago's less-than-savory characters, and Eleanor got to know Johnny Torrio, one of Chicago's vaunted home-bred gangsters.

Twitchell's love of baseball often took him to the White Sox's Comiskey Park, the oldest ball field in the American League. There he rooted loyally for the disloyal Black Sox and made the acquaintance of many players, calling them by their first names and sitting in the park's favored guest pews. When she grew up, Eleanor did not share her father's passion for baseball, but she liked to join him on occasion at Comiskey, for it was exciting to watch so many virile, tanned young men playing under the sun and cavorting on grass that smelled like the countryside.

Eleanor much preferred horseback riding in Jackson Park; she also loved long walks and golf. The Twitchells sent her to public high school at Hyde Park, several blocks away from the high school of Chicago's literary troubadour James T. Farrell. But in short order the Twitchells developed reservations about the education provided for their daughter at Hyde Park, transferring her to St. Xavier's, then the most respected parochial school for girls on the South Side. The change in venue did remarkably little to curb Eleanor's high spirits, for she continued to avoid most of her classes.

Eleanor was too preoccupied with her horses, a new unlady-like addiction to poker, and her golf stroke to waste much time in class. But although she seemed as untamed as a bucking bronco, Eleanor, in her quiet moments, also enjoyed good books, including Theodore Dreiser's gloomy *An American Tragedy* and the positively scandalous *The Well of Loneliness,* which introduced her to sexual mysteries that few of her young friends knew existed.

Eleanor was captivated by the quick crazes and fads that seized the public imagination at the time—Couéism, comic strips, crossword puzzles, vaudeville shows at the decorous Chicago theaters, Mah-Jongg, all the latest romantic melodies of Berlin and Gershwin, dance marathons, flashy automobiles—but she also had an appreciation of Sigmund Freud's theories and had dipped into Thoreau. She had even audited several of Thornton

Wilder's literature classes at the University of Chicago, accounting perhaps for the misrepresentation that appeared years later stating she had attended the University of Wisconsin.

One of Frank Twitchell's many important connections, Harry Grabiner, a prominent Chicago baseball figure, had practically been raised in the bowels of the ancient White Sox ballpark. Born a block outside the Loop in 1890, Grabiner was hired as a little boy to sell scorecards. In short order he became an usher and a ticket seller. At fifteen he was hired to work year-round, mostly as an office boy, then as assistant to the White Sox secretary. By the time he was twenty-five, Grabiner was the right-hand man of Charles A. Comiskey, the founder of the White Sox.

Two attractive sisters, Dorothy and Mary, some fifteen years older than Eleanor, were married to Harry and his brother, Joe, a gambler in a town that venerated the species. But Harry was the guy who went straight. Since neither of the Grabiner women knew how to drive a car, Eleanor got to chauffeur them around town on shopping and sightseeing jaunts. Eleanor developed a great affection for them, and for Anna Torrio, Johnny's wife, who often joined them for poker sessions. Sometimes the Grabiner sisters, Anna Torrio, and Eleanor would drink together, go to the racetrack and bet on the horses, or just sit around and talk about things.

It was also fun to go to Comiskey Park with the Grabiners, for Harry would always arrange for them to sit close to the action, where they could see the color of the players' eyes and the stubble on their chins and hear the often censorable exchanges between them.

In 1928, when the famous Yankees were in town, presumably to demolish the White Sox, fifth-place finishers from 1925 through 1928, Dorothy Grabiner invited Eleanor to join her at the park. Before the game, Harry Grabiner visited them in their box, not far from the Yankee dugout.

At the time Eleanor was not much of a reader of the sports pages in the *Chicago Tribune,* she had never dated a ball player, and she had little interest in them and almost none in the outcome of any particular game. When Dorothy rooted for the White Sox, so did Eleanor, but only to be congenial. However, like anyone else of her generation, Eleanor certainly knew who Lou Gehrig was, just as she'd heard of Knute Rockne, Red Grange, the Babe, Helen Wills, Earl Sande, Dempsey, and Tunney.

When Lou came trotting off the field after Yankee infield practice, Harry Grabiner motioned to him to come over to his box.

"This is Eleanor Twitchell," Grabiner said, introducing her to Lou. "She lives here in Chicago."

Gehrig's discourses with women until that time wouldn't have filled a one-page diary. He perfunctorily tipped his cap, grunted "Nice to meet you, ma'am," and made a quick retreat to his dugout. Years after, Eleanor could scarcely recall that the first time they'd met had been like that, though Lou always insisted that's the way it happened. The mighty sequoia of the Yankees, the first ball player Eleanor had ever met, made as much impression on her that afternoon as some faceless stranger sitting next to her on the Chicago elevated.

When they met the next time, in 1931, Eleanor had been through several jobs. Out of sudden need, she had learned shorthand and typing, for the depression had rolled like a great angry wave over the country and over the Twitchell family as well. Now the once-flighty Eleanor badly needed the $40-a-week secretarial job she had at the Chicago World's Fair headquarters. In 1931 there were no steady beaux in Eleanor's life, though the Grabiner women constantly urged her to meet young men and to make a good match for herself.

On this particular day, on the way home from her job, Eleanor ran into Kitty McHie Perry, whose father published a small muckraking newspaper in Indiana and whose husband was a wealthy plumbing businessman. Kitty's penthouse apartment was often a gathering place for visiting friends of her father and she had always been partial to the ball-player pals of Harry Grabiner.

Kitty informed Eleanor she was having a little party at her

apartment that evening. Would she come? Lou Gehrig would be there, she told Eleanor. Perhaps Eleanor was more interested in the beer that would be served, but it would be false to suggest she had no interest in meeting him, for he was famous, successful, and had that sparkling movie-star grin, attributes that Dotty and Mary stressed were important.

When they met for the second time Lou was twenty-eight years old, Eleanor twenty-five. She was tired of running. He couldn't stop running, for he had his streak to nurture and what he imagined was an unending baseball life still ahead of him.

Joe McCarthy, having just taken over, perceived immediately that it was the perfectionist Gehrig, and not the slowly fading Bambino, who was the conduit to the team's ultimate success. Even if the Babe tied Lou for the American League home-run title in '31, with forty-six, there was no evading the harsh fact that Ruth was thirty-six years old, short-breathed, considerably overweight, and not a particular favorite of his team's new manager.

McCarthy's supportiveness toward Lou, which was quite open on his part, helped to bring Lou out of his shell. Praise from McCarthy for Lou was limitless, even if it was craftily designed to put the free-wheeling Ruth in his place. Such treatment from an authority figure could only increase Lou's confidence level. Most certainly it helped him cope with the newest phenomenon in his life, the unpredictable Eleanor Twitchell.

Love at first sight, or, in this instance, second sight, is more often a novelistic invention, or simply the mushy words of popular songwriters. But, by his own later admissions, Lou was smitten. Eleanor remembered how Lou couldn't take his eyes off her and wouldn't leave her side for one moment during that evening at Kitty McHie's apartment. She was not one to fantasize about such matters—she was too sophisticated and realistic for that. But she knew almost at once that "this beautiful man, sturdy as a rock and innocent as a waif," had, indeed, fallen for her. That he was virtually tongue-tied didn't matter. The fact that he asked to see her home at midnight was what counted, even if he didn't dare to kiss her goodnight.

The courtship, to the amazement of his teammates and the consternation of Mom Gehrig, was on in earnest. When he was in Chicago with his team, Lou never failed to take Eleanor to lunch or dinner. When he was on the road, the long-distance phone became an appendage, even at one o'clock in the morning, long past Lou's usual bedtime. He gave Eleanor a lovely necklace that he'd purchased when he was in Japan. Formerly, it was only Mom Gehrig who received such flattering baubles—Lou had given her thousands of dollars' worth of jewels, ivory animals, and jades, all bought on his Japanese trips.

People would muse about how different Eleanor and Lou were—the early-to-bed fellow in a three o'clock town linking up with an unbridled young woman who had made "Whoopee" her personal theme song. Wasn't this, they said, the perfect mismating, a couple as odd as the patrician President Roosevelt and his tobacco-chewing, hard-cussing vice-president, John Nance Garner? Who ever thought the introverted, reserved Lou would be writing love letters to such an outgoing, worldly woman?

Although Lou had not officially informed his mother of his intentions, Mom Gehrig sensed immediately that her boy was infatuated. What made it so unsettling was that she had as yet never set eyes on the woman.

Eleanor knew Lou's mother would have a difficult time accepting her. But she also knew that Lou was deeply in love with her. The sooner the "triangle" of mother, mother's son, and son's potential wife was ironed out amicably, the sooner life could go on for all of them, without pain or chaos.

When they finally met in Chicago, Eleanor did not find Mrs. Gehrig particularly lovable. In fact, this difficult woman, said Eleanor unkindly of Mrs. Gehrig, was "built like a lady wrestler, with yellowish gray hair snatched back in a bun." There was no humor or understanding in Mom Gehrig, Eleanor complained. She could have added there was little desire on Mrs. Gehrig's part to welcome her into the Gehrig fold.

If Mrs. Gehrig didn't approve of her, Eleanor contented herself with the knowledge that Lou's mother never approved of *any* of Lou's infrequent girlfriends. Mrs. Gehrig felt she had slaved to raise, feed, clothe, and house her boy and she was not about to release him—and release would be the word—to some mindless, carefree flapper. Under her maternal guidance, Lou had evolved into a monument of goodness and perfection, and she was not about to let another woman have him without a fight.

If it remained for the faithful son to set new ground rules for his mother, it was also up to Eleanor to confront her. That she did, by inviting Mom to visit her in Chicago, where the two could take some time to get to know each other. Eleanor entertained Mom Gehrig quite royally. She took her to an expensive supper club and showed her other high spots in her vibrant hometown. But all to no avail. Mom Gehrig was intransigent. She just could not adjust to the idea of her Lou being married, or of his being gone from her household in New Rochelle.

Despite his mother's hostility, Lou was determined to marry Eleanor. The big question remained: How would this chronic wallflower propose to her?

There is confusion as to whether Lou blurted out his proposal in Grant Park, where the two often walked arm-in-arm, or over drinks at Chicago's elegant Drake Hotel. One spy insists Lou actually made his proposal in New York, when Eleanor made a crucial visit to settle the whole affair before Lou's mother could sabotage their plans.

However, by Eleanor's own admission, she carefully guided Lou through his proposal, or what constituted his official terms of engagement.

It began with a rambling talk about baseball on one of their dates. Assessing his qualifications as a potential husband, Lou spoke of himself disparagingly as a ball player. Amid such self-deprecation, Eleanor took matters into her own hands. She asked Lou if what he was trying to say was that he wanted her hand in marriage.

"Yes," he said, blushing. "That's what I'm asking."

He kissed Eleanor and made a hasty departure.

With the engagement set, Lou proceeded to Yankee Sta-

dium, where he hit a majestic home run, befitting a melodramatic
movie scenario. Still playing out the script, Eleanor was there to
watch her hero, sitting in a box near the field, exulting in his
achievement. As he touched home plate, Lou waved to her; she
waved back. Lou said it was the happiest day of his life; Eleanor
concurred.

Plans had to be made for the wedding. It was no chore in
those depression days to find a vacancy, so Lou and Eleanor
located a small apartment in New Rochelle, not far from the nine-
room house that Mom and Pop Gehrig lived in and which Lou
had bought on time. The couple then mutually decided that
they'd marry before the end of the 1933 baseball season, on Friday, September 29.

Not a participant in the decision, Mom Gehrig clung to the
belief that Lou's place was at home with his mother. She insisted
that she'd always made life comfortable for him and could continue to do so. She was actually echoing Lou's oft-repeated remarks to reporters. "You know, guys," he'd say to them, "I don't
really need much else. I get everything I want at home."

Hearing of the date, Mrs. Gehrig expressed herself vehemently to Lou. "I'm not going to be there!" she said. Lou took her
at her word, for he knew how stubborn she could be. He immediately sought the aid of Fred Lieb, who qualified as Lou's best pal
in the press corps, principally because he got along famously
with Mom, to whom he spoke excellent German.

"I'd appreciate it if you'd do me a big favor," said Lou to
Lieb. "Mom insists she won't come to our wedding. Could you try
to get her to come? I hope you and Mary [Lieb's wife] can talk her
into it."

Lieb was astonished that Mom was so adamant. But he promised to make the appeal. That afternoon he walked up to Mom as
she sat in her seat close to the Yankee dugout. Despite the
brouhaha over the marriage, she had continued to attend her
son's games faithfully.

"Mom," began Lieb soothingly, "Lou would like me to bring
you to the wedding on Long Island."

"I have absolutely no intention of going," Mom exploded. She thereupon launched into an especially ferocious attack on Eleanor, so vindictive and personal in nature that Lieb diplomatically refused to reveal to anyone, even in his memoirs, what she had said.

Mrs. Gehrig concluded her angry oratory by assuring Lieb that if she showed up she'd only raise a "lot of hell." So, she said, "it's best that I stay away."

Confronted by such rancor, Lieb tried to talk sense into her. He told her that he knew how close and loving Lou and she were. He warned that if she wanted such closeness to continue, she had to accept her son's choice of a wife. He emphasized that her fierce attitude could lead to a complete break in her relationship with Lou—and she would never want that.

Without waiting for a further diatribe, Lieb informed Mrs. Gehrig that he'd be at her house at 5:30 P.M. on the day of the wedding, in his car, so they could get to Long Island in plenty of time. "When I honk," said Lieb, "I want you to be ready."

As intermediary, Lieb was one of the few privy to Lou's plans. Nobody else on the Yankees, including McCarthy, was aware of the event, except Bill Dickey, who had been invited to be present.

On Thursday afternoon, September 28, Lou connected for one hit in three times at bat as the Yankees beat Washington, 11–9. Lou quietly left Yankee Stadium after the fourth inning, presumably to prepare for what was still a secret wedding day. The Babe, as was his custom, finished the game at first for Lou.

That evening Lou told Eleanor he was pained by his mother's refusal to come to his wedding, but he underlined that he didn't care to risk any unseemly outbursts from her if she actually decided to attend. So, at dawn on a warm, cloudless Friday, Lou made up his mind to get it over with in a secret ceremony that very morning.

He immediately placed a telephone call to a rotund, forty-eight-year-old lawyer named Walter G. C. Otto, the mayor of New Rochelle, asking if he'd kindly come over to their fourth-floor apartment at 5 Circuit Road, close to the Hudson Park boatyard, to perform the ceremony. Lou also invited Fred Linder of Mt. Vernon and Blanche C. Austin, Eleanor's aunt, to stand in as witnesses.

What Lou and Eleanor both wanted was a scaled-down ceremony, without frills. What they got was Mayor Otto, who showed up with a marriage license and a few words to anoint them, and a screeching caravan of motorcycles ridden by cops from the New Rochelle force.

The scene, wryly characterized by Eleanor as "the classiest wedding ever held in Westchester County," saw Lou in his shirt-sleeves, sweat trickling down his back and bulging neck muscles; Eleanor in a besmudged apron; plumbers coming, going, and plumbing; carpenters pounding away with hammers; furniture arriving in trucks; carpet-layers clamoring for space; and an arm-waving janitor attempting to direct activities.

For a few precious seconds, as Mayor Otto reeled off the magic words that consecrated the marriage, the discordant assemblage in the apartment came to a respectful halt. Hats were removed and everyone stood at strict military attention. With the brief rite completed, Eleanor passed around dusty, unwashed glasses of tepid champagne.

Within minutes, Eleanor made a quick change of clothes while Mayor Otto commanded his motorcycle cops to provide a noisy escort for the royal couple down the highway right up to the players' door of Yankee Stadium! After all, what else would Lou Gehrig be expected to do on his wedding day, except devotedly continue his streak!

Instead of going off on a honeymoon, Lou went right to the ballpark, where the Senators would be waiting for him. Eleanor may have longed for a honeymoon cruise to Bermuda on the *Queen of Bermuda*—for $50, with private bath—but she knew where Lou wanted to be that day.

Before the game started, Lou broke the news to the press about his marriage. Then he scrambled into his pinstripes. As the Yanks lost, Lou failed to get a hit in four times at bat, facing his old nemesis, Earl Whitehill, who thoughtfully refrained from throwing at Lou's head on his wedding day. Lou handled eight putouts at first and played errorlessly in the field. "Pretty good for a man who has just gotten married," commented the local Westchester newspaper.

The four thousand fans had to wait for the next day's papers to read the marriage news. The *Daily Mirror* heralded Lou's resignation from bachelorhood with a back-page headline, while the *Times* failed to mention the matter in its game story or even in its society pages, but duly noted the alliance in a three-paragraph story on page seventeen.

Promptly accorded recognition, in an unscientific survey, as being among the "best husbands in the country," Lou was ranked right along with President Roosevelt, the artist Thomas Benton, and Guthrie McClintock, the mate of actress Katherine Cornell. To top it off, Christy Walsh wrote a glowing personal letter to Lou that could have wrung tears out of the worst curmudgeon: "If I had a sister," said Walsh, "and she was getting married, I would sooner see her get Lou Gehrig than any other player in baseball. That is due in large part to the fine, clean example and home life of your wonderful mother and your good father. But it's also because of your own square-shooting, loyal and wholesome disposition."

Lou now realized that he'd have to deal with the fact that his "wonderful mother" detested Eleanor and feared that she would be left high and dry financially after his marriage. He also appreciated how his mother had coped with the chronic unemployment of Pop Gehrig, and remembered, with sadness, how she had given birth to four children with only one—himself—surviving past infancy. He remained very proud of his old-world parents, even if he now sensed that others were often irritated and annoyed by their behavior. At times, he may have been embarrassed himself by their actions and words.

Thus, he performed the ultimate act of loyalty by placing all of his savings into a trust for them. Mr. and Mrs. Gehrig would receive the income for life, a nice monthly sum in 1933 of some $200. Mom also would receive the deed to their New Rochelle home, as well as a brand-new automobile.

"Lou paid the price for the right to our fairy tale," wrote Eleanor some years later.

A day after the wedding a reception was held at the Long Island home of Eleanor's aunt, Blanche Austin. Lieb came by for Mom Gehrig. Reluctantly, she joined him. Despite Lou's fears, there were no heated arguments instigated by his mother.

On the trip home with the Liebs, Mrs. Gehrig was unusually quiet. When the car arrived at her house, she tapped Lieb on the shoulder. "See," she said reassuringly, "I acted like a good girl." Lieb nodded—indeed she had. "I didn't raise any hell, did I?" she added. Lieb smiled at her. No, she hadn't, he said.

19

Happy Days

The world was crumbling by degrees in 1934, as millions of Americans scavenged in garbage cans and the jackboots of Hitler's storm troopers echoed ominously on the streets of Germany. The bank robber John Dillinger was gunned down by FBI agents in July, outside of a movie theater in Eleanor Gehrig's hometown of Chicago. The luxury liner *Morro Castle* went up in flames off the New Jersey coast, with hundreds dying. At Yankee Stadium, the Babe was fading away in everything but poundage. In his farewell season with the Yankees he had twenty-two home runs, the lowest total in fifteen years in New York.

However, one couple striving to forget these public and private troubles was succeeding mightily. Eleanor and Lou, in their first year of marriage, were gloriously happy.

Severing his umbilical cord, Lou soared to a rousing level of productivity on the ball field, in contradiction of the clubhouse myth that women and base hits don't mix. To many of the hard-drinking, tobacco-chewing hooligans who played before and during Gehrig's time, sex could only be depleting. In the prizefight world, there were mountainous intellects among the managers who prohibited the presence of wives or girlfriends at their pugilists' training quarters. But in Lou's case, his union with Eleanor turned out to be invigorating, certainly in the statistical column.

He hit forty-nine home runs, his all-time high, winning his first American League home-run title, as well as leadership of both leagues. Lou batted in 165 runs, also the high in his league, which made the ninth straight year he'd gone over 100 in that department. Plus he cracked out 210 hits and ended up batting .363, which also led the league and thus provided him with the necessary third leg of the Triple Crown, the first time a Yankee had ever won that distinction. During the year he hit four grand slams and had thirty homers at the Stadium, both Yankee marks.

Further demonstrating how inexhaustible he was, Lou wrapped up his batting title on the last day of the year, coming through with three hits in four at-bats against Washington. His last-ditch stand squeezed him past Gehringer of Detroit, who finished at .356.

Despite the Triple Crown, Lou was bypassed when it came time to name the league's most valuable player. Mickey Cochrane, with only 2 homers, 76 RBIs, and a .320 batting average, was selected. That Cochrane was the playing manager of the pennant-winning Tigers was, without doubt, the decisive influence, for the writers determinedly believed their own stories about inspirational value and intangibles of leadership. A mystique also attached to the position of catcher—supposedly the nerve center of a ball club—and Cochrane seemed to fill the role to perfection.

So Gehrig, an acknowledged leader himself, was forced to accept a back seat again, even as the Babe was moving out of the picture. (However, the *Sporting News,* baseball's unofficial bible, did name Lou as the American League's MVP.)

But it was in his life off the field that things changed immeasurably for Lou. The alliance with Eleanor opened up a once-insulated existence. From the moment they were married, Eleanor embarked on a modest crusade to release him from his often sullen preoccupation with yesterday's ball game. She soon learned that Lou had a tendency to brood after "going for the collar" (a hitless day in the jargon of baseball), so she tried to take his mind off affairs of the field.

She knew that her Luke, her favorite name for Lou (she had other nicknames, too, like the Monster, Dracula, and Frankenstein, depending on her playful mood, while he liked to call her Pal or, in lighter moments, Battle-Axe and Old Bat), took his work too seriously. She was aware that he worried, had a ridiculously low estimate of his own value, and in social situations continued to feel inadequate. Eleanor sought to change all these things in Lou if she could.

Without being a nag, Eleanor tried to put Lou in touch with the worlds of opera, good books, movies that featured people other than cowboys, the broadway theater of drama and musicals, and ballet. Wagnerian operas were especially pleasing to Lou, for he discovered that he could follow the plot line in German, his knowledge of which was not as rusty as he'd thought.

He marveled at the athleticism and calisthenics performed by both male and female ballet artists. Attending the Ballet Russe for the first time and sitting close to the stage, where he could see the sweat and hear the effort (Eleanor always knew the right people from whom to get the best tickets), Lou was almost overcome with excitement. Squinting through the darkness in the theater, he turned to Eleanor to register his impression. "It takes only fifteen minutes before a game for me to warm up," he whispered, "but it takes these ballet dancers hours."

As the process of Lou's intellectual renascence went on, Eleanor risked some backlash directed at both herself and Lou. Never overly friendly with the wives of other players, Eleanor was perceived by some of them as a snob, an uppity character. The wife of one of the team's best pitchers charged that Eleanor thought she was too "damn good to socialize with us . . . she thought she was better than we were."

Only a single bond, for example, existed between Eleanor

and Claire Ruth, and that was drinking, a pastime that Claire also shared with her Babe. But drinking was an avocation that Lou didn't indulge in with Eleanor, since he'd never cared much for the bathtub gin and beer that were always available in the saloons of the Prohibition era.

(One tawdry story circulated for years about a drinking bout between Eleanor and the Babe that supposedly took place en route to Japan in the off-season of 1934, in the Babe's stateroom on the *Empress of Japan.* The gossip suggested that the incident ended with the two of them in bed. This tale supposedly contributed to the developing alienation between the Babe and Lou. Eleanor always vehemently denied the rumor, while granting that she'd been drinking with the Babe. She was enraged that anyone would give credence to the story.)

Exposing Lou to cultural pursuits that ball players ordinarily ignored, Eleanor was aware that she was making him vulnerable around the clubhouses. If bench jockeys could mock a man's ethnicity, physical appearance, and religion, they also had little use for those who used their brains for anything more than calculating their batting averages. Eleanor tried to keep Lou's newfound interests a private matter, but that was difficult in a world where photographers and newspaper reporters lurked almost everywhere.

As far as Lou's mother was concerned, Lou tried to separate himself from her as much as discretion would allow. Eleanor and Lou maintained a curtailed social relationship with the aggrieved lady, but things would never be the same again between Lou and Mom.

Mom Gehrig was still a frequent visitor to the ballpark, where she could revel in Lou's emergence as the Yankees' unrivaled hero, but such pilgrimages were limited by her health and attitude. On those occasions when Eleanor was at the ballpark on the same day as Mom, the two rarely sat close together, if they could help it. By this time, of course, Mom had overcome the sense that baseball was a fearful waste of her son's mind and body. After all, it had given her comfort, a house, and respect from the world, even if it hadn't provided her with a daughter-in-law to her liking.

In keeping a safe distance from his mother, Lou still knew she could be a catalyst for trouble. When it appeared after several years that Eleanor and Lou couldn't have children, there was some talk about adoption. But Mom Gehrig could only express horror at such a suggestion. She was so outspoken on the subject that no child was ever adopted.

Although Lou's attitude toward the Babe would never again be as warm and worshipful as it had once been, they managed to remain on fairly genial terms over the years.

In September 1934, when it became painfully clear that the Babe was on his last lap as a Yankee, Lou told Tom Meany, a New York sportswriter, that he'd be very sorry to see the Babe leave. "He meant a lot to me, to the Yanks, and to baseball," said Lou.

However, a rather petty incident served to bring the curtain down on any further civility between the two men. One morning the Babe brought his daughter Dorothy, then twelve years old, to Mom Gehrig's house. Such visits were not unusual, since Dorothy had always adored Lou. On this visit Dorothy was decked out in nondescript clothes, a cross between a ragamuffin and a tomboy. Peering at the unfashionable young lady, Mrs. Gehrig noted acidly that Claire Ruth didn't seem to care how Dorothy looked.

Julia, Claire's daughter by her first husband, was five years older than Dorothy and considerably more favored by Claire. Dorothy was the daughter of Babe's first wife—or perhaps of another woman—and thus not due the love Claire would give to Julia.

"Why doesn't Claire dress Dorothy as properly as she dresses Julia?" Mom Gehrig asked querulously of one of the Yankee players' wives.

Mom Gehrig's remarks inevitably reached Claire's ears. Claire had always had a low tolerance for Mrs. Gehrig, and thought Mom had little use for her. Incensed, she heatedly informed the Babe about the comment. It wasn't long before the Babe blurted out to Lou, in his typical blunderbuss style, that Mom Gehrig should "mind her own goddamned business!"

Lou's attachment to his mother was still so intense that to hear anyone, including the Babe, attacking her was simply not acceptable. The relationship between Babe and Lou, teetering for years over their basic differences in temperament—Lou's frugality, introversion, and need for privacy versus the Babe's prodigality, extroversion, and constant need for acclaim—chilled permanently.

Off the field the two men now scarcely spoke to each other. Occasionally they would shake hands when the Babe, batting ahead of Lou in the Yankee lineup, pigeon-toed across home plate on one of his homers. When photographers asked them to pose together, as they had done thousands of times before, they usually were accommodating. Lou would still grin broadly, playacting his cheeriness and congeniality, while the Babe, hunched and porcine-featured, seemed increasingly gloomy. Indeed, the Babe had much less to smile about at that stage in his life. But only transient exchanges took place between them in the locker room.

When the Ruths and Gehrigs were aboard the *Empress of Japan,* with fellow barnstorming ball players, Lou and the Babe took obvious pains to avoid each other. It was noticeable to the athletes traveling with them. Even Julia, who had accompanied her folks on the trip, spoke of the mutual disaffection. "The Ruths don't ever speak to the Gehrigs any more," she told a friend, when Lou walked nearby.

Once they reached Japan, Lou and the Babe still kept their distance, while Claire and Eleanor barely acknowledged each other. When Lou arrived late for a ceremony that had been scheduled for an early-morning start, and for which Babe himself had gotten up, Ruth went into a rage. "One more time," he barked, "you arrive late again, and you'll go home on the next boat!"

If the Babe was acting completely out of character, he was still the one that the Japanese wanted to see, so his cautionary words had to be taken seriously. Nobody could doubt that his passions had been aroused by Claire.

Anxious at the plate, as always.
(Wide World Photos.)

TIME

The Weekly Newsmagazine

YANKEE GEHRIG AND GIANT HUBBELL
They both work for the I. R. T.
(See Sport)

Volume XXVIII

Number 14

In October 1936, Lou shared *Time*'s cover
with Giants' hurler Carl Hubbell.
(Copyright 1936 Time Inc. Reprinted by permission.)

When Joe DiMaggio (left) became an instant Yankee star in 1936, he took headlines away from Lou. Bill Dickey, Lou's roommate, is on the right. (National Baseball Library, Cooperstown, New York.)

After they became friendly, Lou posed with Detroit's first baseman, Hank Greenberg. (National Baseball Library, Cooperstown, New York.)

Between takes for
Rawhide in 1938.
(UPI.)

Ice skating, Lou's
favorite exercise,
with a young fan.
(National Baseball
Library,
Cooperstown,
New York.)

Detroit, May 2,
1939, the day Lou
benched himself.
(UPI.)

With "Babe"
Dahlgren, his
successor at first
base. (National
Baseball
Library,
Cooperstown,
New York.)

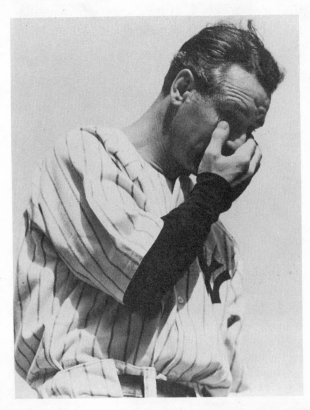

Lou's farewell. (AP.)

July 4, 1939.
(National
Baseball
Library,
Cooperstown,
New York.)

With New York City mayor Fiorello La Guardia. (AP.)

Joining New York's Parole Commission in 1940. (UPI.)

Crowds lined up outside Christ Episcopal Church in
Riverdale to view Lou's body in June 1941. (UPI.)

Babe and Lou, the last time. (AP.)

The Babe and actor Gary Cooper.

The Iron Horse.
(National Baseball
Library,
Cooperstown,
New York.)

In 1989 a Gehrig
postage stamp was
issued, making Lou
the fourth ball player
to be so honored.

But it would be wrong to put most of the blame on Mom Gehrig for the rupture in the relationship between Babe and Lou. Some of it had to do with Babe's bitterness as his flabby body failed him in his efforts to remain baseball's king of the hill. Frustrated with his decline and the refusal of the Yankee management to give serious consideration to his managing the Yanks once his playing days were over, the Babe hit out at a man on the verge of winning the full appreciation of the fans.

While this dramatic subplot coursed through the 1934 season, Lou also coped with other matters that might have abruptly ended his streak.

In June, with Lou's streak at 1,414 games, the club traveled by boat from Washington, D.C., to Norfolk, Virginia, to play an exhibition game against its farm club there. As the team of Ruth and Gehrig, the Yankees were always an enormous attraction in the hinterlands; also, fans, even those in minor league cities, were aware of Gehrig's Iron Horse status.

A young right-hander named Ray White was scheduled to pitch for Norfolk. He had been an excellent pitcher in the Eastern Intercollegiate League, when it also boasted such talented hurlers as Johnny Broaca of Yale and Charlie Devens of Harvard, both of whom graduated to the Yankees. When White pitched for Columbia he had been the team captain.

For a long while Gehrig had remained aloof from his old Columbia roots. Still, he had gotten into the habit each year of paying courtesy visits to his college coach, Andy Coakley, prior to joining the Yankees at their training camp in Florida.

During several of these visits to Coakley in the Columbia gym, Lou had been introduced to White. Coakley felt White had a promising baseball future and was eager for Lou to get to know the pitcher. These meetings with Gehrig turned out to be disappointing for White, who concluded that Lou ignored him and always acted as if they'd never met before.

Earlier in that spring training of 1934, White, as a member of the Newark Bears, another Yankee farm club and one of the mightiest minor league teams ever assembled, faced the Yankees in an exhibition for the first time. Lou promptly hit two long home runs off him, and gave little thought to one White pitch that grazed his head. That is, until Joe Glenn brought it up.

Glenn, with the thankless job of backup catcher to Dickey, was showering next to Lou after the game. A jovial type, Glenn pressed Lou on why he didn't seem friendly toward White, who, after all, had also attended Columbia. Gehrig chose to take the question seriously.

"That guy can go to hell!" Lou growled.

White was on the mound again in the June game for Norfolk, where he had been sent to work out the kinks in a bad back. In the first inning, Lou pleased the fans by hitting a home run into the right-field stands, his third in two exhibitions against White. The Babe led off the second inning with a bullet through the second baseman, bringing Lou up again. This time White reared back and threw a ball that struck Lou squarely on the crown of his head. The ball bounced high in the air behind home plate, thudding against the side of the press box.

As Lou dropped like a deadweight at home plate, McCarthy, sitting in the dugout in street clothes, started to jump up and down as if he'd gone crazy.

"My God, there goes the pennant!" he shrieked.

Dickey and Crosetti led other Yankee players in a worried huddle around Lou as the Norfolk team doctor, S. B. Whitlock, rushed out to attend him. Unconscious for fully five minutes, Lou was then moved to a local hospital.

The drama on the field continued when Chapman came to bat after Gehrig. Always a firm Gehrig loyalist, Chapman yelled out at White that he was a "son of a bitch." Then, on White's first pitch, Chapman hammered the ball right back through the origin.

When X rays were taken of Gehrig's head at the hospital, fears that he might have sustained a fractured skull were allayed. However, he did have a concussion. (Had he been wearing a helmet, Lou would not have been hurt. But such protective devices were twenty years away from being introduced into baseball.)

It was expected that Lou would stay in the hospital at least a couple of days, just to be on the safe side. After all, wouldn't McCarthy want to protect his most precious property? But Lou was adamant. He left the hospital and insisted on playing the next day in Washington, despite a knob on his head the size of a coconut. He couldn't get his own cap over his head, so he borrowed one of the Babe's caps and cut the seams to fit his head into it.

Playing with a severe headache, Lou put on an amazing display of power hitting. In the first five innings he pounded out three straight triples, to left, right, and center field. Suddenly, in the Senators' fifth inning, when a squall hit the field, the game had to be canceled. With the cancellation went Lou's three triples, permanently lost to the record books.

Years later Lou said it may have been a "dumb trick" to have played right after the near-calamitous beaning. He acknowledged that rejecting a doctor's advice may have been foolhardy. "It's just that I had to prove myself right away," he reflected. "I wanted to make sure that big whack on my head hadn't made me gun-shy at the plate."

White, who became a manager in the Yankee farm system, then president of Royal Crown Cola, admitted that he'd had a grievance against Gehrig going back to those unpleasant early meetings. "He might have shown some interest in me as a fellow Columbian and a potential Yankee. But he always seemed cold and unfriendly. He just didn't seem to give a damn about me—that's the impression I got," White insisted.

But White maintained that the "brushback" at Norfolk was more in retribution for Lou's first-inning homer than in retaliation for past slights. "I was glad he wasn't hurt seriously," said White, "because I'd been hit in the head myself. I knew what it was like."

The beaning by White wasn't the only time Lou had been hit in the head. It had occurred twice before. Each time he managed to duck away so the ball didn't smack him with full force. Each time he remained in the game.

But it was a strange episode several weeks after the incident in Norfolk that almost ended the endurance streak. The first man up in the second inning of a July 13 game in Detroit's Navin Field, Lou hit a single. Speeding to first base, he suddenly stumbled halfway to the bag. (Long before Pete Rose made a religion out of running to first base when he drew a walk, Lou had traveled full speed even on easy-out ground balls.) Only with great effort was Lou able to reach first base. When he arrived there he found he couldn't straighten up. Earle Combs, coaching at first base, asked Lou what was bothering him.

"I think I caught a cold in my back," Lou said, breathing heavily. "It hurt me a lot last night and again this morning. But this is the first time I felt it once I got to the park."

The kaffeeklatsch between Lou and Combs was joined by Art Fletcher, the third-base coach, and an anxious McCarthy.

"What's bothering Lou?" Fletcher asked of Combs.

"A cold in his back or something. Maybe lumbago," Combs informed Fletcher. Then, addressing the thirty-one-year-old Gehrig, Combs tried to get a laugh out of him.

"Hey, you're just getting old, Lou," he said.

Lou grinned through his hurt, playing his usual role to perfection. "Let's get on with the game," he said. "It's only a cold in the muscles of my back."

When play resumed, Lou was still having trouble straightening up. Chapman, next up, singled sharply to right and Lou barely got to second base on the hit. Dickey followed with a low line drive to center field, where JoJo White caught it and threw to second, to shortstop Billy Rogell, to double up Gehrig. Starting for third, Lou couldn't reverse himself and was an easy out.

With the inning over, Gehrig assured McCarthy he'd be able to play. But after one out, he waved to McCarthy from first base, indicating he'd had enough. Saltzgaver ran out to replace him.

In the clubhouse, Lou underwent the skillful ministrations of Doc Painter, the Yanks' trainer. While Lou was on the rubbing table, receiving heat treatment and massage from Painter, Babe pumped the 700th home run of his career.

After the game, Gehrig returned to the team's hotel, where he spent a painful night. Painter remained with him, continuing the massages. At dawn Lou fell asleep for a few hours.

When he awoke, Lou was drenched in sweat, an unlikely

candidate to continue the streak. But he stubbornly struggled into his clothes and journeyed to the ballpark, convinced that batting practice would loosen him up. A few tentative swings disillusioned him. McCarthy kept staring at him, waiting for him to say something.

"I don't think I can go nine today," said Lou, finally. "But I'd like to keep the streak alive, Joe, because I'm sure I can play tomorrow. Would you do me a favor? Let me lead off. I'll take my first bat, then I'll get out for the day."

Lou dragged himself to the plate, according to plan. Though he had difficulty coming around on his swing, he lunged at the first pitch. Miraculously, the ball plopped into right field for a single. He jogged at half-speed to first base, an excruciating ninety feet, touched the bag, then left the field. Red Rolfe came in to run for him.

The next day, Gehrig was back in the lineup as if the previous forty-eight hours had never happened. In a bravura performance, he banged out four hits in four times at bat, including three doubles off the Tigers' Lynwood "Schoolboy" Rowe.

Lou suffered similar attacks over the next five years. They escaped accurate diagnosis and usually wore off in a couple of days.

Were such episodes a harbinger of the disease that would ultimately take his life? The current medical understanding suggests that amyotrophic lateral sclerosis was not incubating at the time. But such attacks raised suspicions that there might have been a tragic connection.

20

Captain of the Yankees

I n the winter of 1934 the Babe told Colonel Ruppert that
McCarthy wasn't worth spit as a manager, which was his
way of putting in his application for the job. But the Colonel
wasn't buying. Instead, he suggested Ruth try a minor league
apprenticeship at Newark.

The Babe chose to be seduced by Judge Emil Fuchs, owner
of the Boston Braves. When Ruth signed with the Braves, he
thought in time he would grab off the manager's post. But Fuchs
had other plans. He hoped the Babe might give the team's anemic
attendance figures a shot of adrenaline, since the Braves hadn't
finished higher than fourth since 1916.

Ruth provided, instead, the most prominent silhouette this
side of Alfred Hitchcock, plus a valedictory gasp of three home
runs on May 25, 1935, at Pittsburgh's Forbes Field. Five days later
the Babe, fatigued, fat, and forty, retired.

With the Babe gone, Lou stood alone as the driving force of

the Yankees. If the Yankees were to advance to the head of the class, Lou would have to be their leader. In the decade that Lou and the Babe had formed the most fearsome one-two punch in history—1925 to 1934—they had collectively hit 772 home runs, an average of over 77 homers a season. They hit home runs in the same game 72 times, performing the feat back-to-back 16 times. Their yearly RBI average was 274. No two players ever came close to that.

Many of Lou's friends urged him to accept the leadership of the club. They said he'd earned it, so now he should claim it. Some encouraged him to take on a different personality, a feat that was like transposing Mt. Rushmore to Coney Island.

Lou may have been a skinflint with tips but he did give his time generously for public appearances or to hand out trophies to excited kids at day camps around Westchester. Generally, he was a willing writer of autographs.

Eleanor addressed a letter to Lou, realizing he was under pressure to change. "Be yourself," she wrote. "Just go on being fine, true and simple." She didn't want him to be bulldozed into anything that he might regret. She reminded him, if he needed reminding, that he wasn't Ruth—and would never be.

She joined with her friend Fred Fisher in writing a song "dedicated to Lou." Published in 1935, "I Can't Get to First Base with You," though not exactly evocative of Cole Porter, boasted lyrics ("You got me crying, alibiing, making me blue, I can't get to first base with you," etc.) that brought an appreciative grin to Lou's face. Fisher, a professional songwriter, who also wrote such standards as "Peg O' My Heart," "Chicago," and "There's a Broken Heart for Every Light on Broadway," constantly kidded Eleanor about their masterpiece.

"I wish we'd written 'Take Me Out to the Ball Game' instead," he laughed. Fisher was a colorful man, who had been born in Germany and served in the French Foreign Legion. Sometimes he loved being around gangsters, sometimes politicians like Mayor Jimmy Walker (who also wrote songs), sometimes slapstick comics like Pitzy Katz.

Lou and Fisher enjoyed fishing together and were crazy

about jellied butterfish. They'd often spread newspapers on the living room floor and devour crabs like a couple of overgrown kids. After almost every home game, the two would get together at Fisher's apartment on the Upper West side of Manhattan and carry on like the Katzenjammer Kids. It was a light side of Lou that few ever saw.

After his Triple Crown season of 1934, Lou might have been expected to stage a roaring imitation of a labor organizer. But that wasn't Lou's way. He docilely accepted a raise of $7,000, some $5,000 less than he'd asked for. His $30,000 salary for 1935 was $50,000 less than what the Babe had received in his peak year of plundering Colonel Ruppert's treasury.

"We had no trouble at all signing Lou," said Colonel Ruppert. "He merited a raise in salary on the strength of his wonderful year. He is satisfied and so is the club."

Playing for the highest salary in baseball must have pleased Lou enormously, but his complacency in dealing with the Yankee front office irked Eleanor, although she knew he remained true to form.

Eleanor was now also a strong influence on Lou's finances. "We never try to live up to our income," she said. "We've always gone on the theory that you ought to invest as much as possible." Having control over the Gehrig checkbook, she adopted her husband's philosophy, with financial security being the ultimate objective. If this meant that Lou would continue to shovel out dimes to shoeshine boys and car attendants, so be it.

The Yankees had been without a team captain since Everett Scott carried the title from 1922 to 1925. The Babe was captain for one laughable week back in May 1922, an unlikely assignment for a man who specialized in ignoring training rules.

Before Scott and Ruth held the post, the dependable shortstop Roger Peckinpaugh had been the captain from 1913 to 1921. Now McCarthy awarded the job to Lou. Even though there was scarcely more to it than presenting lineup cards to umpires before games, Lou said he was proud to have the title. He would remain in the post through his final season of 1939.

With McCarthy's contract expiring in 1936, rumors circulated that Gehrig might be in line to succeed McCarthy as a playing manager. Even if Lou had never uttered a syllable about such ambitions, the rumors persisted. In addition, playing managers were not as uncommon in the thirties as they are today.

However, this was as much nonsense as the report of a handwriting analyst named Shirley Spencer, who fanned the flames of managerial speculation with a publicized assessment of Lou's penmanship. "The very even base line of his writing," she wrote, "is proof of his cool composure . . . he has a quality of sincerity that is rare." These did seem like made-to-order qualities for a manager. But Lou's only desire was to keep playing for as long as he could serve the club.

For most players, Lou's 1935 season, when the Yankees ended in second place for the third straight time, would have been more than acceptable. His batting average of .329 was down, as was his home run output, at 30. His RBIs, at 119, were also disappointing, although he led the league in runs scored with 125 and walks with 132.

Obviously, with the Babe gone, more pressure was on him to produce. His high bases-on-balls figure, the most he'd ever coaxed, was a sign that pitchers were not timorous about walking him, since no frightening hitter followed him in the order.

Clearly, the Yankees needed a new slugging partner for Gehrig.

21

New Man in Town

Joe DiMaggio was the rage of Pacific Coast League baseball from the time he was seventeen years old. He hit close to .400 there, playing the outfield with a silky elegance that was astounding in such a youth. Long before he arrived at the Yankees' spring training enclave in 1936, New York fans were exulting in his acquisition.

Now, a year after the departure of the disaffected Babe, captain Lou found himself again about to be nudged from the headlines, this time by DiMaggio. Doggedness and power were just not enough for Yankee fans. It was simply that this stylish youngster from San Francisco had all of Lou's drive for excellence as well as other qualities that gave him, from the start, an appeal that only the Ruths, Mattys, and Cobbs ever possessed.

DiMaggio was as shy and aloof as Lou, but there was an aura about him that caused people to wonder what he was thinking,

even if, in truth, he was thinking very little. Humor was not Di-
Maggio's forte and roiled emotion was something he put on display only infrequently. Injuries plagued him, but he accepted
them stoically, in marked similarity to Gehrig. An intensely private man, like Lou, he chose, oddly, to spend his off-hours in very
public places like Toots Shor's and the Stork Club, where he was
customarily surrounded by courtiers and sycophants.

Lou may have been the captain of this team, but even before
setting foot in the Stadium DiMaggio, by acclamation, emerged as
the team's hope for renewed success. Even as DiMaggio faced
the New York press with sullen indifference, they made him their
favorite immigrant's son—forgetting for the moment Gehrig, that
other immigrant's son!

It had taken years for Lou to register a minor peeve about
salary. But after only two years in a Yankee uniform, DiMaggio
had no compunctions about asking for $45,000, a lot of money in
those days. When Barrow harrumphed that DiMaggio was asking
for more than Gehrig had ever gotten, DiMaggio's poker face
never reddened in embarrassment.

"It's too bad," he said serenely, "that Gehrig is so underpaid."

In the DiMaggio era, starting in 1936, Gehrig, at thirty-three,
was the solid man but DiMaggio was the solid-gold Cadillac. It was
DiMaggio who was now cheered to the echo as he glided on the
plains of center field or stood in his unforgettable spread-out
picture-book stance.

For Lou there were always appreciative cheers, too, but
each game was just another afternoon in the trenches, with dirt
on the Yankee bloomers, sweat on the brow, a hot shower, then
quickly home to the little lady in the suburbs.

The two men never had much to say to each other, or about
each other, even though they had lockers side by side in the
Yankee clubhouse. DiMaggio once remarked that he thought Lou
was the most powerful hitter he'd ever seen; Gehrig was re-
strained in comment about DiMaggio, in the beginning.

"Nice to have you with us, Joe," said Lou, when DiMaggio

showed up for spring training. Later, Lou would have high praise for the newcomer. "I envy this kid," he said. "He has the world before him. He has everything including the mental stability."

The rookie DiMaggio was an intimidating, chilly presence. His face, unlike Lou's, was invariably frozen in a scowl. The young man's tensions were assuaged by endless cups of coffee and packs of Camels. Lou had the cigarette habit, too, even if he tried to hide it when he was around kids.

From the start, DiMaggio was "Dago" to his teammates. But it was intended as an embrace, not what Lou had experienced in his neighborhood with the anti-German needling of "Kraut," "Heinie," and "Dutchman."

Although DiMaggio missed the first sixteen games of his rookie season because of a foot injury, he had already been canonized by the press. "Here is the replacement for Babe Ruth," exulted Dan Daniel. Two years later Connie Mack couldn't restrain himself. If Gehrig was the crown prince to Ruth, the old man said, then "DiMaggio is the heir apparent."

It was remindful of the claims made for Lou when he'd been a thunderous batter at Commerce High. But when Lou came to the Yankees some retreated from their predictions—they saw too much awkwardness and uncertainty in the boy.

Now it was scarcely a secret, least of all to Gehrig's teammates, that DiMaggio's arrival was depriving Lou of the attention he deserved.

"The man I felt sorry for was Lou," said Lefty Gomez, who had become one of those on the Yankees with whom DiMaggio was comfortable. "Joe became the team's biggest star almost from the moment he hit the Yanks. It just seemed a terrible shame for Lou. He didn't seem to care, but maybe he did. Sure, the relationship between Joe and Lou seemed pretty good; they never had a cross word that I heard of. They got along, but how could you ever know how Lou really felt?"

Whether Lou was drowning in sorrow for himself or simply regarded the new man in town as a natural evolution, it didn't stop him from playing every day, as usual. There was no sense complaining about a fickle world.

On the other hand, Christy Walsh, alert to the fans' tastes, thought it was time for Lou to change the public's perception of him. Walsh was fond of Lou, but he was also fond of money, so he made an absurd proposal. Wouldn't it be wonderful, suggested Walsh, if Lou would offer himself to the entertainment world as the newest Tarzan! This assumed, of course, that there was something wrong with the old Tarzan, Johnny Weissmuller, a former Olympic swimming star, who had been carrying off the popular jungle boy role with aplomb.

Lou chose to go along with the "screwy idea," pretending it was a challenging assignment. Walsh encouraged him to pose in a leopard skin while brandishing a bludgeon. Few newspapers passed up the opportunity to run the pictures.

When word reached Weissmuller about his would-be successor, he roared with laughter. "I guess they'll be making me a ball player next," he said. "I'll need some first baseman lessons."

Lou soon regained his senses, convincing Walsh that this wasn't quite the way for him to gain attention. If movies were in Lou's future, Tarzan was just too much to swallow. A few months later, after having suffered enough derisive comment, Lou said "the hell with this Tarzan stuff." The idea of swinging from trees in front of grinding cameras just didn't sit well with him or anybody else. The notion even drew a smile from DiMaggio.

With or without Tarzan, the Yankees were on their way to their first American League flag since 1932. Despite such distractions, Lou again played through the entire schedule without a break. At bat he was devastating. He hit 14 home runs against one team, the Indians, a major league record that will probably stand for all time. His home-run output was a league-leading 49, equaling his highest mark of 1934. He batted .354, with 152 RBIs, marking the eleventh straight year he'd exceeded 100. He also led the league in slugging, with .696, and in walks (130) and runs (67).

The Baseball Writers Association voted Lou the League's most valuable player, which meant that after nine years he'd made it officially again. Other MVP awards to Lou by the *Sporting News* in 1931, 1934, and 1936 never had quite the aura of acceptance as recognition from the writers. To win the 1936 MVP, Lou topped such able players as Luke Appling, who batted a league-leading .388 for the White Sox, and Earl Averill, the Cleveland outfielder, who pounded out an average of .378. Lou took four first-place votes out of the eight that were cast, with Appling getting three.

Lou was one of five players on the Yanks to reach the 100-RBI level that year (DiMaggio, Lazzeri, Dickey, and Selkirk were the others). Such power, plus a well-balanced pitching staff headed by Red Ruffing, helped the club clinch the pennant by September 9, the earliest in American League history.

Had it not been for the puffery that surrounded every move and pout of DiMaggio, Lou would have won considerably more applause. Joe got three hits in his first game, hit two home runs in one inning in a June game, and set an American League record for rookies for most runs scored (132). Batting .323, he knocked out twenty-nine home runs.

Yet Bob Quinn, an official in the Boston Braves organization, wasn't completely taken in by the one-note praise for DiMaggio. Near the end of the season he wired Lou: "In this age of alibis, Lou, when any number of players don't play—the least pretense—the latest excuse being my manicurist files my nails so short and trims the cuticles on my moons so close that I can't grip the ball—you are to be congratulated on your staying qualities. I hope you can continue for 1,800 more."

Grateful for Quinn's attention, Lou still insisted the streak was "luck." But he added, "I'm very proud of it, like a postman might feel after making his rounds for eighteen hundred days or so."

22

Old World Series Rivals

With the 1936 World Series approaching, the baseball cauldron boiled again in New York. The Yankees were going to face their old subway rivals, the Giants, for the first time in thirteen years. But the country had changed since the confident, raucous days of the twenties. Baseball had changed, too.

Giant fans, who once welcomed the combativeness of McGraw, now rooted for Bill Terry, Mel Ott, and Carl Hubbell. Yankee fans, nourished on a diet of Ruth's home runs, now had the Iron Horse and DiMaggio.

Events of minor and major dimension, inside and outside the game, were taking place. News crackled over the radio of the death of King George V of England, bringing Edward VIII to the throne. With Edward's accession came the sticky issue of his enamorata, the American divorcée Wallis Simpson. Bruno Richard Hauptmann was executed for the kidnapping and murder of Charles Lindbergh's baby, as millions listened to Gabriel Heatter's breathless death-house report. Germany's Max Schmeling upended Joe Louis in twelve rounds, and Roosevelt almost pitched a shutout in the electoral college against Governor Alf M. Landon of Kansas.

The singular event in Lou's life was his sharing of the cover of *Time* magazine, prior to the Series, with Hubbell, the Giants' southpaw. Babe had been featured there before; Lou hadn't.

Hubbell was confident that his pet screwball pitch would be able to foil Lou, as it had during the All-Star Game of 1934. His delivery, developed on a pecan farm in Meeker, Oklahoma, was a reverse curve that broke into the hands of left-handed batters like Gehrig. Against right-handed batters it floated away, like an autumn butterfly.

In the '34 All-Star Game Hubbell made consecutive strikeout victims of Lou and four other renowned sluggers in the first and second innings. In the first inning, following a leadoff single by Charlie Gehringer and a walk to Heinie Manush, Hubbell was called on to face the Babe, Gehrig, and Jimmie Foxx, in that order.

The Babe took a called third strike. Then Lou went down swinging at Hubbell's mesmerizing pitch. As he returned to the dugout, shaking his head in disbelief, he stopped in front of Foxx to exchange confidences about Hubbell. Foxx, a first baseman, was in the game at third base, for it was unthinkable that anyone other than Lou would play first on this team.

"You might as well cut away," said Lou. "It won't get any higher. That guy won't give you anything to hit." Foxx listened, then went up and struck out.

Picking up where he left off in the first inning, Hubbell fanned Al Simmons and Joe Cronin in the second. His five straight strikeouts of these Hall of Famers has since been regarded as a landmark of pitching wizardry.

Gehrig was eager to test Hubbell again in the Series, scheduled to open at the Polo Grounds, the scene of Hubbell's All-Star triumph. With forty-two thousand fans sitting under a downpour, Hubbell struck out eight Yanks and walked only one, as the Giants won, 6–1. Lou never hit the ball out of the infield. Batting in the cleanup slot, behind DiMaggio rather than the Babe, Lou failed miserably his first three times up. In his fourth try, Lou was struck by a pitch so soft that a gnat could have survived the impact.

After the game, Hubbell corrected the false impression that he'd purposely hit Lou. "I slipped and the ball got away from me with nothing on it," he said. "Maybe it's lucky it hit Lou, instead of going over the plate."

In the second game, the Yanks exploded for seventeen hits against several Giants pitchers not named Hubbell. They won, 18–4, with the help of seven runs in the third inning. Lou hit two singles, driving in three runs.

On October 3, at Yankee Stadium, the Yanks' Irving "Bump" Hadley won a thrilling 2–1 pitching duel over "Fat Freddie" Fitzsimmons. On this sun-bathed afternoon Lou connected for his fiftieth home run (including post-season play) of the year, in the second inning.

With the Series at two games to one in the Yanks' favor, Hubbell opposed Monte Pearson at the Stadium on October 4, before sixty-seven thousand, the largest Series crowd ever recorded. The Giants pitcher had a record that defied belief. He had won his last sixteen starts of the season, plus his first Series game, adding up to seventeen victories in a row.

When Lou batted in the third inning, he had *never* hit a ball out of the infield against Hubbell. Working carefully, Hubbell went to a three-and-two count on Lou. At this point, manager Terry sidled over from first base to remind Hubbell "not to give him anything good to hit."

True to Terry's instruction, the next delivery was a curve, high and inside. Lou would have walked on it. Instead, he swung, virtually from behind his ear, driving the ball on a line straight into the right-field bleachers. The crowd emitted an enormous roar, for Lou's two-run homer was the *only* homer hit all year with a man on base against Hubbell. Later, Lou added a double against his old nemesis, as the Yanks won, 5–2.

The Yanks lost the fifth game in ten innings, 5–4, as Lou went one-for-four, a single. But in a crucial moment Lou hesitated trying for home on Dickey's grounder that might have scored him from third. Too late, he broke for home and was thrown out. There was some grumbling about Lou's boneheadedness, sadly reminiscent of the days when he'd been painted as slow-witted.

When the Yanks won the Series in the sixth game, with a 13–5 victory at the Polo Grounds, Lou batted twice in a seven-run ninth inning. The first time Lou singled; the second time he came within inches of a "foul" home run.

Although he hit only .292, Lou batted in seven runs, maintaining his reputation as one of the great Series players of all time. However, nothing could deprive him of the pleasure of his home run against Hubbell. It had turned the tide in a game that could have knotted the Series.

"He was all pitcher, that Hubbell," said Gehrig. "If he had stopped us that day, with that incredible pitch of his, he would have been very tough in a seventh game. I've had thrills galore. But I don't think any of them top that one."

Ted Williams once asserted that Yankee Stadium was inordinately "tough on hitters . . . it's the bigness of it . . . those high stands with all those people smoking . . . all those shadows . . . it was always hard to get accustomed to, even after playing a series there . . . even then, you can never be sure."

That Lou could zero in on Hubbell's pitch at Yankee Stadium, when the Giant hurler was the most proficient pitcher in baseball, says much about him when put to the test.

23

Visiting Professor

Occasionally a story would appear that Babe Ruth was about to manage somewhere on the planet, or that he was scheduled to play a charity golf match with Ty Cobb, for whom he nursed an intense dislike. There were also the Babe's infrequent excursions to Yankee Stadium, where an exciting buzz would go up among the fans and autograph seekers. But the Babe was increasingly out of sight, out of sorts, and out of mind. The baseball jury had seconded Bob Shawkey's observation that the Babe could hardly be expected to manage a big league ball club when "he couldn't even manage himself."

In the winter of 1937, in his eagerness to keep his name before the public, the Babe gave an interview that dramatized how his relationship with Lou had gone from bad to impossible. Somehow, Ruth could not cease pondering Lou's dedication to the game. Fully aware of Lou's consecutive-game streak, the Babe chose to characterize it as a useless exercise. He minimized it as a boring statistic, nothing more, and always talked about it with an edge. A few years before he had circulated hostile remarks on the subject. Now he was at it again.

"This Iron Man stuff is just baloney," scoffed the Babe. "I think he's making one of the worst mistakes a ball player can make. The guy ought to learn to sit on the bench and rest. They're not going to pay off on how many games he's played in a row. When his legs go, they'll go in a hurry."

One suspected the Babe was not being very helpful. He sounded like a petulant man, blackballed from his profession, reduced to drinking and talking too much.

In his response to Ruth's public musings, Lou was careful not to get personal, but he showed anger in his words and manner. He might have been sympathetic with Ruth's frustrations but that didn't mean he had to accept his appraisal.

"I don't see why anyone should belittle my record or attack it," Lou said, as he avoided mentioning the Babe's name. "I never belittled anyone else's. I'm not stupid enough to play if my value to the club is endangered. I honestly have to say that I've never been tired on the field."

Lou emphasized that his immediate target was 2,500 games in a row. He also suggested that records by Cobb, Honus Wagner, and Ruth might even be surpassed in the long run. The inclusion of Ruth's name was unusual, for under ordinary circumstances Lou never placed himself on the Babe's level.

It was fine with Christy Walsh if Lou was determined to keep playing but he continued to seek another environment that might be appropriate for Lou—without projecting him as the son of a wild jackass. Both Walsh and Eleanor anticipated that Lou, unlike Old Man River, could not roll along forever, even if he was doing an excellent job of it now.

It would be nice for Lou, thought Walsh, if he could latch on to a compatible movie role, for he had the all-American good looks that would endear him to the public. Walsh was seeking a vocation—in addition to occasional product endorsements— that would assure Lou a means of income after retirement.

"There is a death that waits all athletes, when they quit," the novelist John Updike has written.

Tarzan was now out of the question and the childless Lou was not precisely the person to succeed movie veteran Lewis Stone as Andy Hardy's father. Neither did Lou threaten to be a nimble dancing partner for Ginger Rogers.

So in March 1937 there was Lou in Hollywood, chaperoned by Walsh, where he signed a one-picture contract with a gentleman named Sol Lesser of Principal Productions. The announcement was made at a press luncheon right before spring training. Lesser told reporters—more of the *Variety* mold than the *Sporting News*—that tests would be made of Lou to determine the type of character he should portray on the screen. There wasn't any chance, assured Lesser, that the venture would interfere with Lou's baseball career, for the movie would be shot during the off-season.

Shortly after, when the tests were completed, with Lou being subjected to his first instructions about emoting and projecting for a camera, it was decided he'd play a sort of urban cowboy who goes West, as himself, and gets involved in an adversarial situation with a posse of modern cattle rustlers.

His Hollywood assignment capped off a winter in which Lou basked in the afterglow of his World Series performance. The Young Men's Board of Trade of New York threw a dinner for him at the Harvard Club, where, it is reasonably safe to say, he had never eaten in his life. He was presented with a Distinguished Service Key in recognition of the fine example he set for boys and young men of the big city. As the first athlete ever to win the award, he was traveling in prestigious company, for the previous year District Attorney Thomas E. Dewey had been honored for his efforts in putting many powerful mobsters and crooked politicians behind bars. Dewey wound up as New York's governor, while Lou wound up back on first base for another season.

By late May 1937 the Yankees, with a horde of stars in the lineup, moved ahead of the pack and were never seriously threatened. As if Lou and DiMaggio did not throw enough dread into pitchers, Dickey hit twenty-nine home runs and Rolfe, one of

Lou's bridge partners, developed into one of the best third basemen in the league. The pitching was also extraordinary, with
Gomez and Ruffing winning forty-one games between them.

Prior to the All-Star Game in Washington, D.C., where President Roosevelt became the first chief executive to attend the
mid-summer promotion, Lou was in high spirits. One of five Yankees in manager McCarthy's American League starting lineup,
Lou was hammering the ball with stunning consistency. He was
one-fourth of a remarkably dependable infield (Lazzeri was still
at second, Crosetti was at short, and Rolfe at third), and looked
more fit than ever. "He seemed as strong as a slab of New Hamp-
shire granite," wrote Fred Lieb.

On the morning of the game, when he breakfasted at the
Shoreham with Eleanor, Lou had a premonition he was going to
bust one that afternoon against Jerome "Dizzy" Dean. Baseball's
most magnetic attraction since Ruth's departure, Dean was slated
to be on the mound for the National League team. His pre-game
boasts, typical of the slyly ungrammatical right-hander, promised
that all American Leaguers would fall easy prey to his incomparable "fogball."

"I don't know about that," Lou laughed. "Don't be surprised
if I knock one out of the lot off Diz. I told Eleanor when I got up
this morning that I felt like a million dollars."

In the third inning, with two out and the score tied at 0–0,
DiMaggio singled, bringing Lou to the plate. Dizzy gloried in such
a scenario, for here was Gehrig, the old crown prince "hisself,"
facing the self-confessed greatest pitcher in baseball.

Dean threw five pitches to Lou, sending the count to three
balls and two strikes. Before unleashing his next pitch, Dizzy
rudely shook off catcher Charles "Gabby" Hartnett twice. Hell,
who's out here pitchin' this game, anyway, he seemed to protest.

"What's he want to throw to me?" Lou asked Hartnett. But
the rosy-faced catcher glowered at Lou. He didn't like to be sec-
ond-guessed by anybody, even by Diz.

When Dizzy reared back and finally let his fast one go, Lou
swung viciously and the ball soared the proverbial country mile
into the right-field stands. This home run, Lou admitted later,

ranked right up there with his big blow against Hubbell in the '36 World Series.

The next batter, Earl Averill of Cleveland, sent a bullet back at Diz, who was still plainly upset with himself after the pitch to Lou. Averill's liner hit Dean squarely on the right big toe, fracturing it.

The Cardinal pitcher was never the same again. Trying to pitch too soon after the injury, he put too much strain on his right arm. At twenty-six, at the howling crest of his career, he was through—but didn't know it.

So the summer of 1937, a year of another lopsided Yankee triumph, was also a time of firsts and lasts for Lou. His .351 batting average marked the last time he'd ever hit .300. His hit total of 200 was also the eighth—and last—time he'd reach that coveted level.

But the first in Lou's life was when he got to play the role, however briefly, of professor. Invited to Columbia University, a place about which he still nursed mixed feelings, Lou delivered a lecture sponsored by Teacher's College. He was quite at ease as he talked for an hour before an audience in the Pupin Physics Building. Each of the students—forty athletic coaches from all over the United States—had plunked down a $12.50 fee to hear Lou's discourse.

By the time Lou appeared, in brown slacks and sports jacket, armed with a bat to be used as a pointer to emphasize his strategy on a blackboard, 110 neighborhood kids had sneaked in to hear their hero. Also on hand were two Teacher's College women students, who swelled the female representation to three.

Most of the youngsters in attendance, including the seven-year-old son of Professor W. L. Hughes, who was in charge of the course, were more interested in acquiring Lou's autograph than his batting tips. However, Lou took his mission seriously, as he did everything else in life. Hitting and other baseball problems were not subjects to be treated cavalierly.

"When I hit," said Lou, in a quiet voice, "I come as close to the plate as I possibly can. I try never to lunge at the ball. That's a deplorable error. A great deal of hitting is in the wrists . . . I wait until the ball is over the plate, then I step in just a few inches."

Lou's remarks confirmed the impression, if it needed to be confirmed, that he was a traditionalist in his approach to his occupation. He believed strongly in "percentage" baseball.

"If a play works fifty-three times out of a hundred, it should be used," he said. "That's the only proper and scientific method in playing this game."

Toward the end of the year, when the Yankees were casually tending to their margin over the second-place Tigers, twenty-four-year-old Tommy Henrich appeared on the scene. Henrich was a solid left-handed hitter out of Masillon, Ohio. Commissioner Landis had ruled that Henrich was a free agent, charging he'd been "covered up" in the minors by the Cleveland Indians. Following Landis's decree, there was considerable bidding for the young man before Henrich decided to sign with the Yankees for $25,000.

Henrich turned out to be a winner. He was also a fellow of considerable charm, which caused columnist Red Smith to say once of him that he'd never seen "anyone get more pure joy out of playing the game."

Although the Yankees employed Henrich in the outfield, he liked to work out at first base. One day when a writer watched Henrich scooping up grounders and throwing with accuracy to second and third base in a practice session, he turned to McCarthy.

"Looks to me," he said, "that if Gehrig ever knocks off, you've got a fellow out there to take his place."

Yes, the time would come, and McCarthy knew it. But he didn't like to think about it. Not just yet.

However, with another World Series with the Giants approaching, the prospect of Henrich, or anyone else, picking up Lou's glove at first base was unthinkable. Going into his sixth World Series as a Yankee, Lou seemed as vigorous as ever. He was still important to the club, even with the presence of DiMaggio and the other stellar performers rounded up by Barrow. And here he was about to get still another chance to bat against Hubbell.

24

A Final Series Homer

Compared to the Yankees, their 1937 World Series opponents, the Giants, were hardly more than "Babes in Arms," the popular Rodgers and Hart musical that continued its long run on Broadway. Few thought that the Giants had a whisper of a chance to defeat the Yankees.

Bill Corum, a Hearst columnist who had "marvelled at the sight of Lou's long drives" at Columbia's South Field when they were both students, challenged the Giants' manager, Bill Terry, to a bet. "I'll take the Yanks. A team with Lou can't lose," said Corum.

"What kind of sucker do you think I am," responded Terry.

By the time the Series started, the muggy days of August had turned into a landscape of autumnal rust. The New Deal seemed to be working, business was perking up, stock prices started to climb. But President Roosevelt was not complacent. He still saw "one-third of a nation ill-housed, ill-fed, ill-nourished."

If there was complacency anywhere, it was in the camp of Yankee fans. The notion that the Yanks would demolish the Giants was so widespread that tickets went begging at Stadium games. Among Giant fans defeatism was equally contagious. Even for games on Saturday and Sunday, they stayed away in droves.

For five innings of the first game at Yankee Stadium the doomsayers were put to rout. The gaunt Hubbell was as trickily successful as ever, and the Giants led, 1–0. Suddenly, in the Yankee sixth, the roof caved in, after Hubbell ingloriously walked his pitching rival, Gomez. A few batters later Gehrig was walked intentionally, to load the bases. By the time Hubbell left the scene, the Yanks had scored seven runs. They went on to win, 8–1, reinforcing the pre-Series predictions.

The next day, defying mathematical probability, the Yanks repeated by the same 8–1 score. In the Yanks' four-run sixth, Lou scratched a single to Mel Ott at third base, for his first hit of the Series. Southpaw Cliff Melton, a hillbilly with enormous ears, showed the Giants' continuing respect for Lou by purposely walking him twice.

In the third game, at the Polo Grounds, Gehrig gave a stern pre-game pep talk to Monte Pearson, a pitcher who often complained about minor miseries, illusory or otherwise. The verbal message worked wonders. Pearson won, 5–1.

In the fourth inning, Lou lifted a fly to JoJo Moore in center field, scoring Rolfe from third base. This tied Gehrig with Ruth for RBIs in World Series games at 33.

Desperately trying to get the Giants back into the Series, Hubbell beat the Yanks, 7–3, in the fourth game, working on only two days' rest. Previously hitless in the game, Gehrig connected for a long home run in the ninth. It meant nothing to the outcome of the game, but it provided Lou with another historical footnote. It was his tenth Series homer—his last—and also gave him 34 Series RBIs, sending him ahead of Ruth.

But these personal accomplishments didn't satisfy Lou. His team had lost the game. That always meant more to him. "A fellow has to get lucky some time," said Lou, about his homer. "But it didn't do us much good, did it?"

As the Yanks clinched the Series in the next game, with a 4–2 victory, Lou hit a screaming double down the center of the Polo Grounds fairway in the fifth inning to break a 2–2 tie. In this last game he also hit a triple, walked once, and struck out twice. His .294 average for the 1937 Series was not up to his Series marks of 1928 and 1932, yet his performance was strong at bat and he played flawlessly in the field.

After the Series was over, Lou reacted in traditional fashion. Speaking into a portable mike in the Yankee locker room, he said it "was an honor to be connected with the Yankees." When Lou uttered such phrases, the hardened pros around him didn't snicker. Stan Lomax, a veteran New York sports broadcaster, aware that Lou was given to such orthodox statements, said of Gehrig: "He lived in a rough, tough world, but it never got on him. That's the way he was."

Though the movie deal with Principal Productions may have been ill advised, Gehrig traveled to California after the season to fulfill his commitment. Once in Hollywood Lou obligingly went to all the breakfasts, luncheons, receptions, studio conferences, prizefights, and horse races on the agenda. He drew the line only when he was encouraged to pose for publicity pictures with nubile starlets in their bathing suits. With Eleanor back home, Lou sternly rejected Walsh's entreaties to nuzzle up to these accessible women. It simply wasn't his style.

However, Walsh was not beneath sneaking off with one of Lou's nightshirts and inducing such seductive actresses as Mae West, Jean Harlow, and Joan Crawford to scribble their autographs on it. Walsh then wrapped up the garment and mailed it home to Eleanor. At least, that's what he proclaimed in his noisy press releases. Such a stunt didn't sit well with Lou. But once he'd succumbed to the cinema siren song there was little he could do to rein in Walsh's commercial instincts.

The movie, a horse opera named *Rawhide,* had its premiere in March 1938 in St. Petersburg, Florida, where the Yankees were training. It was clear that Lou represented little threat to matinee idols Clark Gable and Robert Taylor. However, up there on the black-and-white screen he did come off as a boyish Bronx cowboy, showing as little fear of the varmints as he had batting against the fastballs of Bob Feller. The consensus was that Lou hadn't fared much worse than other sports-world icons who had dared to invade the silver screen.

The Yankees and their training partners, the Cardinals, joined in a glittering "Hollywood" premiere for *Rawhide.* There was a parade down Main Street, led by St. Petersburg's mayor and a proud Colonel Ruppert, secretly pleased Lou had found another way to earn extra money. A local high school band tooted away; Pepper Martin's Mudcats played hillbilly tunes; Al Schacht, the well-known baseball clown, rode a trick bicycle. Overhead Roman candles formed silvery snakes as newsreel men recorded the event for posterity.

Rawhide didn't require much from Lou outside of his chucking a bunch of billiard balls off the heads of the villains in one scene. Since the girl in the movie was supposed to be his sister, he was never required to do any kissing. Once he'd rescued the ranch for the good guys, Lou dashed off to training camp, safe once again in the comforting arms of baseball.

"Lou didn't appear long enough to emphasize his talents," wrote his pal Stanley Frank. Wanda Hale, the movie critic of the *Daily News,* thought Lou was "having a good time play acting" (a highly dubious premise), while the *Daily Mirror*'s Bland Johaneson wrote that "he was no mushy actor . . . in fact, he's no actor at all."

Interviewed after the film was released, Lou attempted to be loyal to the project. He made small jokes about never having been on a horse in his life and told about the camera tricks that were used to make it appear that his horse, Snookie, was running fast.

Asked if he had kissed the faithful old pinto when he departed the range to return to the civilization of Yankee Stadium, Lou replied: "That's my own affair. You fellows have no right to pry into my private life."

For Lou, that was levity.

25

"Why Not Stop at 1,999?"

As the 1938 season approached, and with it Lou's thirty-fifth birthday in June, some of the purists wickedly pointed out that Gehrig's streak suffered from a fatal flaw. They said that back in 1931, when Lou was in Tokyo, a pitch thrown by a 135-pound Japanese collegian hit him in the right hand, breaking a bone, and as a result Lou sat out the next game. But since Lou's post-season games were never included in the streak, now at 1,965 games, why should anyone unleash this wet blanket?

At spring training, Lou put on his rubber shirt and sweatpants to prepare for his sixteenth season in a Yankee uniform. His weight was at 212 pounds, just a few pounds over normal.

"Ruth always told me to stop eating," Lou said. "He warned me that when I got into my thirties, I'd put weight on. But I was dumb. I went right on eating."

On his first day in camp Lou amazed everyone by taking batting practice five times and running around the perimeter of the field a dozen times, though not consecutively. When asked if he wasn't going to ease up, now that he was a Yankee senior citizen, Lou answered: "Nope, not a bit. You can't make dough saving yourself. I'll be out there hustling as hard as ever and taking my chances. I'm not trying to be modest or anything like that. It's just that I'm a lucky guy. Ty Cobb once told me something after he retired. To last a long time, he said, you've just got to be lucky enough to avoid serious injuries."

It was no secret Lou was aware that the gravest danger facing a player was being hit by a pitched ball. He could dig down into his own experiences, too. There were those three beanings, with the worst of them the one back in 1934. "That beaning in Norfolk improved my hitting," laughed Lou. "I got three triples the next day." But he always knew that getting hit in the head was a serious matter. Hadn't the career of the Tigers' Mickey Cochrane come to a shocking halt in 1937 at Yankee Stadium when Bump Hadley hit him on the left temple?

As Lou's streak neared 2,000 games, Eleanor found it increasingly worrisome. Maybe, she said to Lou, you should take a rest, take a day off. She reminded Lou that he already owned the all-time record. "What challenge is there for you now?" she asked him. Why keep adding to the numbers, when nobody else will ever come close?

On the morning of May 31, 1938, with the Red Sox in New York to face the Yankees, Eleanor audaciously suggested to her husband that this was the day for him to stay home. "Just skip it," she said flatly. "Stop at 1,999. People will remember the streak better at that figure."

Lou wouldn't hear of it. "You can't be serious," he said. "They've got a little ceremony prepared for me at the Stadium today. I can't just walk out on them." He also reminded Eleanor that Colonel Ruppert got almost as much of a kick out of his streak as he did. "He'd never forgive me if I didn't show up," he added.

There wasn't any doubt who would win this argument. Lou dressed, drove downtown, got into uniform, and played. The Yanks won, 12–5, though Lou was forced to celebrate with one meek single in a sixteen-hit attack. Photographers were on hand to certify the event with lots of pictures.

When Lou returned home to Eleanor, who stayed away that afternoon, he had a huge, aromatic horseshoe of flowers draped around his neck. Yes, the Colonel had wanted him to be there for that. The two of them then celebrated very privately, with lots of bear hugs and glasses full of chilled champagne. Even with her misgivings, Eleanor knew how much it meant to Lou, and she shared his delight at another goal reached: 2,000 games.

If the biggest news of the baseball summer was Cincinnati pitcher Johnny Vander Meer's two consecutive no-hit games in mid-June, Gehrig's arrival at 2,000 did not lag far behind. Within a matter of weeks, unmatchable baseball events had transpired— but, as always seemed to be the case, Lou had to share kudos.

By the time Lou reached the 2,044-game level, he'd been forced from two games that he'd started in. One of those recurrent attacks of lumbago sent him to the sidelines in Cleveland, after five innings. In another game Lou's thumb was damaged on a low throw to first by pitcher Spud Chandler, forcing him to retire in the seventh inning. Dr. Robert Emmet Walsh, the Yanks' club physician, thought the thumb should be X-rayed but Lou wouldn't hear of it.

"I'll shake it off. That's what I've always done." he said. The next day, despite severe pain, Lou was in the lineup.

Such misadventures had occurred before in Lou's career, and none had been able to draw the curtain on his streak. However, something else was happening now. As the Yankees played their way to a third straight pennant, suddenly there was a moratorium on Lou's base hits. Overnight a drought set in. When he started slow, Lou kept hearing that soothing prediction: "When the warm weather comes around, your bat will heat up, too." Ball players have said that to each other for decades.

Rejecting hints that Lou might be showing his age, teammates like Lefty Gomez made light of Gehrig's diminished batting average. "Talk all you want," said Lefty, "but Lou's got a better constitution than the U.S.A." Lou tried to laugh along with Lefty, but he couldn't.

The slump lingered. Occasionally there were long hits, maybe a two- or three-hit day, but going into the last two months of the season Lou's batting average was in the low .270s.

There were times when Lou, worried sick over the dearth of hits, became sullen. He hadn't been in that kind of funk for years. One afternoon the Yankees staged a typical "five o'clock lightning" rally to overcome a three-run Cleveland lead, with the help of a DiMaggio triple and a Henrich double. The losing pitcher was Johnny Allen, who had knocked down more than his share of rival batters and booze in his time.

In the clubhouse Henrich, ebullient as ever, told his teammates that "I'm the happiest guy in the room. It's always great to beat that redneck!" Sitting nearby, Lou snarled out a contradiction. "Hell, *you're* not the happiest guy," he said. *"I* am!"

Allen, once with the Yankees, had constantly squabbled with his teammates and possessed a mean streak that could match Lefty Grove's. Lou had reason to dislike the man, and his shrinking batting average just added to his displeasure with Allen.

Lou never had an easy time facing slumps. His teammates told him to cheer up. But McCarthy, sensitive to Lou's personality, was nearly as distressed as Lou. He looked for flaws in Lou's stance, suggesting to Lou that he try a lighter bat. So Lou shifted to a bat weighing thirty-three ounces, instead of thirty-six ounces. When that didn't help, Lou went back to thirty-six ounces, then began punching at the ball, using his arms and wrists instead of his full body.

For most of the season sportswriters alternately speculated that Lou "was about to break his slump" or was nearing the end of the road. Were the years of playing without let-up hurting him? Or was it the numbers game finally doing him in?

A few didn't think it was any of those things. "I've seen players go overnight, but I think there's something deeper than that in Lou's case," Jim Kahn wrote in the *New York Sun.* "He takes the same old swing, but the ball doesn't go anywhere."

In a close July game with the White Sox, Lou came up with two men on base and laid down a bunt! Nobody could recall Lou ever having done that before. Joining the ranks of the mystified, Red Rennie, of the *Herald-Tribune,* wrote: "Gehrig bunting in such circumstances was as shocking as it would have been to see Jack Dempsey bringing into the ring with him a little sweater he was knitting."

McCarthy, reluctant to talk about his suspicions, said he didn't think Lou was hitting the ball as hard as he used to, though he had no accurate measurement to back up such an idea. In an unguarded moment, McCarthy might reveal more of his concerns. Many of Lou's fellow Yankees gazed at their captain anxiously, talking among themselves and wondering what was happening to the Iron Horse.

"To see that big guy coming back to the dugout after striking out with the bases loaded would make your heart bleed," said Lefty Gomez. "He couldn't understand what was wrong."

Though Lou might fling his bat after one of his frequent failures, he never intimated verbally that anything was bothering him. If something was wrong with his body, he never let on to anyone, including Eleanor. As someone who always casually dismissed injuries, he could easily have ignored the dreaded warning signs that were coursing through his system.

At the beginning of August Lou's average was down to .277, a mark that was foreign to him. "Hell, I'm not hitting with all these changes of stance and other things," he said. "I've tried just about everything. So I might as well go back to my old way."

In a marvelous reversal that lasted until the end of the month, Lou's bat experienced a resurgence of power. He hit at a .400 pace, with 24 hits in 60 times at bat, batting in 23 runs, as the Yanks won a record 28 games for the month.

During those few weeks Lou gave voice to an optimism he hadn't expressed since April. "I must confess that forcing myself to a feverish pitch day after day, I lost some of my zest for play," he said. "But now my confidence is as strong as ever and I can't wait for game time. I may be down, but Gehrig has not quit on Gehrig."

There was some loose babble to the effect that Lou's off-season movie chores under the klieg lights had hurt his batting eye. "Nonsense," said Lou. "My loss of timing had nothing to do with that." He was quick to point out that most of the work for *Rawhide* was done outdoors, with only two days spent in the studio.

On September 27, with only 2,773 fans at the Stadium, Lou hit a home run against Washington's knuckleballer, Dutch Leonard. It was his final home run of the year, and it was also the last home run he'd ever hit in regular-season play. When the season ended the next day, Lou hit a single in four at-bats against Boston. The streak stood at 2,122 games.

26

The Last Series

Despite his rash of base hits in August, Lou finished the regular season of 1938 at .295. It was the first time since 1925 that his average dipped below .300. He had 29 home runs and knocked in 114 runs, his lowest total since 1926, so these numbers, though excellent for other players, were dramatically below his normal production. DiMaggio was ahead of him, with 32 home runs, while Hank Greenberg chased the Babe's record 60 home runs until the final doubleheader of the season. Hank's 58 homers tied him with Jimmie Foxx for most home runs ever hit by a right-handed batter.

"Somewhere in the creeping mystery of that summer," Eleanor remarked later, "Lou lost the power" that had made him the most prodigious hitter in the game after Ruth's departure.

The Yankees facing the Cubs in the 1938 World Series were, thought McCarthy, the best team he'd ever managed. Considering Lou was in decline, that was saying a mouthful. But gazing at the pin-striped line—DiMaggio, Gehrig, Dickey, Joe Gordon (the second baseman successor to Lazzeri), and Henrich, each of whom hit over twenty-two homers—it's understandable why McCarthy made this judgment. Combined with these explosive hitters, McCarthy had a splendid pitching staff of Ruffing, Gomez, Pearson, Chandler, and relief hurler Johnny Murphy.

The Cubs were winners in a National League dogfight with the Pirates, when Gabby Hartnett hit his famous "homer in the gloaming." National League rooters now hoped the Cubs would make a better showing than the Giants did in 1936 and 1937.

The Yanks started by winning the opening game, 3–1, in Chicago, where straw hats were in vogue one day and ear muffs the next. But even under the soothing rays of a straw-hat sun, Lou's bat remained quiet. In the second inning he walked on four straight pitches. In the fourth he nudged a single, but was out trying to stretch it into a double. The other two times he struck out.

In the eighth inning, when Lou went down on a half-swing, umpire Charlie Moran's call was sharply protested by Gehrig. All of the frustrations of a puzzling summer now rose to the surface. When the game was over, Lou delivered an uncharacteristic post-mortem. "I never raised my bat for that one," he insisted.

The next day Chicago's weather changed. Under a brooding sky, Chicago's fans crossed their fingers for Dizzy Dean, who had come to them from the Cardinals in the spring, with an aching arm. Throwing balls that were often softer than a sofa cushion, Dean kept the Yanks at bay for seven innings, as the Cubs led, 3–2. The partisan crowd was with Diz on every pitch. When Lou stepped out on Dean four times early in the game, he was booed harshly. But his dilatory tactics worked, for he singled.

With two out in the eighth inning, it appeared that Dean's "junk" could beat the Yanks. Then the house caved in, as Crosetti hit a two-run homer. With Dean's demise, the Yanks went two games up on the Cubs.

When the scene shifted to Yankee Stadium, home runs by

Dickey and Gordon beat the Cubs again, 5–2. Lou hit a single in four trips, scoring a run. In the fourth inning he unloaded two fouls deep into the right-field stands, the last show of power he'd ever display in Series competition.

The next day, Ruffing took on six Cubs pitchers and won, 8–3. When the Yanks scored four runs in the eighth inning to sew it up, Lou followed a DiMaggio single with a single to right field. It was his final Series hit in a total of 34 games and 119 plate appearances.

As expected, the Yanks had walloped the Cubs four straight times, an echo of their omnipotent Series play in 1927, 1928, and 1932. They became the first team ever to win a World Series three times in a row. By playing through a victorious four-game Series sweep for the fourth time, Gehrig set another mark that will probably never be equaled.

However, Lou's scorecard was a hollow imitation of his halcyon years. He hit just four looping singles in fourteen at-bats, for a .286 average. He scored four runs, walked twice, and struck out three times. For the first time in Series play he failed to bat in a single run. Many great players have performed ingloriously in post-season play—but somehow it wasn't expected of Lou.

As the post-Series festivities went on in the Yankee locker room, with the usual horseplay and gulping of Colonel Ruppert's beer, Lou sat quietly on a bench next to his locker. The leading RBI men had been Gordon and Crosetti, his fellow infielders. How rare it was that Lou was not one of them, for manufacturing runs had always been his specialty.

In the path of the celebrating hurricane, Lou smoked his cigarette and smiled wanly for writers, who probed his feelings. Yes, he said, he knew he'd had a "lousy Series," but there was compensation in being part of a winner. That was vintage Gehrig. How did he think he'd do in 1939, he was asked.

"I think I'll do fine," he said. "This was just a bad year for me."

Several weeks after the Series, Lou was asked to be a guest speaker at the *Herald-Tribune* Forum, as a representative of baseball. He chose the theme "Baseball: The Common Denominator," a little high-flown, perhaps, but a subject he could handle and about which he had opinions.

A man of sound intelligence, Lou was generally underrated when it came to such matters as articulating his philosophy of life, or what baseball meant to him or his country. Such matters, he knew, were better handled by men of politics, religion, or law. Not a poised speaker, Lou was self-conscious and anxious in front of an audience, yet he made such infrequent appearances out of a strong sense of duty. His words before the Forum represented his essence, giving meaning to the drives behind his own career.

Here, in part, is what Lou said:

"I'm not trying to pretend that ball players have any altruistic mission in life. Frankly, we play baseball for a living. It's our job. Yet, I do think we accomplish more than just our own selfish purposes. I do feel we contribute to the spirit of the country and its mental attitude towards life. . . .

"I can remember the reactions of a sweet little old lady I happened to meet in a St. Louis railroad station. As we got off the train, a lot of people recognized our players and stopped to stare. This lady touched me on the arm and asked if I knew who all these men were that everyone was looking at.

" 'Why, yes, lady, those are the Yankee,' I said. She said: 'The Yankees? What do they do?'

"I said they played baseball.

" 'Is that all,' she said, and when I nodded she said, 'Tch, tch, they ought to be ashamed of themselves. Big, strong men like that playing games. They ought to go to work.'

"Well, maybe she was right. But it seems to me there's all kinds of work in this world. It would be a dull place if everyone was a salesman, a contractor, or a politician . . . and how dull it would be without the movies, the theater, the swing bands, even without the funny papers. . . .

"I think baseball plays an important part in keeping this country out of trouble that it might otherwise be in. . . . When the public is busy discussing pennant races and speculating on who is going to win the World Series, they don't have to work out their natural instincts for excitement by starting a war. . . .

"As long as the country can work up such enthusiasm about a game there's no immediate danger of it having much enthusiasm for much less healthy matters."

The words and thoughts were all Lou's, with perhaps a bit of prodding from Eleanor. There was no ghostly presence here of Christy Walsh.

27

Silent Spring

For only the second time in his playing life, through Prohibition, the Roaring Twenties, the Great Depression, and the New Deal, Lou accepted a salary cut in the winter of 1938.

Lou's off year in 1938 (McCarthy often said he'd love to have more players who had such off years!) gave Ed Barrow the opportunity to decrease Lou's pay to $36,000, some $3,000 less than he'd received the previous year. (DiMaggio signed for $27,500 after a squabble with management.) True to his style, Lou didn't battle over it or threaten. He would just strive mightily, he promised, to regain his form of earlier years.

That winter Lou was also saddened by the death of Colonel Ruppert at the age of seventy-one. Although he had never been close to the owner of the Yanks, Lou respected what Ruppert had done to build up the Yankee franchise. Ruppert's ascendancy in the baseball world was bound up with his own progress—and Lou understood that.

What Lou also understood was that others were concerned about him. He knew they thought he was slipping—a notion he publicly rejected—and that to put them, and himself, at ease he should be checked out by a doctor. This he did. The doctor felt Lou had been suffering from a gallbladder condition and recommended a bland diet. Eleanor appointed herself chief cook and guardian for Lou's food intake.

For most of the New York winter, Lou exercised outdoors as he had always done. He fished on Long Island Sound when weather permitted and went ice skating on the frozen lakes of Westchester, with Eleanor as an ever-present companion. He'd often visit the Playland Ice Casino in Rye, where, within a few minutes, schoolchildren would flock around him as if he were a robust Pied Piper.

During several of these outings to the Casino Lou lost his balance on the ice and fell down, rather awkwardly. A strong skater, although not balletic, Lou shrugged off his mishaps. Eleanor was puzzled by them.

In the first days at training camp in St. Petersburg Lou worked hard on his body, in the hope that 1938 was just an aberration. He was convinced that his conditioning program under the Florida sun would heal whatever was ailing him.

But by mid-March, after Lou had played in ten exhibition games, he was barely hitting over .100, with no extra-base hits. His reflexes seemed even slower than they'd been in 1938, and that familiar scythe-like cut of his big bat was missing. Fans sitting in the stands, who had once waited expectantly for Lou's turn at bat, now shouted insults. "One out" or "Two out" they'd jeer when Lou appeared at the plate.

"I've been worried about my hits since 1925," said the downcast Lou. "But you know that I never hit in spring training. I just have to work harder than ever."

Suspicions were rampant that Lou's abilities had retreated so far over the winter that McCarthy might have to think seriously about replacing him. Such a notion was anathema to McCarthy, but he had admired Lou for too many years not to appreciate that something was radically wrong. "You could see his reflexes were shot," said McCarthy. "I feared Lou might get hurt if I didn't get him out of there."

In one spring batting-practice session DiMaggio watched with disbelief as Lou missed nineteen straight swings. "They were all fastballs, too, the kind of pitches that Lou would normally hit into the next county," said DiMaggio. "You could see his timing was way off. . . . Then he had trouble catching balls at first base. Sometimes he didn't move his hands fast enough to protect himself."

In the clubhouse, on another afternoon, as Lou tried to put his pants on after a game, he fell down. Pete Sheehy, the clubhouse attendant, and DiMaggio went over to pick him up. But Lou waved them away.

"Please, I can get up," he said.

Even a little thirteen-year-old boy from New York City named Tom Orr, who was working that spring as a Cardinals batboy, was aware of Lou's difficulties. Each day Lou, in his oilskin jacket, came to Waterfront Park in St. Petersburg to work out in silent desperation. It was maddening trying to figure out what was wrong with his body.

One morning, before the Cards played the Yankees, Lou stopped to chat briefly with the batboy about his new baseball shoes, which he complainingly said had cost him $15. But there was more on Lou's mind than that.

"I'm just not feeling right," said Lou, his face lined with weariness. "But I'll work it out, you'll see."

Wes Ferrell, next to Lou possibly the handsomest man in a big league uniform, joined the Yanks in 1938, near the end of his pitching career. He was in the clubhouse with Lou one day, moaning over the rigors of spring training for veterans like themselves. When Lou tried to get up on a bench to look out of the window, he did so only with enormous effort.

"All of a sudden," recalled Ferrell, "he fell backward, down to the floor. He fell hard, too, and lay there frowning, like he couldn't understand what was going on."

Ferrell asked Lou if he was hurt.

"No, I'm okay," answered Lou, uncertainty in his voice.

The next day Lou went to a St. Petersburg golf course with Ferrell to watch the pros. Ferrell noticed that Lou, instead of wearing cleats, which normally would have been worn for walking across grass, was wearing tennis sneakers and was sliding his feet as he walked, instead of picking them up and putting them down. The effort seemed too much for him. "God, it was sad to see!" said Ferrell.

Previously, Lou's slumps had always engendered good-natured needling from his associates. But now, as if on command, such joking ceased. It was insensitive to shout "Hey, old man" at someone who was obviously suffering.

Though writers tried to be sympathetic, their stories suggested that Lou had aged overnight, that he seemed to be running in swamp water.

Generally, Lou preferred to nurse his wounds in private. Never adept at handling writers, this was a time when he yearned for solitude. However, Vincent X. Flaherty, a sports columnist for the *Morning Sentinel* in Orlando, Florida, attempted to interview Lou on one of those gloomy days of the 1939 spring. When Flaherty started to pump Gehrig with questions, Lou became angry and uncooperative.

"Why in hell don't you leave me alone!" Lou snapped, pounding his glove against a locker.

Flaherty, who never before had had any trouble with Lou, became vengeful. He wrote a piece denigrating Gehrig, adding that he resented all of the "maudlin slobbering" that had been written about Lou during spring training. "I'm not in St. Petersburg to praise Gehrig," he continued. "I'm here to bury the bloke . . . when Gehrig goes, I'll be sitting in on the requiem of a selfish, surly tightwad, who milked the game of all he could and who walked through his career filled with the self-sufficient philosophy that the world owed him everything."

Writers and players who had known Lou for years were shocked by Flaherty's intemperate attack. You're writing about someone else, they insisted. This is not Lou Gehrig you're portraying.

Not long after, Flaherty felt repentant enough to make an apology to Lou in a column. "He's a man of matchless spirit," wrote Flaherty, "a team man, with wholesome good character . . . the terrific strain of long and hot seasons is enough to burn out the filaments of the strongest human."

Even a rookie like Charlie "King Kong" Keller, not long out of the University of Maryland and in his first training camp, knew all wasn't well with Gehrig. Keller had his own hands full in his first year, but he could see that Lou was struggling as he put on his heavy clothes to sweat. Lou looked so bad, recalled Keller, that you couldn't help feeling he was going to get hurt even in practice.

In spite of such ominous circumstances McCarthy was reluctant to jettison Lou from the Yankee lineup. As far as McCarthy was concerned, the Iron Horse himself would have to ask to be relieved.

As the Yanks broke Florida camp and headed north before opening the season, Lou had played in twenty-seven games without hitting a home run or a triple. The club had four games left with the Brooklyn Dodgers, who were touring with them.

In the first of those games in Norfolk, Virginia, Lou cracked out four hits, including two homers off Freddie Fitzsimmons. When the team arrived in New York, the news of Lou's "revival," dutifully reported in the papers, raised hopes that Lou's silent spring of '39 had been a bad dream.

But McCarthy was a realist. He put Lou's Norfolk home runs in perspective. "They were balls hit over a short right-field fence," said the manager. McCarthy then paid close attention as Lou went out for infield practice. Lou always enjoyed these sessions, the scooping up of ground balls, the hustling in on bunts, the long throws across the diamond to third base, the chirpy camaraderie of the infielders.

A writer sitting next to McCarthy watched, as Lou appeared sluggish and feeble. "He looks much worse than I thought he would," the writer said. McCarthy remained silent.

"What's the matter with him?" the writer continued.

"I don't know," said McCarthy at last.

"Do you think Lou is through?"

McCarthy shrugged, adding that Lou would open the season at first base against the Red Sox. Perhaps better than anybody else, McCarthy could recite Lou's spring training figures: a .215 batting average in 31 games; 26 hits in 121 times at bat; no triples, no doubles; two "short" homers in Norfolk; 13 runs scored; 21 runs batted in (6 in one game); and 8 glaring errors in the field.

With the stylish team he had—DiMaggio, Henrich, Dickey, Rolfe, Keller, Gordon, Crosetti—McCarthy felt he could afford to be patient with Gehrig. He would wait for some miracle to resuscitate Lou.

When the season began at Yankee Stadium on April 20, Lou was at first base. But what the fans saw, in Lou's 2,123rd straight game, was a scarcely recognizable athlete. His performance confirmed those dreadful suspicions that people had. Almost overnight, Lou seemed to have lost everything.

The first time Lou batted, he received a rousing round of applause, almost as if the fans were telling him how much he was appreciated. When the applause died down, Lou lined out to right field, with Jake Powell and DiMaggio left stranded on the bases. The right fielder who caught the ball was twenty-one-year-old Ted Williams, the rookie Red Sox outfielder, who represented a new generation of titans ready to step in and replace old heroes like Gehrig.

A more distressing episode occurred in the fifth inning. With Powell on third and one out, Lefty Grove, who had always treated Lou with great respect as a hitter, chose to walk DiMaggio intentionally in order to face Gehrig. This was the ultimate indignity for Lou. What was worse, Lou then hit into a double play, though the Yanks did go on to win their opener.

On April 21, Lou scratched his first hit of the year, as the

Yanks won, 6–3, behind Gomez. But Lou also committed an error on an easy ground ball. When the Yanks lost their first game on April 22 against Washington, Lou failed to hit in four at-bats.

The Senators won again the next day, as Lou was again hitless. On April 24, the Athletics lost at Yankee Stadium, 2–1. Lou had no hits. The A's fell the following day, too, 8–4, as Lou experienced his last two-hit game. But in the field Lou had no more elasticity than an old rubber band.

During the Series with the A's, Philadelphia's right-hander George Caster declined to pitch inside to Lou. "I was afraid if I pitched him tight, he wouldn't have the reflexes to jump out of the way," said Caster. "His body suddenly seemed to have slowed up."

There were no games on April 26, 27, and 28, giving Lou a chance to rest and McCarthy time to ruminate. Before the schedule resumed on April 29, there were those who theorized that without "strange interludes" (skipping of games), Lou might have caused some damage to his body.

But Lou remained adamant on the subject. "What do you mean about consecutive games," he repeated, in an old refrain. "It rains now and then, doesn't it? I don't play that day. Isn't that a day off? What's the difference between taking the day off, or having the day off because it's raining? Why, I've had lots of days off over the years."

On April 29 the Senators beat the Yankees, 3–1. Lou had a single in three at-bats against southpaw Ken Chase. It was the 2,721st hit—the final one—of Gehrig's career.

The next day, Sunday, April 30, President Roosevelt was in New York to open up the New York World's Fair, situated on 1,216 acres that had once been the dismal swamp of Flushing Meadows. At Yankee Stadium twenty-four thousand fans chose to watch the Yankees and the Senators, instead of going to the Fair. Lou arrived at the park early to work on his hitting. He had produced a puny four singles in the first seven games, with only one run batted in. Although the Yanks had won five of those seven games, Lou's failures were mounting.

In batting practice he hit several balls that barely reached the lower right-field bleachers. When he moved around the bases, he appeared to be shuffling, instead of running. During infield practice the team's little mascot, Timmy Sullivan, worked faithfully with Lou as he shakily tried to field ground balls.

McCarthy did some improvising with his lineup that afternoon, for DiMaggio was out with torn muscles in his right ankle. So Dickey batted fourth, ahead of Lou. For the fifth time in eight games Lou went hitless, as the Senators beat the Yankees 3–2. John Kieran wrote that Lou looked "like a man trying to lift heavy trunks into a truck."

After the game there was a buzz of disgruntlement in the Yankee clubhouse. Some players openly expressed doubts that the Yanks could keep on winning with Lou in the lineup. Lou overheard some of the remarks and was shaken by them. that night, deeply troubled, he talked about the situation with Eleanor.

"These fellows don't think I can do it anymore," said Lou. "Do you think I should quit?"

Eleanor tried to be politic.

"All that matters," she said, "is if you still get satisfaction out of playing."

"How can I get satisfaction, when I'm hurting the club?" Lou responded.

A day off was scheduled before the Yanks opened a series in Detroit on May 2, so McCarthy went home to Buffalo. That gave Lou another day to contemplate his future in his room at the Book-Cadillac hotel in Detroit.

After a decade of gloom, 1939 seemingly dawned as a year of hope. President Roosevelt assured the country that no American boys would be sent into any foreign wars, Clark Gable and Vivien Leigh glorified the Old South in *Gone with the Wind,* and Judy Garland wondered in *The Wizard of Oz* why she couldn't fly over the rainbow. Big bands belted out a driving beat and the Inkspots crooned "If I Didn't Care."

In this pre–World War II cocoon of surface serenity and mass-produced happiness, sports-loving America was about to suffer a body blow, for Lou had decided to limp away from the playing field after 2,130 straight games.

His mind made up, Lou waited for McCarthy in the hotel lobby. The two then went up to the manager's room. McCarthy was already anticipating what Lou was about to tell him. But he hated to hear it.

Lou got right to the point.

"I'm benching myself, Joe," he said.

After a moment's silence, Joe asked, "Why?"

"For the good of the team, Joe. Nobody has to tell me how bad I've been and how much of a drawback I've been to the club. I've been thinking ever since the season opened, when I couldn't start as I hoped I would, that the time has come for me to quit," Lou said disconsolately.

"You don't have to quit," said McCarthy. "Take a rest for a week or so, and maybe you'll feel all right again."

"I just don't know," said Lou. "I can't figure what's the matter with me. I just know I can't go on this way. Johnny Murphy told me—"

"What do you mean Murphy told you?" McCarthy asked, angrily.

Lou explained that Murphy, a relief pitcher, as well as the other Yanks, hadn't said a word to hurt his feelings. But in the last game at the Stadium something happened that convinced him it was time to quit.

In the ninth inning a ball was hit between the pitcher's mound and first base. Fielding the ball cleanly, Murphy had to wait for Lou to get over to first to take his throw. It should have been a simple play for Lou—but it wasn't. He should have been there in plenty of time, but the play was unnecessarily close.

"When Murphy came over to me, as we left the field, to tell me what a nice play I'd made," said Lou, "I knew then it was time for me to get out."

McCarthy understood what Lou was telling him. After all, he'd been seeing it with his own eyes for several months.

"All right, Lou, take a rest," said McCarthy. "But any time you want to get back in there, it's your position. I'll put Dahlgren in at first today."

As much as McCarthy loved Lou, he felt that Lou was doing the right thing. What irked him additionally was that his nominee to replace Lou was someone he didn't particularly like. Ellsworth "Babe" Dahlgren, a slick-fielding San Franciscan, had arms "that were too short," according to McCarthy. Dahlgren once tried to rebut such disparagement by having his picture taken with Gehrig. According to Dahlgren, it proved his arms were longer than Lou's!

On that May 2 afternoon the Yankee clubhouse, under the stands at Briggs Stadium in Detroit, was like a graveyard. Even before coach Art Fletcher tapped Dahlgren on the shoulder to inform him he was playing first base, the melancholy grapevine had reached the players. Most of them spoke in whispers as they started to dress for a game they wished would never take place.

"Good luck, Babe," said Fletcher to Dahlgren. In a state of near-shock, Dahlgren suited up, picked up his first baseman's glove, and went out on the field to warm up. He noticed Lou, dedicated to the end, in the outfield chasing fungoes with the pitchers.

For a half-hour Lou worked hard with his reluctant body, as if he were trying to shake the demons loose. When the practice period was over, he walked dejectedly toward the dugout.

With photographers clamoring for pictures, Lou remained on the field to pose with his successor. Dahlgren knew Lou's heart had to be breaking: When he looked into Lou's eyes and saw tears there, he regarded himself as a culprit. Yet he also knew this was the time for him to make his own reputation.

"Come on, Lou," said Dahlgren. "You better get out there! You've put me in a terrible spot."

Lou tried to smile reassuringly at Dahlgren. But he couldn't. Instead, he slapped him on the back. "Go on out there, Babe, and knock in some runs," he said.

When the game was set to begin, Lou walked slowly up the dugout steps with a Yankee lineup card in his hand that excluded his own name. Umpire Stephen Basil accepted it. Then the announcement, to the 11,379 people at the game, came over the public address system: "Dahlgren, first base." For seconds there was a powerful silence, then the fans in the park—these were Detroit fans, but they were also baseball fans—stood up spontaneously and applauded. It went on for almost two full minutes. Lou tipped his cap and, head down, disappeared into the dugout.

That Sunday's *New York Times* ran a photo of Lou sitting on the dugout steps, gazing wistfully out at the diamond. The headline over the picture said "PITCHERS ONCE FEARED HIS BAT."

28

Farewell to Baseball

The long streak had ended. But the mystery of Gehrig's rapid decline remained unsolved. Lou continued to hope that rest might do him some good. "Maybe it will, maybe it won't," he said. "Who knows?"

There were times in those first few days after Lou quit that he cried in the dugout. When he did, his teammates looked the other way. Lefty Gomez groped for a laugh by quipping that it had "taken fifteen years to get Gehrig out of the lineup, while it takes only fifteen minutes to get me out." Strangely, at other times, Lou seemed relieved, almost buoyant.

McCarthy was equally relieved. "It's just as well he made up his mind to get out," he said. "I never wanted to hear people shout at him 'Ya big bum, ya' if Lou made an out or messed up a ball. Lou's been too grand a fellow, too big a figure in baseball for that sort of thing."

With his active career over, Lou chose to remain with the team as the summer wore on. Staying around the comforting environment of ballparks was the best therapy for him, thought Eleanor.

Each day Lou struggled into his Yankee uniform and sat in the dugout. Before game time he'd perform the ritual, as captain, of walking, sometimes falteringly, out to home plate. When he got there, he would hand that day's Yankee lineup card to the umpire. This symbolic mission, with crowds warmly applauding him wherever he went, reminded Lou that he was appreciated and remembered.

Marius Russo, a Brooklyn-born southpaw who became a Yankee in 1939, scarcely knew Lou. But he was touched, as were others on the team, by Lou's plight. "When he took that lineup card to the umpire," said Russo, "Lou was usually accompanied by a coach or player, so he wouldn't stumble or fall. It wasn't much fun watching his daily struggle with his body and emotions. Most of the time he sort of walked with a dogtrot, so his limp didn't seem so noticeable."

With each passing day Lou's hair was graying at the temples, his face looked more drawn, and he was losing weight. But he rarely complained and always had a cheery grin for those who approached him.

On railroad trips between cities, Lou traveled with the team. He was never asked to sleep in an upper berth, for there were fears he might fall out. He had always loved playing bridge in the old days with the Babe, Dickey, Combs, or a sportswriter or two. Now he played with Dickey, who was still his roommate, Rolfe, and writers Tom Meany, Kieran, and Grantland Rice.

Lou's hands had lost so much of their dexterity that he couldn't deal the cards properly. He'd clench the cards so tightly that they became bent and distorted. A new deck had to be called on after almost every rubber. Those who played with him never remarked on his difficulties with the cards—it was no time for unthinking wisecracks. Listening to Lou discussing the hands, no one would have suspected the heavy load in his heart.

That summer the Yankees' triple-A farm team, the Kansas City Blues, was having a brilliant season. Phil Rizzuto, the mite of a shortstop who later would spend a lifetime in the Yankee organization as player and broadcaster, teamed with Jerry Priddy, the second baseman, to form one of the best double-play tandems in minor league history. Vince DiMaggio, Joe's brother, was in center field for the Blues.

The Blues were to play their parent club in an exhibition game on June 12, at Kansas City's Ruppert Field. The next day Lou was scheduled to visit Rochester, Minnesota. Eleanor, becoming increasingly concerned that Lou had a brain tumor, had arranged for him to be examined at the world-famous Mayo Clinic. Lou consented, for he was eager to learn what was wrong with him.

There was little reason to think that Lou would play in the exhibition, or even climb into uniform. But with twenty-three thousand fans on hand, most of whom had never seen Lou or a big league team, Gehrig decided to play, even though players on both teams tried to talk him out of it. He insisted because he said the fans wanted to see him. "He played by popular demand and because he was an obliging fellow," wrote the *Kansas City Times*.

Lou was in the starting lineup at first base, batting eighth. In the second inning he grounded gently to Priddy at second base. After he caught a line drive that literally knocked him on his back, Lou left the field in the third inning. Within a few minutes he was on his way back to his hotel, with the crowd's ovation still ringing in his ears.

In this farewell appearance, many on the field were aware of Lou's difficulties. Several of the Blues players have recalled, with poignancy, how Lou struck them. Buddy Rosar, the KC catcher, said it was "hardly a pleasant day to play a game of baseball." He knew Lou simply could not perform anymore as a player. Johnny Sturm, the Blues first baseman, chatted with Lou in German before the game. His parents, like Lou's, had come from Germany. When Sturm asked Lou how he felt, Lou responded wearily that he felt *schlect,* which means "terrible" in German. The

KC catcher, Clyde McCullough, who went on to a long career in the majors, observed that Lou looked so weak in going to home plate with the lineup card that he appeared to be "staggering." KC's right fielder, Bud Metheny, remembered that Lou told him "I feel like hell."

The next day, an anxious Lou entered the Mayo Clinic for a battery of tests. Within a week, the Clinic issued its official report, in the bloodless language of medical public relations. It read:

> To Whom It May Concern:
>   This is to certify that Mr. Lou Gehrig has been under examination at the Mayo Clinic from June 13 to June 19, 1939, inclusive.
>   After a careful and complete examination, it was found that he is suffering from amyotrophic lateral sclerosis. This type of illness involves the motor pathways and cells of the central nervous system and in lay terms is known as a form of chronic poliomyelitis (infantile paralysis).
>   The nature of this trouble makes it such that Mr. Gehrig will be unable to continue his active participation as a baseball player, inasmuch as it is advisable that he conserve his muscular energy. He could, however, continue in some executive capacity.
>   Signed
>   Harold C. Habein, M.D.

At last, the reason for Lou's baffling deterioration had been offered by knowledgeable doctors. Lou's motor neurons, responsible for carrying motor impulses from the brain through the pencil-thin spinal cord, then to the muscles, had degenerated. When this happens the muscles, even on such a powerful individual as Gehrig, atrophy and paralysis sets in.

ALS, as the doctors disclosed to Eleanor, is an insidious, progressive disease of the central nervous system. She soon learned that what makes ALS especially cruel is that its victims are fully aware to the end of what is happening to their bodies. At the start, one may hardly be cognizant that anything serious is going on: There can be a temporary weakness in a hand, a twitching of muscles, a sudden difficulty in walking. Curiously, the disease is painless.

(A French physician, Dr. Jean Charcot, first described ALS in the late nineteenth century. In a few places in the world, including western New Guinea and among the Chamorro people in Guam, the incidence of ALS is a hundred times higher than any other place—but nobody knows why. Science has still failed to discover many clues that might lead to a better understanding of ALS, either in those afflicted areas or elsewhere. Today ALS is also known as Lou Gehrig's disease, making Lou possibly the first victim to have a disease named after him, a macabre form of immortality.)

Shortly after their examination of Lou was completed, the Mayo Clinic doctors phoned Eleanor with the verdict: They had handed Lou a death certificate, with a date certain before 1942. June 19, the day the dire news was delivered to Eleanor, was Lou's thirty-sixth birthday.

According to Eleanor, Lou never knew he had an incurable disease that would soon kill him. She had made up her mind never to tell him what the doctors had told her and she had requested that the doctors not tell Lou. But there is reason to feel that Lou sensed he was engaged in an uphill battle. In the first few months after the diagnosis Lou expressed an interest in the available research and literature on ALS, corresponding with many other victims. He even underwent a series of injections of vitamin E directly into his muscles, an experimental treatment proposed at the Mayo Clinic.

Sitting on the bench that year, Lou acknowledged seeing things he hadn't seen before. As a player, he said, he was preoccupied with the results of each game and his own performance. He had never really gotten to see how others performed.

"Now I get a chance to look at a complete game," he said. "I'd much rather be in there. But it's really a delight to watch those two guys out at short and second [Crosetti and Gordon] do tricks and make the plays. You'd be surprised how different a slant you get of a ball game sitting on the bench."

Being with the players, as the team battled for another flag, was the best place he could be. The Yankees, even without him, were still very much the cream of ball clubs. As they increased their lead over the Red Sox daily, Lou looked forward to another World Series.

Day after day, Lou sat on the Yankee bench, a perch that increasingly represented his security. Living vicariously through his teammates was better than being home, preoccupied each day with his eroding strength. One afternoon, with Dahlgren near him in the dugout, a photographer asked Lou if he could take a photo of the two of them. Lou agreed, until the photographer suggested that Dahlgren pose in a fielding position at first base, with Lou cheering him on.

"I'm not cheering him," said Lou, ruefully. "This is still *my* job!"

Always believing he could conquer his ailment, Lou had hopes, however slim, that others were writing him off too soon.

"I thought to myself," said Dahlgren, "that here I'd been rooting for this guy all these years, and now he refuses to root for me. Then I realized his resentment was based on what an intensely competitive guy he always was. He just refused to give up, as sick as he felt."

The players tried to kid Lou, suggesting he was "faking" it, or "jaking" it. They made a standing joke out of the fact that Lou really was on an extended vacation, getting all the free railroad trips and meals without ever having to pick up a bat on all those hot, muggy days.

Lou watched George Selkirk step into the batter's box for a few practice swings one afternoon.

"Hey, George, I want to see you hit one today," said Lou.

"If you had any guts, Lou, you'd be the one hitting a couple, instead of me," Selkirk yelled back.

"I wish to God I could, George," Lou responded.

Such exchanges were rare, for Lou went out of his way to keep things comfortable between himself and his buddies. He wanted to make his presence natural, not an imposition.

"I never realized," Lou said one day, "how much I'd miss the clubhouse atmosphere and my roommate, Bill Dickey. I guess my life is bound up with baseball and this ball club."

Lou continued to hope that his creeping paralysis could be halted. What kept him going was the belief that he had a fighting chance to beat the disease. Several years before Lou contracted ALS, Bruce Campbell, a Cleveland outfielder, came down with spinal meningitis. After missing parts of two seasons, Campbell returned to play full time and did well enough to bat over .300 each year. Gehrig was aware of Campbell's recovery and though the case was hardly the same as his, he took heart from Campbell's successful battle and tried desperately to relate it to his own struggle.

Though Eleanor kept to her resolve never to tell Lou he was doomed, he gave out hints, from time to time, that he realized his chances for survival were slim. Once, when a small crowd of admirers gathered around him outside the Stadium, he turned to a writer companion and whispered, "These people are yelling 'Good luck, Lou' and are wishing me well, and I'm dying."

Dickey hadn't been informed that Lou was in a terminal stage of ALS. But even if he didn't understand all of the nuances of Lou's disability, he was convinced it was serious. He could observe Lou daily and was shocked at what he saw: things like Lou's legs suddenly buckling for no apparent reason or Lou having trouble bending down to tie his shoelaces, with fingers that shook alarmingly. Although Dickey rarely heard Lou complain, on one occasion, when the Yankee team stopped at a small town and some kids gathered around seeking autographs, Lou said to Bill: "These boys have a whole life to live—but I don't have long to go."

Shortly after Lou's return from the Mayo Clinic, the Yankees, reacting to widespread sympathy for him, arranged a Gehrig Appreciation Day, to be held on July 4, when the Senators would be in New York for a doubleheader.

However, behind the scenes, Barrow, a man who wasted little sentiment on players who had outlived their usefulness, chillingly informed Eleanor that "it was about time for Lou to get himself another job." Having always assumed that Barrow (who lived near him in Larchmont) would reward his loyalty by provid-

ing him with a post in the organization, Lou couldn't believe it.
Eleanor was even more bitter than her husband, refusing to forgive Barrow for his coldness. She regarded Barrow as a sanc-
timonious hypocrite and scoffed at his gesture to retire Lou's
number 4 permanently. To her it was just empty window dressing
that would do little practical good for Lou.

In preparing for Gehrig Day, some in the Yankee hierarchy
speculated on the possible negative impact such a highly
charged experience might have on Lou's physical and emotional
well-being. McCarthy, in particular, was concerned it could further damage Lou's health.

Despite such reservations, when the event was held it
evolved into one of baseball's most memorable episodes,
though, indeed, it was agonizing for all of those present.

Many of Lou's tough old squadron from the Murderers'
Row club of 1927 were there, including Lazzeri, Meusel, Flet-
cher, Combs (now a Yankee coach), Pennock, Koenig, Bengough,
Dugan, Hoyt, and Pipgras, who was umpiring that afternoon.
Wally Pipp and Everett Scott, who had played watershed roles in
Lou's career, were also on hand. Mayor Fiorello La Guardia stood
next to Postmaster General Jim Farley, who had started out life in
upstate New York wanting to be a ball player. Eleanor sat next to
Mom and Pop Gehrig, for Lou's sickness had brought them all
closer together. The Babe showed up, too, arriving late, as usual,
and looking tanned as a lifeguard. Until this moment he hadn't
exchanged a word with Lou for years.

With over sixty-two thousand fans sitting under blue skies to
pay their respects, the ball games with the Senators were all but
ignored. When the first game ended, the Yankee players of yesterday, graying at the temples and in their street clothes, joined
the current crew in a loose circle around Lou near home plate.

They listened as McCarthy, barely able to control his emotions, assured Lou "it was a sad day in the life of everybody when
you told me you were quitting because you felt you were a hin-
drance to the team . . . My God, man, you were never that!"

When McCarthy finished, Sid Mercer, a veteran sportswriter

serving as master of ceremonies, presented Lou with gifts from his fellow players, from the writers, from the club's employees, from the Harry M. Stevens concessionaires—even some from the enemy New York Giants. Then he leaned over to catch what Lou, his face twitching and jaws contracting, was saying to him. Mercer stepped to the microphone and relayed the message.

"Lou has asked me to thank all of you. He is too moved to speak," Mercer said.

At that moment the chant "We want Gehrig, we want Gehrig" started to rumble from every corner of the big ballpark. The fans who had come to pay their respects wanted to hear from their hero.

As he listened to the beseeching chorus, Lou drew a handkerchief from his pocket, blew his nose, wiped his eyes, and advanced unsteadily to the microphone. (McCarthy, fearful that Lou might fall, had whispered to Dahlgren, "Catch him if he starts to go down.") His cap in hand, Lou briefly scanned the packed stands, now silent as if on cue. Then he began to speak:

Fans, for the past two weeks you have been reading about a bad break I got. Yet today I consider myself the luckiest man on the face of the earth. I have been in ballparks for seventeen years and I have never received anything but kindness and encouragement from you fans. Look at these grand men. Which of you wouldn't consider it the highlight of his career just to associate with them for even one day? Sure, I'm lucky. Who wouldn't consider it an honor to have known Jacob Ruppert? Also, the builder of baseball's greatest empire, Ed Barrow? To have spent six years with that wonderful little fellow, Miller Huggins? Then to have spent the next nine years with that outstanding leader, that smart student of psychology, the best manager in baseball today, Joe McCarthy? Sure, I'm lucky. When the New York Giants, a team you would give your right arm to beat, and vice versa, sends you a gift, that's something. When everybody down to the groundskeepers and those boys in white coats remember you with trophies, that's something. When you have a father and mother who work all their lives so that you can have an education and build your body, it's a blessing. When you have a wife who has been a tower of strength and shown more courage than you dreamed existed, that's the finest I know. So I close in saying that I might have had a bad break, but I have an awful lot to live for. Thank you.

With the conclusion of Lou's words, the crowd let out a deafening roar. The Babe walked over to the stooped figure at the microphone and threw his arms around Lou's neck. The embrace was frozen in time by photographers.

Lou's valedictory has been acclaimed, without sarcasm, as baseball's Gettysburg Address. It's remarkable, too, that during his delivery, Lou showed no significant signs of slurred speech, often so characteristic of ALS.

The words had been written down by Lou, as he worked on the speech the night before. But when it came time to deliver them, he spoke from memory. "He was groping for some way to phrase the emotions that usually were kept securely locked up," said Eleanor. If the reaction to his simple, honest words by those who listened in over the radio or later read the lines in the newspapers was any indication, Lou had succeeded more than he could have imagined. Lou's few sentences were certainly the most memorable he'd ever uttered, for he was a man who, by common consent, didn't speak often or loudly.

By summer's end the Yankees had captured their fourth pennant in a row, leaving the Red Sox in the dust. The achievement was a record at the time. With Lou gone from the lineup, DiMaggio rose to the occasion, winning the batting championship with a .381 mark, higher than Lou had ever hit in a single season. Dahlgren had 89 RBIs and 15 home runs, which was a productive season but proof he was not ready to make people forget Lou.

The Cincinnati Reds were the Yanks' foes in the World Series, having surprised many by inching out the Cards for the National League flag. They were led by two talented pitchers, Bucky Walters and Paul Derringer, who won fifty-two games between them.

Having traveled with the Yanks all year, Lou remained with

them throughout the Series, including the train trip to Cincinnati. How it must have ached him to be a spectator at a World Series! The Yanks, displaying power from King Kong Keller, who hit three homers, again won four games in a row. The last two games were played in Cincinnati, so the trip back to New York in a special train was joyous—for everyone except Eleanor, who thought such excitement might drain her husband's vitality.

Celebrating still another Yankee victory was Mayor La Guardia, who had accompanied the players to Cincinnati and was returning with them. In six years as the bustling, unorthodox mayor of New York City La Guardia had proved himself equally at home at City Hall and in baseball parks, especially Yankee Stadium. Earlier in the summer, after it had become clear that Lou's playing days were over, La Guardia had made him a proposal. Would Lou like to become a parole commissioner for the City of New York? The mayor, an astute politician, thought Lou could prove an inspiration to many youngsters in trouble.

When Lou reminded the mayor that he knew nothing about the law or the workings of the Parole Commission, La Guardia was insistent. "All you need is common sense. You have that," said La Guardia. "I have confidence in you. I'll send you some books and reports to study. Then if you want the job, it's yours." Included among the books were studies on psychology and criminology.

While traveling with the Yanks, Lou diligently read what the mayor had passed along to him. He thought back to his own youth as a kid, drifting on the streets of New York, and reasoned he might be useful to the city's young people.

On the victory train from Cincinnati, La Guardia, a man of endless curiosity about others, watched Gehrig intently. Lou played some bridge with Dickey, John Kieran, and Grantland Rice. However, most of the time he spent reading the newspapers, puffing on his pipe, and trading small talk with La Guardia. The mayor was impressed with Lou's courageous, cheerful attitude in the face of everything that had happened to him. Lou told La Guardia about a visit he'd once made to New York's Sing

Sing Prison, where he played an exhibition game against the inmates.

"A lot of those fellows up there," he remarked, "kept yelling at me, 'Hello, Lou. How are you, Lou?' And I thought they were just fans. But when I looked close at them I realized a few of them used to run around with me when we were kids."

After considerable thought, and with Eleanor's encouragement, Lou decided to accept the challenge with the Parole Commission. Eleanor laughingly warned him that some youngsters might do something wrong in order to get to meet him. Nevertheless, Lou elected to try it, after he was also assured by the mayor that it would not be a ceremonial position.

By December 1939 the Baseball Writers Association voted Lou into baseball's Hall of Fame, waiving a rule that said no player could be eligible until he was retired for at least one year. His election was unanimous. Public sentiment for such a summary move was as equally persuasive as Lou's brilliant record. At the same time the Yankees retired Lou's uniform, making him the first major league player to be honored in such a way.

Once Lou made clear to La Guardia that he preferred public service, rather than more lucrative commercial opportunities, a day was earmarked for Lou's induction. He was sworn in on January 2, 1940, at 139 Centre Street, for a ten-year term, with the mayor on hand to give his official blessing. Gehrig's pay was $5,700 a year, a solid salary at that time, but only a few dollars more than he had received as his 1939 World Series share.

In his new job Lou's primary function was to make judgments about the time of release for prisoners who had been sentenced to indeterminate terms in the city's penal institutions. The caseload of the Commission came to about six thousand a year.

When Lou accepted the mayor's assignment, Eleanor emphasized that they both thought "it was a real chance to do something for the old hometown." The Gehrigs also felt strongly that it would be only proper for them to move into New York City from Larchmont, to satisfy the residency law requirement that made it mandatory for city employees to live within the metropolitan area. Within days, they rented a white frame home on the edge of Fieldston, in the Riverdale section of the Bronx. Nearby was Christ Episcopal Church and the newly completed Henry Hudson Parkway. Without doubt, the Gehrigs could have won an exemption from the law. Lou just didn't choose to play it that way.

For the next twelve months Gehrig had almost daily contact with street criminals, hoodlums, vagabonds, pimps, prostitutes, and con artists, a rung of society that as a ballplayer he had known relatively little, if anything, about.

"Only a small percentage of men have to go back to prison," said Lou, reflecting on his role. "It seems to me that many convicted fellows deserve another chance. But we not only have to play fair with the fellow who got bad breaks, but we must also consider the rights of the taxpayers and our duties towards them. We don't want anyone in jail who can make good—but we don't want people out there who are a danger to the rest of the community."

One of the individuals who came before Lou was nineteen-year-old Rocco Barbella, who had been incarcerated in the Tombs on a charge of statutory rape. When Lou first confronted Barbella, Rocco was a tough, Lower East Side punk with little respect for the law or Gehrig. Later, as Rocky Graziano, he was to fight his way to the middleweight championship of the world.

As a kid, Barbella had gone to the Stadium a couple of times, primarily to see if he could swipe some gloves, bats, and balls. "Maybe I even got one of Gehrig's gloves," he said, after he became Graziano. "We'd just run down on the field, pick the stuff up, and run off with it."

As the door to the hearing room opened, Barbella, having heard that the great Yankee player was going to review his case, was curious to see what Lou looked like. What he saw shocked him. Lou had lost considerable weight and, as he walked, his body leaned heavily on crutches. The simple process of moving toward his desk took enormous effort, causing him to breathe stertorously. When Lou settled in his chair, sweat rolled off his forehead. It was difficult to hear his husky, muted voice. To start,

Lou asked the young man his age. Then he informed Barbella that
he'd gone over his probation record carefully.

"You've been in your share of trouble, haven't you?" asked
Gehrig, staring at Barbella. Rocco nodded.

"You've caused your mother a lot of grief, haven't you?"
asked Lou.

"Yes, sir," answered Barbella, who was not aware of the im-
port of such a question, for he knew nothing about Lou's devotion to his own mother.

When Lou asked Rocco to identify his favorite sport, Rocco
quickly responded "Baseball," though clearly he preferred street
brawls at the time.

Looking Barbella straight in the eye, Lou pronounced he was
going to send him back to a New York City reform school for
parole violation.

"Go to hell, you bastard!" Rocco exploded. This cripple,
thought Barbella, was pulling his whole world from under him. "I
felt like killing him," said Graziano, recalling the incident.

When he'd had a chance much later to think about what
Gehrig had done, Barbella thought he "probably should shake
Gehrig's hand for straightening me out. But it was too late. I found
out he was dead."

On most days, until the last months of his life, Lou was driven
downtown from Riverdale to his office in lower Manhattan by
Eleanor. He spurned official license plates for his car. Some days
he visited Rikers Island or the Tombs. When he tried to walk, his
legs usually didn't respond. In signing official documents Eleanor
had to hold his trembling fingers as he affixed his signature. He
took his daily injections of vitamin E after arising at 7:30.

When reporters asked him to pose behind his desk, he
would remove his pipe from view. He told newsmen he thought
the pipe, or cigarettes, might encourage young people to smoke.
A little black-and-white mutt named Yankee was a constant companion for Lou when he was at home.

There were only a few visits to Yankee Stadium in the last
year of Lou's life. One afternoon he sat in the dugout and talked
to Babe Dahlgren.

"How are you doing?" asked Lou.

"I'm coming along okay," answered Dahlgren. "How are things with you, Lou?"

"I miss all this," said Lou, wearily, as he pointed to the flags flying above the Stadium.

On those infrequent occasions when Lou showed up at the Stadium, the players would engage him in clownish repartee, and he would sit, unmoving, in his business suit.

"Did you ever try getting Gehrig on the phone at his office?" kidded Lefty Gomez, always the ringleader in needling. "The first girl who answers the phone wants to know your name. The second one wants to know how old you are. The third one asks if you've ever been arrested." It would go that way, somewhat self-consciously, but it served to perk up Lou's spirits.

Each time Lou came to the ballpark, walking unsteadily into the clubhouse, he was mobbed by his old friends. On another afternoon, when the players clattered out of the dugout for their pre-game batting and fielding practice, Gehrig found himself alone with Mel Allen, the Yankees' radio broadcaster, who admired Lou almost as much as McCarthy did.

After a long silence, which made Allen uncomfortable, Lou turned toward him and patted him on the knee. "You know, I never really got much of a chance to listen to your broadcasts," he said, hoarsely, "because I was playing every day. But I want you to know you're the only thing that keeps me going."

Allen got up and walked away from Lou, for he didn't want Gehrig to see the tears in his eyes. From that moment on, Allen believed Lou knew he was dying. He was also convinced that Gehrig's words were not meant to be patronizing or a conversational device. "Lou never said anything he didn't mean," said Allen.

On Sunday, August 18, 1940, the New York *Daily News* published a shocking article written by its sports editor, Jimmy Powers. The story suggested that the Yankees, many games behind Cleveland and occupying fifth place in the American League, had been hit by a "mass polio epidemic." A man with admittedly sparse medical knowledge, Powers charged that Lou's "infantile paralysis" had infected the other Yankees, thus accounting for the team's shocking reversal of form. The article immediately caused a sensation among readers and fans, who knew little more than Powers did about the details of Gehrig's illness.

At Lou's request, Milton Eisenberg, a Brooklyn attorney, brought suit for $1 million against Powers and the Daily News Syndicate Company in the Bronx Supreme Court. The suit charged that Gehrig's reputation and credit had been hurt and that the article had caused him considerable mental anguish.

Other angry Yankees, including Bill Dickey, also filed suit against the *News,* causing the newspaper to issue a public apology on September 26, 1940. The three-and-a-half-column story appeared under the headline "OUR APOLOGIES TO LOU GEHRIG AND THE YANKEES." It was defensive, but contrite.

In his apology, Powers admitted he had no business getting "snarled up in medical controversy." He wrote, "Gehrig has no communicable disease and was not suffering from the mysterious polio germ that supposedly played havoc with the Yankee ball club." Lou was a personal hero, Powers added. "Hurting his feelings was far from my mind."

29

Last Days

In one of Lou's final visits to the ballpark, he collected various parts of his teammates' equipment and presented them to Tom Horton, the nine-year-old son of Dr. Bayard Horton, who had treated him at the Mayo Clinic. Crosetti's pants, Rolfe's shirt, pitcher Ernie Bonham's spiked shoes—all ended up in the grab bag for the little boy. To a ball player such items are as precious as a scalpel to a surgeon. But Lou pried them loose because he promised Tom he would.

"He was like a Boy Scout doing good deeds, even when he was dying," said Tom Horton many years later.

As it became increasingly difficult for Lou to travel into the city, he stayed at home, where many friends gathered around him. Dickey came often, as did Barrow, despite Eleanor's feelings about him. Pitzy Katz, the comic, was a constant visitor, trying to brighten Lou's last days with jokes and imitations. The Giants' manager, Bill Terry, went to see Lou several times.

"I was shocked at how he looked," said Terry. "It made me want to cry. He must have lost eighty or ninety pounds. But he never talked about dying, even though I'm sure he knew what was happening."

A host of show-business people, famous and obscure, maintained the vigil, including actress Tallulah Bankhead, who had a great passion for baseball. Lou's neighbor, John Kieran, came frequently during the last month of Lou's life.

"One day poor Lou said to me, 'This is the crisis, Jack. After this, I'll gradually get better.' At the time Lou could hardly move his head. I nodded agreement and was overwhelmed by sadness as I walked home," said Kieran.

Fred Fisher, the songwriter, was very attentive to Lou, despite the fact that he was suffering from a stomach ailment that caused him great pain. The mutuality of agony increasingly drew the two men close to each other. Lou made certain that Fisher was referred to the Mayo Clinic. Less than a year after Lou died, Fisher took his own life.

At Christmastime in 1940, Lou tried to remain comfortably cheerful to the outside world. He sent a message to his friends: "These are times," Lou wrote, "when we have much to be thankful for . . . so this Christmas, more than ever, we say Merry Christmas."

The time had come for Eleanor to confide to Mayor La Guardia that her Luke could no longer competently perform his job. She informed the mayor that Lou probably was in the terminal phase of ALS and asked that Lou be given a leave of absence. La Guardia, never fully appreciating how ill his appointee was, was shocked.

In mid-April 1941 Gehrig wrote what was probably his final letter as a member of the Parole Commission, in answer to an invitation to attend a Health and Recreation Week function at the Jacob M. Schiff Center. He had always been an obliging guest at such affairs. Now it was too much for him.

"I know you will appreciate that I am undergoing an intensive course of medical treatment at the present time," he wrote, "so my physicians have advised that I make no personal appearances."

By the end of his life Lou had been robbed of everything he'd always cherished. He couldn't walk, run, or fish. The hands and arms that had propelled so many home runs out of ballparks were useless to him. He couldn't light his pipe or his cigarettes without help from Eleanor. When he played bridge he couldn't grasp the cards. He could barely utter a word or swallow a drink of water. Through it all, his mind remained active and untouched, so typical of the dreadful disease. He reaped his only enjoyment listening to music and opera, tastes he'd acquired from Eleanor. ALS, doctors have said, is like being a participant at your own funeral.

On Monday afternoon, June 2, 1941, DiMaggio got two hits off Bob Feller in Cleveland, as he moved one-third of the way through the fifty-six-game hitting streak that captivated America the summer before Pearl Harbor.

That evening, seventeen days before his thirty-eighth birthday, Gehrig died in his sleep at home. Eleanor was at his bedside. The news stunned the Yankees, who had just arrived in Detroit. Even those, like McCarthy and Dickey, who had suspected how desperately ill Lou was found it hard to accept that he was gone.

Tributes to Gehrig poured in from all over the country. Over 1,500 telegrams were sent to the Gehrig home, signed by everyone from New York governor Herbert Lehman to the redcaps at Grand Central Terminal. President Roosevelt sent flowers. At Mayor La Guardia's instructions, New York City's flags drooped to half-mast. Thousands of fans, forming a line over four blocks long, filed past his body at Christ Episcopal Church in Riverdale. The ceremony was simple and private. There was no eulogy. Reverend George V. Barry said softly that there was no need for that "because you all knew him." Lou's body was cremated, in accordance with an agreement that existed between Eleanor and himself.

One of the mourners, Bill Dickey, said: "Lou doesn't need

tributes from anyone. His life and the way he lived were tribute enough. He just went out and did his job every day."

In a touching, final remembrance, Fred Fisher wrote, in a letter to Dr. Horton, how the Gehrig house had been crowded with friends, "the rich and poor." McCarthy, looking drawn and morose, "shook Lou's hand in his coffin," said Fisher. "The fans lost a great player and I lost a pal that I loved."

Lou left a gross estate of $171,251 to Eleanor. He bequeathed life use of his trophies to his mother and father, plus a shared income of $205 a month. The trophy that was presented to him on July 4, 1939, with a soaring eagle atop a baseball, was originally appraised at five dollars.

In ensuing days, newspapers around the country extolled Gehrig on their sports pages and in their editorials, a place not customarily reserved for ball players. A bronze bust by sculptor William Westcott was cast of Lou, and this along with a Gehrig memorial plaque were placed in center field of Yankee Stadium. An army air base in Texas named its athletic field after him and a World War II Liberty ship carried his name.

Lou's remains lie in Kensico Cemetery, in the hamlet of Valhalla, New York, some forty-five minutes from Manhattan. His modest headstone states that he was born in 1905. This is in error, for he was actually born two years earlier. But the mistake has never been rectified.

Eleanor, who died in 1984, shares Lou's final resting place. The Babe's body is only a few minutes away, at Gate of Heaven Cemetery.

Pride of the Yankees

S amuel Goldwyn, whose artfully crafted malaprops have become as much a part of American folklore as Gehrig himself, had never been much of a baseball fan. "If people want to see a baseball game, they should go to a ballpark," the producer said when a Lou Gehrig movie was first proposed to him by Niven Busch.

But Busch, Goldwyn's story editor and executive producer, insisted that Goldwyn sit down long enough in his screening room to watch the Paramount newsreel of Gehrig's farewell speech at Yankee Stadium. When the lights came on, Goldwyn sat there unashamedly sobbing. "Run it over again," he commanded. Busch did. Within minutes, wheels started to turn to make the movie.

Goldwyn's ignorance of baseball was so complete that he literally thought there were ten bases on a diamond, and that a player had to work his way around from first base to tenth base. When Goldwyn asked Busch what position Lou played, Busch responded by holding up one finger to denote first base. Goldwyn thought that was terrible. Wouldn't it be better if Gehrig was a third baseman, or maybe a fourth baseman, he protested. "Why pay so much money just for a first baseman?" Goldwyn argued.

But Goldwyn recognized that Gehrig's career symbolized more than a dramatic baseball story. It was the "American immigrant tale writ large, Horatio Alger on the hoof," as Mark Harris would later write. To Goldwyn it represented a poignant fable of perseverance and humility, qualities that Goldwyn, an immigrant from Poland, had long admired and believed were firmly rooted in the America he loved.

So Goldwyn produced his sentimental motion picture, *The Pride of the Yankees,* with actor Gary Cooper, a Montanan who had barely heard of the ball player, portraying Gehrig. Any number of other actors, including Eddie Albert, William Gargan, and Dennis Morgan, were said to be eager to play Lou's role. Their press agents spread the word they'd do it for nothing. However, Goldwyn preferred Cooper, whom he had to pay. The price was said to be $150,000, about four times Lou's final salary with the Yankees.

Teresa Wright was cast as Eleanor, despite the fact she admitted knowing "almost nothing about baseball." But, added Wright, "I still know more about it than Mr. Goldwyn." During the filming of the movie, Eleanor spent some time on the set with Wright. She was pleased with Wright's version of herself. "But I'm no Teresa Wright, that's for sure!" she said.

One of Irving Berlin's popular songs of the twenties, "Always," said to be a favorite of both Eleanor and Lou, ran incessantly on the movie's soundtrack, providing a suitable romantic ambiance. The story treatment was by Paul Gallico, a New York sportswriter and Columbia graduate, who had often written about Lou's exploits. Herman Mankiewicz, later best known as co-author with Orson Welles of *Citizen Kane,* worked on the screenplay. A hard-nosed sports buff, Sam Wood, was the director. The movie became an immediate box-office success, making it to the top ten in 1942, only a year after Gehrig's death. One bemused critic rated it a "three handkerchief film" that could have been retitled "Mr. Deeds Goes to Yankee Stadium." However, the *New York Times* adjudged it a "real saga of American life—homey, humorous and sentimental."

Cooper had always been perceived by his fans as a decent, somewhat gawky, dignified guy, qualities that he projected onto the screen version of Gehrig. But in real life Cooper threw a ball, when he bothered to throw at all, with his right hand. Playing a southpaw like Lou became much too awkward for him, so an old Brooklyn Dodgers' favorite, Babe Herman, was recruited to stand in for Cooper in some of the batting sequences. Lefty O'Doul, twice the National League batting champion and a player who had been to Japan with Lou, also was hired to attempt a workable left-handed conversion of the actor. However, Cooper's coordination was so embarrassingly limited as a lefty that they filmed him as a righty and then reversed the negative.

"He threw the ball like an old woman tossing a hot biscuit," remarked O'Doul about his disciple.

Another flaw in the movie was its inaccuracy in depicting how Gehrig's streak ended. The movie suggests that the Yankees and Tigers were locked in a close game when suddenly the ballpark announcer intoned: *"Your attention, please, Dahlgren now playing first base for Gehrig."* A radio announcer then appears, proclaiming lugubriously that Lou's streak has been terminated.

This scenario was pure Hollywood flummery. It just didn't happen that way. And even if it had, Gehrig's streak would not have been cut short, for using a pinch hitter would not have disrupted his flow of consecutive games. Gehrig, of course, would have gotten credit for a game in which he had already taken part. In addition, despite the way the movie kept score, the game was never close. After Gehrig removed himself, the Yanks proceeded to win a laugher by the grotesque margin of 22–2, hardly a cliffhanging script.

Selected to play himself, and looking more than ever like "a truant from an 'Our Gang' comedy" (as author William Barrett notes), the Babe gave the movie some hearty validity. Dickey also played himself in a brief walk-on, and Koenig, the old short-stop, too appeared briefly.

On the giant-sized posters advertising the movie, only Ruth's name appeared. Goldwyn, subscribing to the conventional wisdom that the Babe had universal appeal, insisted on leaving Lou's name off, even though the movie was based on Lou's life.

Pride of the Yankees continues to be a perennial on the television circuit. Each baseball spring it pops up on programming schedules, one index of the grip that Lou's story has on the general public, even those who have never bitten into a hot dog at a ballpark.

Cooper was nominated for an Academy Award for his portrayal of Gehrig. James Cagney, though, took the Oscar that year for *Yankee Doodle Dandy,* so that two Yankees and two Columbians advanced to the spotlight, for Cagney had also attended classes at Morningside Heights.

During World War II, when Cooper toured military installations in or near combat zones, GIs frequently requested that he recite Gehrig's July 4 speech. When first called on to "do the speech," Cooper fumbled his lines. Thereafter, whenever implored by the soldiers to repeat Lou's words, he made sure he was properly prepared.

The legendary oration became an essential part of Cooper's repertoire, never failing to evoke a respectful silence from habitually raucous GI audiences. It was even said that the normally unemotional star choked up almost every time he recited it.

Gehrig, who excelled at a game foreign to Cooper, had become Cooper's greatest role.

Appendices

Appendix A: Gehrig's Lifetime Record

Year	Club	League	Pos.	G	AB	R
1921	Hartford	East.	1B	12	46	5
1922	(Not in Organized Ball)					
1923	New York	Amer.	1B-PH	13	26	6
1923	Hartford	East.	1B	59	227	54
1924	New York	Amer.	PH-1-O	10	12	2
1924	Hartford	East.	1B	134	504	111
1925	New York	Amer.	1B-OF	126	437	73
1926	New York	Amer.	1B	155	572	135
1927	New York	Amer.	1B	155	584	149
1928	New York	Amer.	1B	154	562	139
1929	New York	Amer.	1B	154	553	127
1930	New York	Amer.	1B-OF	154	581	143
1931	New York	Amer.	1B	155	619	163
1932	New York	Amer.	1B	156	596	138
1933	New York	Amer.	1B	152	593	138
1934	New York	Amer.	1B-SS	154	579	128
1935	New York	Amer.	1B	149	535	125
1936	New York	Amer.	1B	155	579	167
1937	New York	Amer.	1B	157	569	138
1938	New York	Amer.	1B	157	576	115
1939	New York	Amer.	1B	8	28	2
	Major League Totals			2164	8001	1888
	WORLD SERIES RECORD					
1926	New York	Amer.	1B	7	23	1
1927	New York	Amer.	1B	4	13	2
1928	New York	Amer.	1B	4	11	5
1932	New York	Amer.	1B	4	17	9
1936	New York	Amer.	1B	6	24	5
1937	New York	Amer.	1B	5	17	4
1938	New York	Amer.	1B	4	14	4
	World Series Totals			34	119	30

H	2B	3B	HR	RBI	BA	PO	A	E	FA
12	1	2	0	—	.261	130	4	2	.985
11	4	1	1	9	.423	53	3	4	.933
69	13	8	24	—	.304	623	23	6	.991
6	1	0	0	6	.500	10	1	0	1.000
186	40	13	37	—	.369	1391	66	23	.984
129	23	10	20	68	.295	1126	53	13	.989
179	47	20	16	107	.313	1565	73	15	.991
218	52	18	47	175	.373	1662	88	15	.992
210	47	13	27	142	.374	1488	79	18	.989
166	33	9	35	126	.300	1458	82	9	.994
220	42	17	41	174	.379	1298	89	15	.989
211	31	15	46	184	.341	1352	58	13	.991
208	42	9	34	151	.349	1293	75	18	.987
198	41	12	32	139	.334	1290	64	9	.993
210	40	6	49	165	.363	1284	80	8	.994
176	26	10	30	119	.329	1337	82	15	.990
205	37	7	49	152	.354	1377	82	9	.994
200	37	9	37	159	.351	1370	74	16	.989
170	32	6	29	114	.295	1483	100	14	.991
4	0	0	0	1	.143	64	4	2	.971
2721	535	162	493	1991	.340	19511	1087	193	.991
8	2	0	0	3	.348	78	1	0	1.000
4	2	2	0	5	.308	41	3	0	1.000
6	1	0	4	9	.545	33	0	0	1.000
9	1	0	3	8	.529	37	2	1	.975
7	1	0	2	7	.292	45	2	0	1.000
5	1	1	1	3	.294	50	1	0	1.000
4	0	0	0	0	.286	25	3	0	1.000
43	8	3	10	35	.361	309	12	1	.997

Appendix B:
The Lou Gehrig Award

An annual Lou Gehrig Award to the major league player judged by the Lou Gehrig Award Committee to best exemplify Gehrig's personal character and playing ability has been given since 1955 by the Phi Delta Theta Fraternity in Oxford, Ohio. Following are the recipients:

1955: Alvin Dark, *Giants*
1956: Peewee Reese, *Dodgers*
1957: Stan Musial, *Cardinals*
1958: Gil McDougald, *Yankees*
1959: Gil Hodges, *Dodgers*
1960: Dick Groat, *Pirates*
1961: Warren Spahn, *Braves*
1962: Robin Roberts, *Orioles*
1963: Bobby Richardson, *Yankees*
1964: Ken Boyer, *Cardinals*
1965: Vernon Law, *Pirates*
1966: Brooks Robinson, *Orioles*

1967: Ernie Banks, *Cubs*
1968: Al Kaline, *Tigers*
1969: Pete Rose, *Reds*
1970: Hank Aaron, *Braves*
1971: Harmon Killebrew, *Twins*
1972: Wes Parker, *Dodgers*
1973: Ron Santo, *Cubs*
1974: Willie Stargell, *Pirates*
1975: Johnny Bench, *Reds*
1976: Don Sutton, *Dodgers*
1977: Lou Brock, *Cardinals*
1978: Don Kessinger, *White Sox*
1979: Phil Niekro, *Braves*
1980: Tony Perez, *Reds*
1981: Tommy John, *Yankees*
1982: Ron Cey, *Dodgers*
1983: Mike Schmidt, *Phillies*
1984: Steve Garvey, *Padres*
1985: Dale Murphy, *Braves*
1986: George Brett, *Royals*
1987: Rick Sutcliffe, *Cubs*
1988: Buddy Bell, *Rangers*
1989: Ozzie Smith, *Cardinals*

Acknowledgments

In the preparation of this book many kind people graciously prodded their memories for me about Lou Gehrig. Former teammates, associates, and fellow ball players, including Tommy Henrich, Joey Sewell, Babe Dahlgren, Charlie Keller, Billy Werber, Ben Chapman, Marius Russo, Mel Allen, Charlie Devens, Jimmie Reese, Frankie Crosetti, Charlie Gehringer, Luke Appling, Mark Koenig, Phil Rizzuto, and Ray White, all contributed anecdotes and insights. Bill Dickey, Gehrig's roommate, was too ill to render assistance but I spoke briefly with him on the phone.

I was also fortunate to chat with Lefty Gomez, Waite Hoyt, Spud Chandler, Bill Terry, Johnny Neun, Bob Fishel, and Andy Cohen before they died. None of them was reluctant to give time and energy, despite their frailty.

The Baseball Library at Cooperstown, under Tom Heitz and his assistants Bill Dean and Pat Kelly, was a rich source of material, as were the bound volumes of the *New York Times* at the New York Society Library. Back issues of the New York *Daily News* were made available to me through the kindness of Vic Ziegel and Faigi Rosenthal. Peter Miller at *Sports Illustrated* permitted me to stroll through *SI*'s files. Holley Haswell of Columbia University's Low Library and Bill Steinman and Carole O'Donnell of the Columbia Sports Information Office put their Gehrig research at my disposal.

An article appearing in the *Missouri Historical Society Magazine,* written by Professor Arthur S. McClure II, was revealing about Gehrig's last game in 1939.

Others who patiently talked to me or wrote to me about Gehrig were Dr. Michael Sesit, Louis J. Lefkowitz, Adie Suehsdorf, Jack Orr, Alan M. Moss, Henry Stern, Rocky Graziano, Jeffrey Lyons, Tom Horton, Lee Lowenfish, Harold Rosenthal, Steve Robinson, Bob Smith, Leo Trachtenberg, Eliot Asinof, Don Honig, Jim Ogle, Niven Busch, Teresa Wright, Dr. Lewis Rowland, Leslie Slote, Dr. Morton Nathanson, Kathryn S. Dohr, Robert Creamer, Bartram Sarason, Doris Fisher, Dan Fisher, Marvin Fisher, Mollie Silverman Rosoff, Al Yudkoff, Graham Gardner, Fred Frick, David Halberstam, Ralph Nader, Edward Rosenthal, Joe Hyams, Louis Muschel, Warren J. Cowan, Robert A. Biggs of Phi Delta Theta Fraternity, Jerome S. Solomon, Jacques Barzun, George T. Moeschen, Art Rust, Joe Gergen, Bill Elster, W. P. Hamilton, Arthur Pincus, and Vincent Tedeschi.

George Pollack, the lawyer for Eleanor Gehrig, was especially cooperative and writer David Noonan generously provided me with a cassette of Gehrig's movie, *Rawhide.* Marty Appel guided me to Gehrig's resting place.

There is a body of baseball literature that was of help. Of them all, Frank Graham's *A Quiet Hero* was invaluable, as was *My Luke and I* by Mrs. Gehrig and Joe Durso. Other important research books were *The Yankee Encyclopedia,* by Mark Gallagher; *Baseball When the Grass Was Real,* by Donald Honig; *The New York Yankees,* by Frank Graham; *The Yankee Story,* by Tom Meany; *The Fireside Book of Baseball,* edited by Charles Einstein; *Murderers' Row,* by G. H. Fleming; *Babe,* by Robert Creamer; *Baseball for the Love of It,* by Anthony J. Connor; *Ty Cobb,* by Charles C. Alexander; *John McGraw,* by Charles C. Alexander; *From Cobb to Catfish,* by John Kuenster; *"Where Have You Gone, Joe DiMaggio,"* by Maury Allen; *The Lawless Decade,* by Paul Sann; *Somebody Up There Likes Me,* by Rocky Graziano with Rowland Barber; *Babe Ruth,* by Kal Wagenheim; *Baseball,* by Robert Smith; *Baseball's Famous First Basemen,* by Ira L. Smith; *Baseball America,* by Donald Honig; *The All-Star Game,* by Donald Honig; *A Farewell to Heroes,* by Frank Graham, Jr.; *The Greatest of All: 1927 New York Yankees,* by John

Mosedale; *Six Parts Love: A Family's Battle with Lou Gehrig's Disease,* by Roni Radin; *Gary Cooper,* by Hector Arce; *The Last Hero,* by Larry Swindell; *Insider's Baseball,* by L. Robert Davids; and *American Baseball,* Volume II, by David Q. Voigt.

A boy's Gehrig scrapbook, conscientiously assembled by Alex S. Kole, was a delight to peruse. My thanks to Sandy Schwarz for steering me to it. It was also a pleasure to view Abe Sukenick's harvest of Gehrig memorabilia.

The ever-ready Xerox machine of Bob Witten, presided over by Marianna Sorshek, was indispensable to me.

A thank you to the U.S. Post Office for issuing a 25¢ stamp of Gehrig during the gestation of this book, making Lou the fourth ballplayer to be so honored. Babe Ruth (as ever, preceding Gehrig), Jackie Robinson, and Roberto Clemente were the others.

To Hilary Hinzmann, the "hard-nosed" editor at Norton, my gratitude for his strict attention to detail and an unswerving commitment to the project.

Finally, to Phyllis, who lovingly shared the ups and downs of *Iron Horse,* with typical optimism, and to my little Norfolk terrier, Penrod, who, from his daily perch under my chair, remained curious about what I was up to until the end of his life.

Index

italicized page numbers refer to photographs